W9-CCA-834

INSTRUCTORS
AND THEIR JOBS

THIRD EDITION

AMERICAN TECHNICAL PUBLISHERS, INC.
HOMEWOOD, ILLINOIS 60430-4600

W. R. Miller
M. F. Miller

© 2002 by American Technical Publishers, Inc.
All rights reserved

3 4 5 6 7 8 9 – 02 – 9 8 7 6 5 4 3 2 1

Printed in the United States of America

ISBN 0-8269-4165-6

made in
USA

CONTENTS

INTRODUCTION

Instructors and Their Jobs, 3rd Edition is a comprehensive reference for instructors, trainers, and human resource development (HRD) specialists. The book can be used as an instructional text for those new to the role of instructor, or as a guide for integrating new techniques for experienced instructors. Theoretical concepts are complemented with practical applications for use in a variety of instructional settings. Topics covered in the book include the role of the instructor, learning theory, learner assessment, instructional methodology, instructional technology, and learning environments.

Instructors and Their Jobs, 3rd Edition is organized into 15 chapters with illustrations and tables. Each chapter contains questions and activities for reviewing content covered. A comprehensive bibliography and index are provided at the end of the book. A new chapter, Industry-Based Instruction, covers topics relevant to industrial training environments including assessment of functional skills, soft skills, and technical skills; instructional planning and methods; models for industry-based instruction; and typical skill requirements of the HRD specialist. Additionally, information related to instructional media and applications has been updated throughout the book.

This book is one of several products available from American Technical Publishers, Inc. To obtain information about related learning material, visit the American Tech web site at www.go2atp.com.

The Publisher

Author Information

Dr. Wilbur R. Miller is eminently qualified as a teacher, teacher-educator, researcher, administrator, consultant, and author. He has taught at the secondary and postsecondary levels. He also served as Department Chair of Practical Arts and Technical Education and as Dean of the College of Education at the University of Missouri-Columbia.

Dr. Miller has been involved in many professional organizations including the American Association of Colleges for Teacher Education, Missouri Association of School Administrators, National Association of Industrial and Technical Teacher Educators, and the Association for Career and Technical Education. He has received numerous awards and citations including the Distinguished Service Award from the National Center for Research in Career and Technical Education and the University of Missouri Alumni Faculty Award.

Dr. Miller serves as a consultant to schools and industry in the U.S. and other countries. He has authored or co-authored eight books and many periodicals, monographs, and bulletins. Currently, Dr. Miller is Vice-President for Development at Auburn University.

Dr. Marie F. Miller is a Professor in the Department of Educational Foundations, Leadership, and Technology at Auburn University. She has conducted numerous research projects, developed proposals, consulted, and participated in a variety of workshops, seminars, and conferences while teaching a wide range of professional courses. Dr. Miller has received many awards and citations for her professional contributions including the Distinguished Alumni Award from the University of Wisconsin-Stout and the Undergraduate Teaching Excellence Award from the Auburn University Alumni Association. She served as President for Iota Lambda Sigma, an honorary society for career and technical education.

Dr. Miller received a PhD in Technical Education from the University of Missouri-Columbia. In addition to her many other professional duties, she also serves as Test Center Coordinator for Alabama for the National Occupational Competency Testing Institute.

Dr. Miller has authored or co-authored four books and has written numerous articles and papers. Currently, Dr. Miller serves on the Board of Editors for the Journal of Technology Studies.

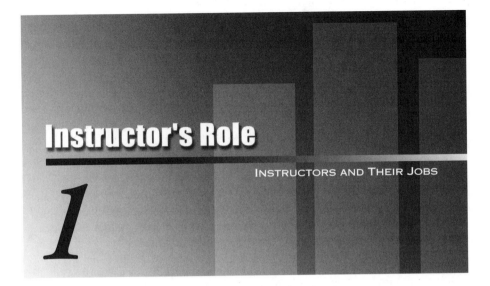

Instructor's Role

1

INTRODUCTION

Facilities, instructional materials, and equipment designed to meet student needs are basic requirements for educational and industrial training programs. However, effective instructors are vital to dynamic, successful training programs. Without instructors who are fully competent in their subject and the teaching process, no educational or industrial training program can be completely successful.

At any level and in any setting, the key variable in effective educational and industrial training programs is the instructional leader – the instructor. This book focuses on professional competency, which is the knowledge and skills essential for instructors to perform their professional tasks effectively.

Two other competency areas equally important to the teaching-learning equation are technical competency and personal competency. These two competency areas plus professional competency provide the balance and harmony required for effective instruction. All three are essential, like the three legs of a stool.

The objectives of this book are to:

1. summarize systematically the existing body of knowledge related to instructional theory and practice;

2. present these concepts, principles, and practices in a practical and straightforward manner;

1

3. show the range of applications of instructional theory and practice; and

4. encourage the formulation of new instructional strategies.

While the applications of instructional theory and practice presented in this book are drawn from the world of work, the principles of instructional planning, execution, and evaluation are universal. The vocational-industrial thrust of this text narrows its focus to the role of the instructor at the upper secondary, postsecondary, apprenticeship, and industrial training levels.

Competent instructors in school, apprenticeship, and industrial training programs are builders of bridges between expanding and changing technical knowledge and a wide range of personalities of individuals who must learn new concepts, develop new attitudes, and acquire new technical skills. Teaching is an incredibly complex task requiring innumerable decisions during each class session.

Instructors are successful only to the extent that they enable their students to learn at the right time, rapidly, and well. The measure of the instructor's success is the learning that results from instruction. Student learning is a direct result of the quality of the instructor's decisions as instruction is planned, executed, and evaluated.

With this concept in mind, educational researchers and scholars examine the personal qualities and professional practices that contribute to instructional effectiveness. Through systematic observation of skilled instructors in action and an analysis of their techniques, a body of knowledge that can be used for self-evaluation and professional development emerges. This knowledge can guide those who select, develop, and supervise instructors.

Personal qualities desirable in instructors may be identified in several ways. Long lists that include such hints as stand on both feet, look at the class, and keep shoes shined have been prepared. Little is gained by listing such items that vary from person to person and are accepted by students as part of the instructor's total personality. Many of these variables have little impact on learners. Most personal qualities and mannerisms become important only in extreme cases.

Competency areas that determine the effectiveness of instructors are:

1. *technical competency* (knowledge and skills to be taught);

2. *professional competency* (knowledge of instructional planning, execution, and evaluation); and

3. *personal competency* (personal characteristics and behaviors that impact the teaching-learning process).

TECHNICAL COMPETENCY

Knowledge of the subject matter to be taught and the skills involved in its application are the key ingredients to effective teaching. To paraphrase Will Rogers, you can't teach something you don't know any more than you can come back from a place you haven't been. In the past, a person's work experience was accepted as verification of his or her technical competence. Today, that is no longer the case. Many states require teachers to take an occupational competency examination in the area in which they are teaching. Such examinations consist of a written component and a performance component. Some states require the written component only, while others require the written and performance components. Occupational competency examinations are available from different sources. The National Occupational Competency Testing Institute (NOCTI) is perhaps the best known source for experienced worker competency examinations. NOCTI provides occupational competency tests for vocational and technical education teachers and industrial workers, and job readiness tests for students.

Benefits

Instructional effectiveness is a unique blend of scientific knowledge and artistic expression. There are many variables involving the subject matter, environment, instructor, and learner. Therefore, it is difficult to make absolute statements about the impact of these interacting variables on learner behavior. However, there is no substitute for knowledge and skill in the subject being taught. Knowledge and skill can be acquired in a variety of ways, and the value of certain types and amounts of experience can be debated. What is not debatable is the need for basic competence. Learners should never need to ask, "Is the instructor competent in the subject matter?"

An instructor's work experience increases credibility and provides examples that can be used to make instruction interesting and meaningful. Additionally, instructors' knowledge of and experience in their subject matter creates a level of confidence that contributes to instructional effectiveness. The nature and extent of an instructor's background provides an additional level of credibility that leads to student respect, especially in the skilled trades and technical areas. However, if that experience is not backed up with evident knowledge and skill, the advantage will be lost. Even the beginning instructor with work experience to support detailed knowledge and skill in the subject is more at ease with students than an instructor with limited experience related to the subject matter.

Limitations

The instructor's skill and knowledge of the subject to be taught are important, but such skill and knowledge alone are not sufficient. Many people have substantial knowledge as well as a high degree of technical skill, but are not effective in the instructional role. The instructor's role requires the transmission of knowledge and skills to the learner. Knowledge and skill are of limited value if the instructor does not have the ability or patience to assist a beginner. Instructors must analyze their competencies and structure the subject matter so that learners can develop their own competency in the subject. Often, basic performance elements are so well-integrated into the total movement pattern of a highly skilled instructor that basic steps are not recognized for instructional purposes. When this occurs, the instructor's high level of competency may interfere with instructional effectiveness rather than contribute to it.

Instructors must make a continuing effort to maintain a high level of competency through additional study and experience with the subject matter. This is particularly true for those students being prepared for positions involving specific and specialized tasks. Students are alert and capable in appraising the competency of their instructors. Respect and credibility are important elements. They can be earned by instructors competent in their field.

Students are also quick to spot bluffing or faking and are likely to be suspicious even in those aspects of the subject in which the instructor is well-prepared. The instructor who attempts to bluff when uncertain of what to say or do is not respected by students. No instructor can know everything about the subject. It must be expected that students may ask questions that the instructor cannot answer. When this happens, the instructor should not feel threatened and display, either through verbal tone or expression, disgust, frustration, or irritation that might prevent future questions. The instructor should compliment the students for raising the question and proceed as follows:

Situation	Proper Technique
Information that should be known and taught in the lesson.	Offer to find out. Keep the promise and relate information to the class.
Material of interest to advanced students but beyond the scope of the course.	Identify source of information and help locate.
Something for which there is no exact information.	Inform the class the facts are not known. Discuss work that has been completed in this area.
Material that is too advanced or complicated for the students at this time.	Briefly describe the technique or process and indicate its complexity. Suggest that the question be asked again in a later lesson or course. If appropriate, make a note to include it later.
Material that is not related to the topic being studied.	Indicate the question is outside the scope of the course. Offer to help locate information after class.

PROFESSIONAL COMPETENCY

Professional competency may be conceptualized in a variety of ways. However, this text focuses on three major areas of the instructor's professional role as they relate to instructional planning, instructional delivery, and instructional evaluation.

Instructional Planning

The essential element of instructional planning is the content of the instructional process. Identification of the skills and knowledge to be acquired by the learner cannot be taken for granted or passed over lightly. Systematic procedures have been developed by educational researchers and scholars that can answer the fundamental question, "Have the appropriate attitudes, knowledge, and skills been identified for inclusion in an instructional program?" One should not think of course content as simply what is to be taught. While curriculum specialists and teachers agree that the student should be able to know or do something or behave in a certain way, the question remains: what kind of learning or knowing, doing, or behaving is important? For example, knowledge and application demonstrate two very different levels of learning, yet each is important in the learning process.

There are many issues related to content in the instructional process. Control of the curriculum and the responsibilities of governments, regions, institutions, administrators, teachers, parents, employers, and other interest groups vary in the identification and planning of content for individual programs of study. In some cases, content may be the result of political bargaining rather than rational thinking. A common concern is the relationship between content and gender. Although the gender issue is not so prevalent in general studies, vocational, technical, and technology curricula may have a marked gender stereotype. Most instructors, especially new ones, are not involved in the content identification process as this is typically accomplished when the curriculum for the program or school is established. However, instructors are frequently involved in updating and verifying the content, especially in occupational areas subject to rapid change. The need to include state-of-the art content in instructional planning is obvious; however, the manner in which this is accomplished ranges from minor revisions based on regular consultations with business and industry to completely new courses that attempt to "overhaul" existing practices. In either case, the instructor must be prepared to make content decisions that give credibility to the instructional program.

After the occupational area has been analyzed and the inherent skills and knowledge have been identified, the portion of that knowledge to be included in a given course must be selected. The selection process involves a number of factors, such as objectives to be met at a given level and the background and experience of the learners.

After selecting the content to be included in a given program or course, the instructional planner focuses more directly on units and lessons to be experienced by students. The instructor makes decisions regarding specific objectives to be met during a specified time period, learning activities that lead to achievement of the objectives, and evaluation procedures that assess the extent to which students have mastered the objectives.

Instructional Delivery

After the instructor has planned the course of instruction and made detailed plans for specific lessons, the plan must be delivered. The fundamental task is facilitating student learning. This may involve direct presentations of content through such general methods as lecture, demonstration, or assigned readings. It may involve the supervision of students as they conduct a laboratory exercise, watch a film, prepare a diagram, or engage in other activities designed to help them develop competencies specified in the instructor's plan. A variety of instructional materials, techniques, and aids are available for use as the instructor guides the learning process.

Instructional Evaluation

Instructional evaluation is typically viewed as a systematic means of assessing the extent to which a student meets specified objectives. This process is also an indirect assessment of the instructional process designed to facilitate student achievement.

Evaluation can be conducted in a variety of ways. Competent instructors select the appropriate evaluation procedure for a given group of learners at specific points in the instructional process. Some procedures are precise and objective, while others are based on the instructor's observational and judgmental abilities. Regardless of the specific procedures used, the process is continuous as it provides information about student achievement and the effectiveness of instruction. Instructors must be sensitive to student response. A continuing effort, both informal and formal, is required to assess students' progress. In formal evaluation, examination questions are used to determine whether or not students have met specific objectives. The students must demonstrate the level of skill, knowledge, or attitude for which the instructional program was designed. In informal evaluation, instructors read the facial expressions of students and listen to their questions to determine the extent to which students have assimilated a particular idea, process, or skill.

⋏ *The primary purpose of student evaluation is to monitor the amount or quality of learning, not to rate or grade the student.* The process of thinking through the material and helping students organize it in their own way is of tremendous value in fixing the important ideas and relationships in the students' memory. Examples of this strategy include the review preceding an examination or the discussion following an examination.

PERSONAL COMPETENCY

People have different characteristics and learned behaviors. No two people are alike. The diverse characteristics of instructors and students and the absence of absolutes or predictable outcomes make the educational process challenging, complex, and interesting. Instructors possess certain characteristics and behavioral patterns that influence their performance and the performance of their students.

Personal Characteristics

An individual's personal characteristics determine the way that person is perceived by others. Physical characteristics are obvious, but there is very little relationship between an instructor's height, weight, color, or sex and instructional effectiveness. Psychological and emotional characteristics influence instructional effectiveness more directly, yet there is a broad range of variability within which little difference in effectiveness is noted.

Attitudes. An instructor possesses both general and specific opinions or feelings about people, things, and events. A person's behavior and comments often reveal either a positive or negative attitude. Attitudes, often reflected through behavior, typically result from life experiences and interaction with others. By the time a person reaches adulthood, changes in attitude are difficult to achieve.

People with positive attitudes are generally more effective instructors than those whose general outlook is negative. Specific examples of attitudes that impact on instructional effectiveness are the instructor's feelings toward students and the learning process. Instructors who use their position to gain attention or impress their students have ego needs that interfere with their effectiveness. An attitude of caring must be projected to students. Students are more motivated to learn under the direction of an instructor interested in students as individuals and in the particular subject.

The instructor with a positive attitude toward teaching sends a reinforcing message to the student, which has a positive impact on learning. Encouragement and expectation are factors that enhance learning. The instructor behaves in ways that make student development a self-fulfilling prophecy. Students think, "I believe I can because you believe I can." "I kept trying until I did it because you convinced me that I could do it."

Instructors who do not like their jobs or the organizations in which they work frequently project a negative attitude in their classrooms. Their attitudes have a significant impact on the learning environment, which affects student learning and student attitudes as well. The role of the instructor demands involvement with students. It is a contradiction for instructors to say they like teaching but are unwilling to assist students in the learning and development process.

Intellectual Abilities. An instructor must read, write, reason, synthesize, solve problems, compute, formulate and express ideas, and make decisions with a reasonably high level of competency. These are tasks of the mind that require facility with the symbols used to communicate about ideas, people, and things.

Good communication is essential for an effective instructor. Individuals wishing to teach must have above-average cognitive abilities. Various terms such as intelligence, cognition, and perception are used to indicate the mental abilities essential to an effective instructor. In conjunction with the ability to speak clearly and distinctly, instructors must possess the intellectual abilities that provide the substance for oral expression.

Creativity. While current research and theory contend that creativity is a part of intellectual functioning, it does deserve some separate attention as it relates to the role of the instructor. Creativity and resourcefulness are qualities that tend to distinguish outstanding instructors from average instructors. Creativity produces the novel idea, strategy, or approach that gets the job done. A creative instructor thinks of ways to describe or illustrate subject matter so that it comes alive for the learner.

Poor instructors often use the same method of presentation regardless of the topic. However, the method that works well for one individual, one class, or one lesson may not be satisfactory in another situation. The effective instructor is alert to the slightest evidence of confusion, misunderstanding, or lack of interest among the students, and is able to adjust the presentation to correct the difficulty.

A primary reason for varying instructional procedures with different classes or students is that individuals differ in native capacity, experience, and learning style. The rapidity with which students learn a particular subject depends to a large extent on their ability to adapt their learning pattern to the instructor's teaching method. This instructor-student relationship should work both ways, and the effective instructor must be quick to modify instructional procedures so that learning is aided. Understanding the principles of learning allows the creative, resourceful instructor to design a new instructional aid to illustrate a principle, use a current event to emphasize a concept, or develop more effective methods of measuring the progress of each student.

Interpersonal Skills. The ability to interact with students, administrators, parents, employers, and community leaders is vital to the effective instructor. It is often said that educators are in the people development business. While good interpersonal skills do not ensure learning, the research evidence is quite convincing that students' learning is adversely affected by negative feelings toward the instructor. A student who is afraid, angry, or worried cannot learn effectively.

A central factor affecting the learning environment is the instructor's self-concept and confidence. People's personalities are the total of their personal, social, and emotional traits. Some of these personality factors are hereditary, while others result from environmental conditioning and experiences over a lifetime. As adults, instructors can anticipate little change in personality. However, awareness of characteristics and behaviors that have an adverse effect on learning can be helpful. Negative feelings about self are often reflected through sarcasm, defensiveness, insults, hostility, aloofness, and overreaction to student behavior. These negative instructor behaviors interfere with the development of good personal relationships.

Although a clear understanding of the instructor's role is necessary to establish a professional distinction between instructor and student, this professional distance must not be viewed as uncaring, uninterested, or a distinction based on human value. An important line exists between a close friendship or social relationship and a professional relationship based on the mutual respect and concern of individuals engaged in the teaching-learning process. The instructor must maintain a positive relationship with students that contributes to the primary goal of learning rather than detracting from it.

The instructor must work in harmony with fellow instructors and supervisors. Willingness to do more than is required helps earn the respect of one's associates and superiors, unless this willingness is accompanied by aggressiveness or lack of consideration. Interpersonal skills are important in the classroom and in all areas of the educational enterprise.

Behavior

Personality, which is largely determined by adulthood, is the primary variable in establishing relationships with others. This complex integration of characteristics is largely responsible for presenting the instructor to others. Some of the ways one presents oneself and is perceived by others occur naturally without any conscious decision making. Nevertheless, much of the instructor's impact on learning is a result of behavior, both word and deed. Obviously, instructor behavior that is consistent with one's feelings and value system seems most believable to students. However, appropriate behavior is important at all times. The appropriateness of a specific behavior depends upon the time and conditions and cannot be determined by someone else in advance. This is a part of the complex decision making process that happens continuously in any teaching-learning environment. General principles of behavior are applicable and appropriate in most situations.

Considerate. Consider the feelings of others. Since one cannot know how others feel about many things, instructors should be cautious in situations that may possibly be embarrassing. Dogmatic statements about such issues as politics, racial and cultural differences, or the value of one school subject over another are best avoided.

Controversial matters can be discussed, but the instructor's behavior should be tactful and considerate. Instructors should react to ideas or statements in a manner that is not demeaning to the person. Think first and talk second because meaningful discussion is difficult if the instructor seems unreasonably opinionated. Honesty with students and colleagues is most appreciated when one seems willing to listen and consider other points of view.

When students present an incorrect response, the instructor should avoid demeaning them. Whenever possible, build on a portion of the incorrect response. For example, "Joe, I believe you may be on the right track, but there are some problems with your answer. Jane, what can you add?" or "Joe, elaborate a bit more. Why do you believe this is true?" Short responses like, "No, you are dead wrong." or "Joe, how could you possibly think that way?" or "Jane, where were you when we talked about this yesterday?" can embarrass students and may be perceived as demeaning. Sarcasm and ridicule have no place in teaching. They have a negative impact on learning and often result in undesirable behavior as the student tries to save face.

Cooperative. Instructors should be sensitive to the total school program and keep their own teaching responsibilities in perspective. Other activities in the school and in the lives of students may be more important than a given class period in a particular course. The understanding instructor should avoid being dogmatic and inflexible in these situations.

It is essential for instructors to cooperate as they work together for the benefit of students. The instructor should discuss noninstructional responsibilities with the administration to clearly understand the expected role. An instructor who carries out this role in a friendly, cooperative manner develops a positive reputation and can expect a high degree of cooperation from others.

Complimentary. A significant factor in human achievement is positive reinforcement. Compliments spur people to increased productivity and satisfaction. Showing interest in a student's or a colleague's accomplishment is a form of compliment. Instructors who achieve unusual success with a class or a particular approach to a student's problem should be complimented sincerely. Avoid flattery and too frequent compliments about inconsequential matters.

Friendly. The instructor who meets both students and associates with a smile and a word of greeting finds it easier to work with them. A free and natural relationship should be maintained with fellow instructors as well as with students. The age old advice to new teachers, "Be fair, be firm, and be friendly," is still relevant today. It is important for students to perceive their instructors as approachable and pleasant. Positive rapport is built on a number of factors, including a smile, an exchange of greeting, and acknowledgment of another's worth.

An instructor may establish a reputation for being unfriendly by any of these methods:

1. using aggressive behavior;

2. speaking in a commanding tone of voice;

3. frowning constantly;

4. displaying an inflexible attitude;

5. bragging or threatening that few A's are given;

6. stating that extraordinary effort is required to pass the course;

7. refusing to repeat instructions or questions;

8. acting as though students must be driven rather than led; and

9. showing little consideration for students.

Instructors who use these tactics seem to believe that students can be bullied into learning. Such techniques discourage students from cooperating with the instructor and fill them with fear or disgust. Little learning occurs when the student feels fear, disgust, or resentment. The effective instructor develops patience, tact, and self-control while exhibiting maturity to facilitate learning.

Involved. The instructor should be involved in the total school program. Interest in and attendance at school functions helps develop rapport with students and colleagues. Participation in appropriate recreational and social activities better acquaints the instructor with other faculty and administrators. The instructor should not limit social contacts to fellow staff members, but should interact with them to develop a congenial, informal relationship within the group.

Professional Organizations. Membership in professional organizations such as the American Vocational Association (AVA) and the state vocational association qualifies instructors to receive newsletters, bulletins, journals, special announcements, and other related materials. This information helps instructors stay abreast of the latest developments, issues, and trends in their fields of expertise. Often new products or services are announced and discussed in literature available to members. Upcoming events, such as district, state, regional, or national meetings and conferences and a preview of the program are often included in membership materials. Simply holding a membership in professional organizations is not enough. It takes active participation if the instructor is to reap the full benefits of the membership cost. Conferences offer a host of guest speakers, seminars, and other professional development sessions and activities. State, regional, and national conferences often feature exhibits where representatives of companies that provide publications, equipment, tools, supplies, and services are available to provide information and answer questions. In fact, one or more of the exhibitors representing private industry may sponsor or assist in sponsoring a particular event or a professional association.

In addition to the AVA, examples of other professional organizations of interest to vocational, technical, and technology teachers include the National Association of Trade and Industrial Educators (NATIE), the National Association of Industrial and Technical Teacher Educators (NAITTE), and the Technology Education Association (TEA). These associations often conduct their annual meeting during the state or national conference. It is at such gatherings where instructors have an opportunity to meet face-to-face with their colleagues from across a state or the nation to share and learn from one another. Interacting with colleagues and private industry representatives in vocational and technical education is particularly important in this day of rapidly-changing technology.

Professional. Professional instructors take pride in their role and are highly ethical in dealing with others. They also take pride in being competent and in using that competency to help students become competent. As a professional educator, an instructor values education and reinforces all parts of the curriculum. For example, the teacher of computing must recognize and reinforce the value of correct English usage, good communication skills, and other elements of the total educational program. According to the Carnegie Foundation for the Advancement of Teaching, the educated person is intellectually curious, thinks critically, weighs evidence dispassionately, is tolerant, temperate, mature, is not intellectually lazy, and does not permit rational processes to be at the mercy of fears and prejudices.

To paraphrase a familiar advertising jingle, the professional instructor needs to look sharp, feel sharp, and be sharp. A clean, neat appearance is an asset in any job, but an instructor is in a position to be observed closely, and poor grooming can have an adverse influence on students and colleagues alike. Associates gain their first impression from general appearance. Such impressions are very strong.

Education is a complex and important area today. With each new scientific and engineering breakthrough, people must learn new skills and adjust to new situations. These changes are escalating at an increasingly faster pace. Corporate expenditures are increasing for employee training because of the skills employees must have. By adding the cost of public and private secondary and technical schools and other government training, it is evident that education and training are part of the nation's major activities. It is also evident that poor methods of instruction are an inefficient use of scarce resources. Without effective educational programs under expert instructors, much of the large investment will be lost.

The need for more and better educational programs for people of all ages is alarmingly evident. Because so many people must learn throughout their working careers, it is imperative to use only the most effective instructional procedures. The progress and well-being of individuals and of the nation depend on how well they learn.

An instructor's effectiveness is determined by technical competency, professional competency, and personal competency. Inadequacy in any one of these areas will have an adverse impact on student learning. A professional instructor's responsibility is to facilitate student learning. Consequently, instructors must eliminate or minimize weaknesses and maximize strengths.

An instructor's role is a challenging one that demands lifetime commitment to learning. However, there are rewards that justify the effort. One of the most satisfying experiences instructors have is knowing that through their efforts someone has become more competent, more confident, a better human being, and a more useful citizen. Through the application of good teaching skills, an instructor brings new opportunities to others.

Good instructors discover dormant talent in students. To motivate students, develop their skills, and see the pleasure that results from newfound competencies is a reward unique to teaching.

Contacts made with students often develop into strong, lifelong friendships because of the mutual respect and understanding gained through working and learning together. Instructors also enjoy exchanging ideas with fellow instructors and developing new ideas and interests.

It has been said that the only way to know something is to teach it. Since this is at least partly true, instructors often find themselves studying the things students must learn from a new, more analytical point of view. Such study adds to an instructor's knowledge of the subject.

REVIEW

Questions

1. List three competency areas essential for an effective instructor.
2. What is the primary criterion by which an instructor's effectiveness must be judged?
3. Why is it difficult to predict the amount of learning that occurs as a result of proper instructional techniques?
4. Why are knowledge of the subject area and the skills to be taught inadequate to successfully fulfill the role of an instructor?
5. What is likely to occur in instructional settings if instructors pretend to know their subject matter or engage in bluffing?
6. What are the primary benefits of an instructor having a substantial amount of teaching and trade experience?
7. What is the difference between content identification and content selection in the instructional planning process?
8. What is the relationship of instructional objectives to instructional planning, execution, and evaluation?
9. To what extent are evaluation and testing synonymous?
10. What are three personal characteristics that significantly influence the instructor's level of effectiveness?
11. To what does the statement, "Instructors are in the people development business" refer?
12. What is the relationship between an instructor's level of self-confidence and student learning?
13. What is the implication of the statement, "Attitudes are better caught than taught"?
14. What is the difference between an instructor's personal characteristics and personal behavior?
15. How do instructors benefit from involvement in school activities?

Activities

1. List the qualities of a former instructor whom you judged to be effective.
2. List the qualities of a former instructor whom you judged to be ineffective.
3. List several factors that may cause students to lose interest in a class.

4. Identify three conflicts you have observed between students and instructors. Indicate your perception of the cause of each conflict and steps that could have been taken to prevent it.

5. Identify limitations you have that should be eliminated or minimized in order for you to develop as an effective instructor.

6. Identify strengths you have that should contribute to your effectiveness as an instructor.

7. Explain the professional relationship that exists between the instructor and students.

8. List professional organizations in which you currently hold membership. List those that you plan to join.

Learning Process

INSTRUCTORS AND THEIR JOBS

2

INTRODUCTION

An electrician can wire a house or a technician can repair a personal computer without knowing all the theories of electricity or electronics. Likewise, a chef may use correct ingredients and procedures to produce a culinary delight without knowing all of the theories involved in cooking. In the same way, an instructor may use good techniques of instruction without knowing, in great detail, the theory of learning. However, the electrician, technician, chef, and instructor will be more effective if they have an understanding of the basic theory related to specific job techniques.

People learn in many different ways – by reading, listening, watching, do-ing, thinking, and solving problems. The success of these learning processes depends on several elements, of which intelligence, attention, and interest are overriding forces. The intellectual abilities through which one acquires, proc-esses, and applies information play a central role in learning. The ability to reason, see relationships, and solve problems can be facilitated by in-struction, but people differ in their intellectual abilities and learning po-tential. Regardless of the student's learning potential, no instructional approach can succeed if it fails to hold the student's interest and attention. It is much easier to learn when the learner is interested; it is most difficult when interest wanes. The learner's attention varies depending on the subject, the level and quality of instruction, and the learner's previous experiences in and out of the classroom. Realizing that students have varying attention spans and that some learn more rapidly than others, the effective instructor varies instructional strategies. The instructor must use techniques that interest the largest possible number of individuals.

The exact nature of the learning process that occurs within the brain is unknown. However, a substantial body of knowledge gained by observation and research provides insight into the conditions facilitating the learning process. The effective instructor operates at a high level of problem solving and should know much of the body of knowledge related to learning. This knowledge enables the instructor to establish the conditions essential for efficient and effective learning.

LEARNING THEORY AND PRINCIPLES

Learning occurs as an individual develops new associations based on experience. The associations involve a mental process, although in many cases there is also a physical component. Though learning is affected by many external factors, it is primarily an internal event occurring in the brain. The chemistry and neurology are not completely understood, but it is known that all of the associations (learning) are stored individually in brain cells.

Early psychologists such as Ivan Pavlov, Edward Thorndike, Robert Gagné (gon-yea), B. F. Skinner, and more recently Jean Piaget (pia-zhay), and David Ausubel have developed substantial knowledge through years of research. Additional research has been conducted relating to the chemical and neurological structure of the brain, connections with the nervous system, and relationship of the left and right halves of the brain. Volumes of literature are available to the instructor who wishes to understand more about the learning process. For the beginning instructor, it is important to understand the basic theory and principles related to learning.

Learning Through Experience

Learning is a dynamic process in which the learner is the central figure. The instructor can help the learner develop new associations, but the instructor cannot learn for the student. Learning through experience involves the acquiring of information and associating it with previously gained information. Educational programs are systematic efforts to facilitate learning and affect behavioral changes.

Learning is not limited to school or other structured learning environments. Associations result effortlessly from experience, and learning can be incidental. For example, the advertising industry is built on the premise that individuals behave on the basis of learning. Nevertheless, instructors should recognize that direct attention and deliberate effort result in the most thorough learning. The instructor directs the attention and effort of the learner so that the individual learns efficiently.

People develop learning skills gradually. They encode and decode information according to individual learning styles. Group instruction is therefore difficult as the instructor's presentation style may not be equally beneficial for all learners.

People respond to new stimulation as it relates to existing knowledge. The person's learning style and previous knowledge influence associations and learning. Learning often involves proceeding through various levels of knowledge, starting with simple elements and building gradually to complex systems. Frequently, progress at higher levels is not possible until certain lower level skills are mastered. For example, a student who cannot subtract efficiently will be continually frustrated by attempts to learn division.

Learning Related to Behavior or Performance

Instructors must distinguish between the learning process and student behavior or performance that indicates learning has taken place. Instructors may be too quick to judge learning by inadequate observation of the student's performance, *performance* being broadly defined in this context as anything the learner does to indicate that learning has taken place. The absence of a correct behavior does not necessarily mean that no learning has occurred. For example, people may forget the name of someone they know quite well. Everyone experiences this inability to retrieve information stored in long-term memory. Therefore, an individual's performance at a particular time may not be a clear indicator of knowledge. Many things are retained for only a few moments in our short-term memory before being lost altogether. Even those that are retained in long-term memory may be difficult to recall in certain situations. Learning that has a substantial physical or motor component presents fewer problems of retrieval than abstract learning.

Psychomotor Learning

Psychomotor learning is the development of associations that have a substantial physical or motor component. This mental-physical learning involves gross motor skills including the general coordination and balance involved in walking or running. Psychomotor learning also involves fine motor skills that are more specific and differentiated and require substantial hand-eye coordination. Fine motor skills are needed for writing, carving, or making electrical connections. Psychomotor skills typically develop gradually, and their refinement requires practice. Most skills require a standard set of manipulations with slight variations based on physical differences among individuals. This sequence of motions allows an individual to become highly efficient in performing a given task. One of the instructor's primary challenges is to determine and relate the sequence of movements that will develop the learner's skill to the highest possible degree in the shortest period of time.

Cognitive Learning

Cognitive learning is the development of associations that have minimal physical involvement outside the brain. It includes everything from complex insights to the simplest associations between *stimuli* (things brought into the learner through the sensory mechanism, for example, sight, touch, or hearing). Cognitive learning is often classified according to complexity. These levels of learning and chaining of associations have substantial implications for instructional sequencing. Cognitive learning includes simple associations between stimuli, such as smoke and fire, or between responses, like inserting a key in a lock and turning it. Cognitive learning also includes complex sets of associations. Bits of information are not individually stored but are part of a complex system of coding, sorting, filing, and cross-indexing.

While the instructor can help students form new associations, new learning can only result from thinking. New associations develop from thinking about past experiences as connections are made between bits of information already stored in the brain. In this regard, thinking is similar to behavior because it leads to or results from learning rather than being learning. Nevertheless, thinking does involve active use of previous knowledge; it does not occur in a vacuum. It must be recognized that people vary considerably in their ability to learn from both external and internal stimuli.

Role of Memory in Learning

Memory is a key factor in learning because information received by the learner must be organized, or mapped, into the memory. Learning theorists disagree on the different processes involved in short-term versus long-term memory. However, it is generally agreed that associations must first be stored in short-term memory before being processed and stored in long-term memory.

Some associations that are stored briefly in short-term memory are not retained. Forgetting is an interesting phenomenon that occurs when one is unable to retrieve a previously learned association from long-term memory. The association is not gone, but it is not retrieved because of strong confusion with other, similar associations. For example, a common spelling rule states, "i before e, except after c." There are exceptions to this rule, and when the learner becomes aware of the exceptions, some confusion may result because of the strong association previously learned. This confusion may affect the spelling of words that follow the general rule. Therefore, confusion between competing associations can cause one to fail to retrieve information stored in long-term memory.

Everyone has experienced reading a page and suddenly realizing that the material being read was not being processed. This happens when thoughts or other stimuli such as sounds, smells, sights, or pain sufficiently distract the reader so that some of the words do not register in short-term memory. When this happens, information does not enter into long-term memory until it is reread or encountered in another way.

This happens because the brain exercises a gating function in dealing with incoming stimuli. Although the chemical and neurological process is not completely understood, it is known that all incoming stimuli are screened for relevance. Neuro-mechanisms close the gate on most stimuli and open the gate for stimuli sufficiently important to enter the consciousness. These stimuli make connections (synapses) in the midbrain that result in the stimulation of the higher brain, or cortex. Only stimuli that reach the cortex become part of the person's conscious awareness. When concentrating on material to be learned, the individual deems it relevant and, as a result, other stimuli are gated out.

A significant implication for teaching is that the attention and interest of the learner are central factors in transferring information into conscious awareness and ultimately into long-term memory. Material mapped into memory is systematically selected because it can be used for future reference. This material is systematically filed just as items in a warehouse are stored according to size and color so that they can be found quickly and easily. Information transferred into long-term memory is organized on the basis of associational patterns.

Each person's associational patterns are unique, although many patterns are similar. This similarity can be observed in word-association games. Most individuals in a given culture respond the same way when presented with one part of an association. For example, most Americans respond with the word "blue" when given cues of "red, white, and _." The dissimilarities in associational patterns can be observed when considering words that do not have a single, expected association such as the words "mountain," "river," "sky," and "dog." Terms of this type reveal differences in the way associations are mapped.

The role of memory in learning has important implications for the effective instructor. Since information is stored in an organized rather than random way, instruction is most effective if new information can be related to existing associations. Also, learners are most motivated to learn something that is relevant to their current interests or future needs. Motivation is important for short-term attention and even more so for the active information processing that leads to long-term memory.

LEARNING PROCESSES

People learn in numerous and varied ways. Because learning is a complex, individual process, the effective instructor must understand the various steps involved in order to select strategies that facilitate learning for each student. Most instruction takes place in group settings where facilitating individual learning becomes an obvious challenge for the instructor.

Learning by Trial and Error

A baby responds to discomfort by kicking and crying. If the discomfort is caused by hunger, the kicking and crying stops when the child is fed. After a few weeks the child learns that a particular cry brings food. Of course, the mother learns that cry too. Later the child and mother learn that other activities, such as reaching for a cup, indicate the desire for food. The baby and the mother have learned to communicate by trial and error. The baby makes all kinds of movements and noises until the food comes. Eventually the baby selects one kind of behavior to bring about the desired response from the mother.

Adults also learn by trial and error, although the trials are seldom random. Because of past experiences and their ability to reason, adults do not have to make as many trials before acquiring the necessary results. Everyone uses trial and error to some extent. However, contrary to popular opinion, learning things the hard way is not necessarily the best way. In a humorous vein, it has been said that good judgment comes from experience and that experience comes from using bad judgment.

Trial and error learning is obviously inefficient, even though the experiences involved may create strong associations. When correct information is available, learning can proceed much more efficiently. A direct learning process is generally more effective than several trials leading to limited or no success before the correct association is made.

Learning by Observation

Watching others can provide visual cues that help eliminate some of the trials a beginner might take. However, many things cannot be learned by observation alone. No amount of watching a pilot would provide the skills needed to fly an airplane properly. Observing behavior aids in developing the physical movements required, but the mental processes cannot be observed. Even narrow motor skills with few informational components, such as tying a shoelace or riding a bicycle, cannot be learned by observation alone. The general idea may be clear, but the skill cannot be acquired by observation. The acquisition of motor skills, such as using hand tools, walking, or throwing a ball, requires a change in the muscle and nervous systems. This is often referred to as psychomotor learning. This kind of learning comes only through doing and practicing over a period of time.

Activities such as using a computer or operating a lathe are usually too complicated to be learned by observation alone. However, observation is a central feature of demonstrating or modeling, which is one of the most efficient methods of teaching. Learners watch the instructor exhibit certain behaviors, and they can sometimes readily imitate these behaviors. In addition to physical skills, generalized attitudes or values can be taught through modeling as the learner gains insight by observation. Especially when combined with verbal instructions and mediation, modeling facilitates learning that otherwise might require long, frustrating trial and error.

Learning by Doing

Many instructors are too verbal. Words are important, and no instructor can do without them, but words usually convey only part of the meaning. Students must participate to completely understand. A city youngster's concept of a farm can never be accurate without some direct involvement such as visiting or working on a farm. Lectures, television, and films cannot take the place of real experience.

Acquiring physical skills obviously involves learning by doing. People learn to drive a nail or hit a ball by executing correct movements and repeating these movements until they become habit. Therefore, the instructor's demonstration should be followed by direct, hands-on experience by the learner.

Although often neglected, the principle of learning by doing also applies to nonphysical learning. Each major concept in a lesson should be followed by carefully prepared student assignments that apply the new concept. Students must summarize, review, and discuss new material. Frequently, they should translate new ideas into their own words. Working models and performance or achievement tests that require application of facts are effective learning by doing techniques.

While lecturing, it is possible to have the mental participation of learners as they relate new ideas to previously learned facts. The skilled instructor gets students to learn by doing through mental as well as physical activity.

The skilled lecturer applies this principle of learning by doing by challenging students with rhetorical questions and allowing time for them to:

1. answer questions silently;

2. critique ideas;

3. disagree and try to defend their ideas; and

4. see specific applications of principles.

Transfer of Learning

Transfer of learning is the learning of something in one setting or situation that permits one to gain insight or solve a problem in a similar situation. Since learning involves associations, transfer involves the association of a new stimulus or response with a familiar one. This generalization of the old association is what occurs when a learner applies a previously learned mathematics formula to a set of variables in electronics.

Transfer is not necessarily automatic, although persons of high intelligence can generally transfer more quickly and effectively than persons of low intelligence. Teachers can facilitate transfer by continually asking students to think of alternatives, to question, and to apply knowledge.

A noted educator once said that there is no single subject that has the key to rational thinking. Any subject can make a contribution, but the way the subject is taught may make all the difference. Unfortunately some people think the mind is like a muscle that can be strengthened by mastering certain difficult subjects and then applied to other subjects with greater intellectual force. This concept of learning is not generally accepted by psychologists, and careful experimentation has failed to support the theory. Knowledge of geometry does not help solve problems of human relations, for example, nor does a knowledge of human relations help in learning geometry.

Learning one specific task or subject can certainly help in learning another if the student recognizes the similarities and common elements between the two. Knowledge of one language is helpful when learning a related language. A knowledge of Latin is helpful when learning English because some English words come from Latin. Of course, it is also true that a mastery of English helps in learning Latin. Mathematics helps in learning electronics because mathematical principles are a part of electronics. Simulators, such as computerized trainers used for pilot training, have great transfer value because they mimic the exact performance of an airplane and provide realistic training exercises. The more the learning environment resembles the actual occupational environment, the easier it is for transfer to occur. Use of these simulation techniques is increasing at all levels of education.

If a student learns that 3 × 8 = 24, this knowledge can be transferred to learn 8 × 3 = 24 without further instruction. With minimal instruction, the student can then learn that 30 × 8 = 240, 8 × 30 = 240, 30 × 80 = 2400, and 80 × 30 = 2400, etc. If such transfer does not occur, it could be because the instructor failed to illustrate the principle in a way that brings it to mind in new but related situations. The instructor may not have emphasized the universality of the principle or taught for transfer.

Practice is essential, but so is an understanding of the principles involved. Much unproductive student homework can be avoided by teaching principles well and using examples to show how the principles can be applied. Homework, however, is extremely important, and its value should not be underestimated.

Value of Transfer. Teaching principles of learning to potential instructors does not have much effect on their performance unless (1) the principles are applied in a variety of practice teaching situations, and (2) the relationship between the principles and specific teaching situations is evaluated and emphasized.

Some people believe that in vocational and technical education there is little need for transfer as specific techniques are taught and used on the job as soon as the student completes the course. However, with today's rapidly changing technology, knowledge of principles rather than just procedures allows students to adapt to changing situations.

All courses should develop the student's ability to see the relationship between basic principles and practical uses. Most of the emphasis in transfer of learning is on positive transfer in which previous learning facilitates new associations. However, transfer may also inhibit learning. Negative transfer is the interference of something already learned with new learning. This often occurs when elements of learning are similar and become confused with one another instead of being associated. *Negative transfer* may also occur when students have learned to do something incorrectly, and the instructor tries to teach them the correct procedure. The old learning gets in the way of the new procedure.

Teaching for Transfer. Instructors can aid the positive transfer of learning by:

1. making sure underlying principles are fully understood;
2. helping students see the relationships between various parts of a subject and between two different subjects;
3. letting students know when to expect transfer and how to facilitate it and benefit from it;

4. using projects, problems, and questions to give practice in transfer; and

5. giving attention to individual learning styles.

Learning Curves and Plateaus

A *learning curve* is a two-dimensional description of the gradual progress made as one learns a skill over a period of time. See Figure 2-1. Since the changes are gradual, the points on the two-dimensional graph reveal a gradual curve when linked together. During the trial and error stage of learning, little progress is made as trials produce errors. With continued practice, instructor feedback, increased understanding, and improved linkage between the neural and muscular systems, the learner begins to progress more rapidly.

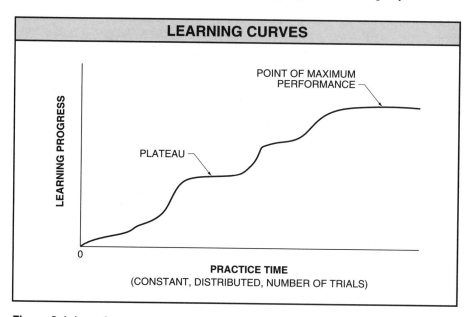

Figure 2-1. Learning curves reveal an irregular pattern of improvement by the learner over time.

Progress continues until performance gradually levels off at a plateau, after which increased learning may occur. However, at some point, individuals reach the upper limit of their ability in a given area. It is difficult to distinguish between a plateau with the potential for additional progress and the point of overlearning beyond which further practice does not lead to improvement. If horizontal and vertical connecting lines are drawn between the points, the lines form steps instead of a smooth curve. The terms *learning curves* and *learning steps* describe graphic representations of the progress an individual makes in the process of learning.

Learning plateaus are like landings in a long flight of stairs. They are particularly evident in the development of psychomotor skills, which are complex combinations of physical coordination and mental processes. After mastering the steps of a skill, students may become discouraged because they appear to be making little progress toward a higher skill level. One cause may be that the learner knows how to perform the skill or task but has not practiced it enough to make it a habit. The learner must think about each step of the procedure as it is performed. At this point, the learner may feel that further progress is impossible and may wish to give up. Golfers and other athletes experience plateaus in developing their game. Students should be informed of this characteristic of learning so they will recognize it as common to everyone who strives for perfection.

Learning plateaus are typically overcome by continued practice, assuming the physical movements are correct. Specialized instruction may be required to overcome the plateau if performance techniques are flawed. As practice and efforts to learn continue, the process gradually becomes as automatic as walking is to most people. Then progress is again possible, just as running is possible after walking has become automatic.

Delays in progress often occur as one strives to develop an additional level of skill. Once the procedure is thoroughly understood, the solution is generally to continue practice until the movements become automatic, and the procedure can be done without thinking. The mind is then free to concentrate on adapting to changing conditions.

Several plateaus may be encountered in learning procedures requiring a high degree of skill. The instructor should:

1. recognize the existence of plateaus;
2. teach students about plateaus in learning;
3. analyze student performance to detect flaws that require remedial instruction;
4. help increase the learner's understanding of the task;
5. emphasize the need for additional practice;
6. recognize that emotions such as fear, hate, and boredom may create plateaus in learning because the student's mind is not free to concentrate on the task being learned; and
7. provide encouragement and continued practice so the steps of a procedure become automatic and the student can concentrate on the next phase of achievement.

Plateaus of long duration may mean that (1) improper habits have been formed, (2) material being studied is beyond the student's ability, or (3) the instructor has failed to give needed assistance and motivation.

Repetition or Practice. Cognitive learning and psychomotor learning are bolstered by frequent repetition of the same pattern of relationships. While a single trial can result in learning, most instructional strategy recognizes the value of repetition or practice. For example, only one trial may be required for a child to learn that a stove is hot even though no flame is present. Obviously this is a dramatic event in which a strong sense of pain is associated with an event. Most classroom events are not this dramatic or sensory; therefore, most learning takes more than a single trial.

As the learning task becomes more complex and involves more associations, repetition becomes increasingly important. Little or no repetition may be needed for simple or isolated behavior like verbalizing the names of objects or pronouncing words. However, practice does become important in applying abstract theories, using mathematical or statistical principles to solve problems, or developing such higher level skills as playing a musical instrument or learning to use a personal computer.

Too frequently there is not enough time for the needed repetition or practice in school settings. As a result, the learner may not develop the necessary level of skill. Usually, frequent, short periods of repetition are better than long periods of repetitive practice, especially if the learner begins to tire or lose interest. This is why review sessions, frequent quizzes, and drills are so important in the learning process.

Feedback and Reinforcement. Both the instructor and the student assess learning by observing the student's behavior or performance. These evaluations provide important feedback regarding the teaching-learning process. Practice does not involve precise repetition of the same behavior. Instead, behavior varies slightly with each trial and may yield different results. These different results teach learners about the relationship between specific behaviors and results. By using this feedback, learners gradually become more skillful. As a result, performance increases with practice until a plateau is reached, or the skill is mastered, or the learners reach their maximum performance level.

All behavior produces some outcome, and therefore individuals receive feedback that creates positive or negative reinforcement. Reinforcement guides behavioral change and provides motivation for continued action. Reinforced behaviors tend to be repeated, and behaviors that are not reinforced tend to be extinguished. Reinforcement is usually effective when it is immediate. Self-instruction materials make use of this principle by presenting learning tasks that can be completed successfully. These correct responses provide immediate feedback and reinforcement in the form of success. Incorrect responses are not reinforced since the immediate feedback spells failure.

LEARNING TYPES AND CONDITIONS

Learning results from associations within the brain. It is primarily an internal process, though it may include motor or physical components. These associations may be simple and involve only two or three elements, such as the relief of pain by wearing earmuffs on cold ears. More complex associations involve retrieving previous associations from long-term memory and using them to solve a new problem.

Learning is different from the natural changes created by human growth and development. The fact that a six-year-old child can jump twice as high as a four-year-old child is more a result of growth than learning.

Educational psychologists refer to this range of learning as types or levels of learning. Although there are many explanations of levels of learning, one of the most comprehensive is provided by Dr. Robert Gagné in the publication *Conditions of Learning*. The levels of learning classified by Gagné fall into eight categories. These include signal learning, stimulus-response learning, chaining, verbal association learning, discrimination, concept learning, principle learning, and problem solving. See Figure 2-2.

Learning is not synonymous with performance, but a student's performance may be the instructor's only means of judging how much that student has learned. To think about the eight levels of learning, it is useful to consider the stimulus (S) to learning as input and the response (R) from learning as output. A *stimulus* is anything brought into the learner through the sensory mechanism, for example, sight, touch, or hearing. A *response* is an observable behavior resulting from a stimulus. Responses permit the instructor to judge the extent to which an individual has changed or learned. In its simplest form, a system consists of input-processor-output. Using a systems analogy, learning occurs in the processor. The association and mapping that occur cannot be observed directly. As a result, the instructor infers learning by observing the learner's performance. Educational psychologists diagram the process as S-R or some variation of this symbolism.

Instructors must focus on the internal and external conditions that facilitate learning to apply the simple to complex levels of learning categorized by Gagné. Instructors who use repetition and reinforcement, teach for transfer, and allow students to learn by doing can influence external conditions.

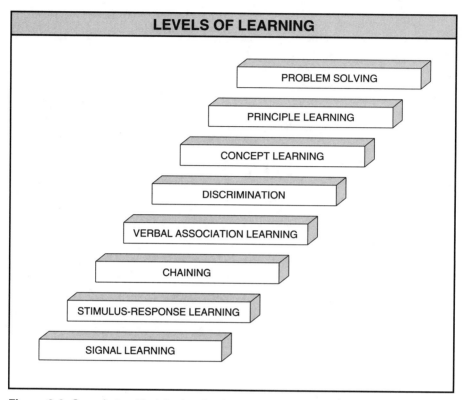

Figure 2-2. Gagné classified the levels of learning into eight categories.

Levels of Learning

Regardless of the level of instruction, the conditions under which learning takes place largely determine the extent to which mental or mental-motor associations are mapped into memory and coded into the central nervous system. To facilitate learning at this level, instructors should (1) specify the content structure, (2) identify prerequisite capabilities, (3) plan instruction carefully, and (4) assess learning. The fundamental question related to learning is, "What new capability was created?"

Signal Learning. Signal learning takes advantage of involuntary responses like eye blinking, nerve reflex, or salivation. The most frequently cited example of signal learning is Pavlov's experimentation with dogs. When feeding was accompanied by a given sound, such as a bell, the dogs would begin to salivate when they heard the sound, even though no food was present. The signal or stimuli produced an involuntary response. Another example is the increased heart rate and tingly feeling associated with fear of heights, water, or the dark.

Stimulus-Response Learning. This type of learning is more important to the typical instructional process than signal learning because it involves voluntary response to a stimulus. Typically the responses are motor responses such as moving a part of the body or speaking. In fact, the stimulus itself is generally motor-related. For example, a parent may teach a child to say "daddy" or "mama" by presenting the stimulus (the word itself) immediately followed by reinforcement (praise, hugging, a pat on the head) for any sound that is close. Learning to type involves stimulus-response learning since one learns to press keys when the letters or numbers are presented visually.

Chaining. This simple, common level of learning involves the connection of two or more previously learned stimulus-response patterns. The English language is replete with verbal chains as revealed in studies of word association. Examples such as "table and chair," "horse and buggy," or "lock and key" imply two different objects that one has learned about and chained together. In this type of learning, two separate association patterns, or links, are prerequisite to the chaining. For chaining to occur efficiently, the two links should occur close together in time. This timeliness or close sequencing is *contiguity*.

Verbal Association Learning. When adults with a sizable vocabulary encounter a new word, the chaining process occurs with ease. However, individuals with limited vocabularies may not know the prerequisite root word, prefix, or suffix that would enhance the verbal association. Previous knowledge of the prefix *bi* and the word *cycle* greatly facilitates an understanding of the word *bicycle*. The presentation of visual stimuli, such as a picture, facilitates verbal association between words. For example, a picture of a bicycle clearly shows two wheels.

Discrimination. Learning to classify and make multiple discriminations is a complex task involving a host of variables and associations. It requires differentiation among similar stimuli and the responses assigned to each group of stimuli. An example is the learning that allows many young people to easily identify new car models. Each year brings changes in body styles, motor sizes, and accessories. Young people who fervently want to own a car can soon identify and name both this year's models and older ones. Each model contains a complex set of stimuli that evokes a response (model name). When a number of these S-R connections are brought together, multiple discrimination is involved.

Interference (an increase in the number of associations with previous S-Rs) occurs as the learning task becomes more complex. The new chain or set of associations interferes with the retention of a previously learned set of associations. This interference is the basis of forgetting something previously stored in one's memory.

Concept Learning. Higher levels of learning distinguish the human from other species. Abstract representations such as up and down, near and far, between, or beneath are concepts formed through an internal neural process. A concept is a class or group of stimuli that have common characteristics. The stimuli may be ideas, persons, events, or things; however, all stimuli do not refer to concepts. For example, book is a concept, while *Instructors and Their Jobs* is not a concept. It is a specific book or stimuli. Tasty food is a concept, while chocolate ice cream is a particular food. Baseball is a concept, while the College World Series is a particular event. In other words, a concept refers to a whole class of stimuli rather than to a particular stimuli. For example, when students learn the concept of cubic shape, variables of color, size, or material will not alter the basic concept. Likewise, when the concept of middle is grasped, the learner can identify anything (animal, vegetable, or mineral) in terms of its position in the middle. Concepts represent human attempts to classify experiences, even though individuals differ in their conceptual thinking. Concepts are important to learning because they help one to group or categorize stimuli.

Unique features of a concept vary from one concept to another. Such variations are known as attributes. Concept attributes are important to learning because they provide detail and description that help one to differentiate between two or more concepts. For example, the concept of town may be differentiated from a city, on one hand, and from a village, on the other hand. A town is usually less populated than a city and usually more populated than a village. Other characteristics of town may also be evident, such as square miles, but population is one of its major attributes, since population can vary from town to town.

A concept may have one, two, or more attributes. For example, an apple may have five attributes such as: color, size, form, texture, and taste. Some complex concepts, however, may have a dozen or more attributes. Think about the concepts of equality, democracy, and happiness. Listing the attributes for any one of these concepts is no easy task! As the number of attributes increases, the difficulty in learning the concept increases. In learning complex concepts, students tend to reduce the number of attributes by learning some attributes and ignoring others, by combining attributes into a smaller number of clusters or patterns, or by giving attention to the dominant or more obvious attributes. Teachers should use a variety of instructional methods and techniques to teach complex concepts. Repetition, diagrams, demonstrations, and drills may help to emphasize obscure, yet important attributes of a concept. If teachers do not provide the emphasis needed to learn important attributes of a concept, students may learn only the most obvious attributes, thereby failing to understand the concept completely.

Principle Learning. Formal education is highly dependent upon the learning of rules or generalized principles upon which future action is dependent. These principles involve chaining two or more concepts, for example, round objects roll; gases expand when heated; fire burns things. This form of learning involves more than memorizing these principles; it requires understanding the inherent ideas. In fact, one can know the idea of the principle without saying the words. From a practical standpoint, the instructor must be certain that the learning observed is really a conceptual chain of understanding as opposed to a verbal chain. In the evaluation process, the student should be required to apply a principle instead of merely reciting it.

Problem Solving. *Problem solving* is the thought process in which previously learned principles are applied to a new situation. Problem solving involves the application of principles to make decisions or control circumstances. Because a lengthy chain may be involved in each of several principles applied to a given problem, the learner must first define the goal or problem. Once the goal is clearly in focus, the relevant principles must be recalled. The next step is the critical thought process through which the human mind combines or interrelates the principles. Sometimes a flash of insight reveals the solution, and a new higher order rule emerges for the individual's use.

As instructors gain insight into the ways people learn, they become increasingly effective. Because learning depends on experience, teachers do more than dispense information; they facilitate learning.

The principles and theory of learning are incomplete and, at best, can only provide guidance. Educational psychology is not an absolute science based on consistent, predictable laws like those that govern chemistry or physics. Nevertheless, instructors can use basic principles and processes to create instructional strategies that do facilitate learning. Effective instructors understand that learning must directly involve students, enabling them to gain a depth of understanding that maps the associations into long-term memory. In order to function effectively and make wise decisions, instructors must also understand the various levels of learning through which students progress and the part that repetition, reinforcement, contiguity, and prerequisites play in education.

Variables involved in instruction include (1) learners and their assets and liabilities, (2) instructors and their personal and professional differences, and (3) the instructional setting. Instructors must take these variables into account as they apply the theory and principles of learning. Teaching involves a substantial amount of decision making. Successful instructional decisions result from (1) knowledge of the subject being taught, (2) knowledge of the principles of learning and instruction, (3) an understanding of the learner's interests, abilities, and limitations, and (4) a careful consideration of timing and appropriateness under a given set of circumstances.

Questions

1. What are three primary factors that control an individual's learning?

2. In what way is learning defined as a mental process?

3. To what extent can learning occur in the absence of experience?

4. Must an individual's experience be purposeful for learning to occur?

5. How does prerequisite knowledge or skill influence learning?

6. What is the difference between learning and behavior or performance?

7. What distinguishes psychomotor learning from cognitive learning?

8. How can the thinking process result in learning?

9. How is forgetting related to long-term memory and the learning process?

10. What limitations are faced when attempting to learn to play a game by observation only?

11. How can learning by doing be incorporated into the lecture method?

12. Define transfer of learning.

13. Define negative transfer.

14. To what extent can an individual be taught to transfer?

15. What is the difference between a learning plateau and an individual's upper limit of ability?

16. To what extent is feedback and reinforcement possible without an instructor present during the learning process?

17. What is the principal factor that distinguishes a lower level of learning from a higher level of learning?

18. What type of learning takes advantage of involuntary responses?

19. What learning principle is applied when an instructor compliments a student?

20. What level of learning is exhibited when learners name and describe tools used in their area of specialization?

21. At what learning level does thinking result in new associations based on the relationship of two or more principles being applied to solve a given problem?

Activities

1. Describe a learning event that involves the association of some new knowledge with information previously acquired.
2. Discuss factors that should be considered by an instructor helping a student develop a psychomotor skill.
3. Ask three or four of your classmates to describe their visual image when you say "mountain," "sky," "dog." Record their responses and indicate the instructional implications.
4. Describe the impact that observation has upon trial and error learning.
5. Discuss how an instructor teaches for transfer.
6. Make a sketch of a learning curve showing that the learner overlearned a skill. Label the horizontal and vertical axes and parts on the curve.
7. List three examples of positive reinforcement.
8. List three examples of negative reinforcement.
9. Describe a learning event diagrammed S-R.
10. List eight levels of learning as categorized by Gagné and explain the concept of prerequisite learning as it relates to these levels.
11. Describe learning as an input-processor-output system.

Influences on Learning

INSTRUCTORS AND THEIR JOBS

3

INTRODUCTION

The instructor's knowledge of principles that influence the learning process is of little benefit without an understanding of key variables in the application of educational theories. Three sets of primary variables that influence learning are those related to the learner, the instructor, and the instructional process.

Variables that relate to the learner have the greatest influence since the individual learner is the central figure in the teaching-learning process. Each individual is made up of a myriad of physical, emotional, and intellectual characteristics as well as interests, attitudes, and experiences that influence the outcome (learning) resulting from a given educational experience.

The instructor introduces another set of variables to the teaching-learning equation. Just as no two individuals are alike, no two instructors are alike. Interaction between one instructor and a learner or a group of learners differs from the interaction of another instructor and other learners. While some principles of human interaction can be used by all instructors, the exact manner in which these principles are applied varies with each instructor.

For purposes of discussion, the instructional process is described separately for learners and instructors, but in reality these three sets of variables interact in the teaching-learning interface. The instructor's technical competency and manner of executing and evaluating instruction exert a substantial influence upon the learner's success.

INDIVIDUAL DIFFERENCES

While no two individuals are alike, from an instructional standpoint, it is important to recognize which differences among individuals cause them to learn differently. Individuals differ in their physical characteristics, such as height, weight, and color of eyes and hair. These physical characteristics have little or no effect on learning.

The instructor must be sensitive to an individual's other, less obvious differences, which have a tremendous impact on learning. These differences include mental ability, personal interests, emotional stability, experience, and knowledge. As a result of basic potential, training, and experiences, learners differ widely in what they have learned and the level of competency they can reach in a given period of time.

Certain learners respond best to one approach while others respond best to another approach. For example, some learners respond to visual materials while others respond better to materials presented orally. Genetic differences lead to differences in learner capacity and potential. Likewise, individuals develop differently because of their environment and their experiences. These differences cause differing responses to instructional strategies.

The fact that individuals differ provides a significant challenge to an instructor. The effective instructor consistently observes, listens to, and tries to understand each student. In casual observation of an instructor and a group of learners, one tends to notice an instructor teaching and a learner learning. The instructor, however, must understand and teach each individual in the group, as only individuals within the group learn. Some members of the group will need guidance, encouragement, extra instruction, more practice, or more challenging assignments than others. Decisions must be made regarding each individual's level of achievement, and ways must be found to help learners achieve maximum potential.

Individuals differ in emotional maturity, ability to understand complex concepts, physical coordination, learning speed, and in other ways that may influence their performance in a learning situation. The instructor must know each member of the group as a unique person in order to facilitate individual learning. This is one reason why large classes are often unsuccessful and why mass media, such as radio and television, can only supplement the instructional process.

Diversity

In the years ahead, instructors can expect to have a greater number of students from a mix of ethnic and racial backgrounds. Judy and D'Amico, authors of

Workforce 2020, discuss gradual changes in the ethnic and cultural composition of the American population. Based on Census Bureau projections, Judy and D'Amico report that the proportion of African-Americans, Asians, and Hispanics is increasing gradually yet steadily in the American population. In fact, by 2020, white non-Hispanics will comprise little more than 64% of the total population, down from 80% in the 1980s; African-Americans will comprise almost 13%, up from 11% in 1980. In terms of percentage growth, Asians will be the most rapidly growing minority group in America. Asians will represent more than 6% of the total population by 2020. In terms of numbers, Hispanics will far exceed all other minority groups, increasing from 9% of the population in 1990 to more than 37% by 2020. The diversification of America's ethnic and racial composition is more noticeable in some geographic regions than in others. While ethnic and racial changes appear to be slow in the Northeast and Midwest, changes in the western and southern regions of the country are occurring rapidly. In fact, Judy and D'Amico report that by 2020 individuals of Hispanic origin will comprise 42% of California's total population; Asians will comprise 18%, and white non-Hispanics will comprise about 33%.

Another factor impacting the learning environment may be the gender composition of individual classes. The number of males and females enrolled in courses and programs nontraditional for their gender is expected to continue to increase. In particular, as the number of females entering and remaining in the workforce continues to increase, so do the numbers of females preparing for traditionally male-dominated occupations. It is not unusual for females to be enrolled in programs such as agriculture, automotive mechanics, computer technology, or welding. Likewise, an increased number of males are opting for work and study in traditionally female-dominated occupations such as vocational business education and healthcare. Regardless of the age, racial, ethnic, cultural, gender, or educational background of learners, the instructor should develop ways to manage student behavior effectively.

Educational and Economic Disadvantages. Various labels have been used to identify students who are at risk of failure or dropping out of school. These learners are in an environment or have certain characteristics that impede learning, and they require special services and assistance in order to succeed in vocational and technical education programs. Two of the most commonly served groups are students with educational disadvantages and those with economic disadvantages. Students whose overall grade point average is less than a 2.0 on a 4.0 scale, who fail to pass a minimum high school competency examination, or who have standardized scores in the lower 25th percentile of their class are generally referred to as having educational disadvantages. Individuals whose family incomes are at or below the poverty level as determined by the Secretary according to the latest available data from the Department of Commerce are said to be economically disadvantaged. Such individuals qualify for the free school lunch program and are eligible for Aid to Families with Dependent Children (AFDC). A student who is educationally disadvantaged may not necessarily be economically disadvantaged; and the converse is true, a student who is economically disadvantaged may not necessarily be educationally disadvantaged.

Today, more than ever before, instructors can expect a disproportionate number of students from special populations in their classes. Because of the differences in cultural and socioeconomic factors, ethnic background, values, abilities, and other factors, it is difficult to impossible to develop a comprehensive list of characteristics that apply to all learners who are educationally or economically disadvantaged or to predict their success or failure. However, as a group, students who have educational disadvantages and students who have economic disadvantages are more at risk of failure or dropping out of school than their peers. Research reveals that some of the characteristics of learners with educational disadvantages may be a lack of self-confidence, a poor educational background, low scores on intelligence tests, no parental guidance, disruptive behavior, and easy discouragement. Learners with economic disadvantages tend to lack interest in steady employment, have low expectations for achievement, depend on public assistance programs, have poor health and nutrition, have poor personal hygiene habits, have no entry-level employment skills, and lack opportunities for employment training. Due to previous failures and dissatisfaction with school, many of these students enroll in vocational and technical education programs in hopes of finding relevant instruction that will prepare them for a job. Such students pose challenges and opportunities for the instructor. They may require remedial or developmental work before they are able to achieve the program objectives.

Basic vocabulary lists, practice problems with sample solutions, clear and simple written and oral directions for assignments, and various types of instruction sheets can help give all students an added measure of confidence. Some of these students need only a little extra coaching from a competent and caring instructor and an opportunity to be successful. Student organizations, school clubs, or classroom teams that require active student participation are ideal for developing leadership and followship skills. This is especially true when students are involved in a project where they perceive some intrinsic or extrinsic rewards.

Inclusion. Federal laws mandate that all students be educated in the least restrictive environment to the extent possible. The regular classroom is the least restrictive environment for many students. The Education for All Handicapped Children Act guarantees that all children with disabilities are entitled to a free, appropriate public education and that an individualized education program (IEP) be developed for each child. An *IEP* is a written plan that specifies instructional goals, related services, and any special education or accommodations the student may need. Instructors are expected to serve on the IEP team, along with other school representatives, the child's parents (or a legal guardian), and the child, if possible. Instructor participation in the IEP process can help to answer questions and alleviate many concerns regarding the inclusion of students with disabilities in the regular classroom.

Instructors can communicate the prerequisite knowledge, skills, attitudes, and behaviors necessary to acquire employment in a given occupation, and they can use occupational analysis, commercially prepared materials, and advisory committees to identify logical exit points in their respective programs that offer potential employment for program completers. As a member of the IEP team, an instructor has an opportunity to provide valuable input for the annual goals and short-term instructional goals for a student. Specific course requirements, expected outcomes, beginning dates and the duration of special services, and tests or other information to be used in identifying whether or not the student has achieved the prescribed goals are included in the IEP.

Instructors have legitimate reasons to be concerned about the inclusion of students with disabilities in their classrooms and laboratories. The definition of "disabilities" in the legislation is very broad. The Americans with Disabilities Act (ADA) defines an individual with a disability as a person who has "a physical or mental impairment which substantially limits a major life activity, has a record or history of such an impairment; or is regarded as having such an impairment." For example, individuals who have been evaluated as being mentally retarded, hearing impaired, speech impaired, visually impaired, emotionally disturbed, orthopedically impaired, or who have specific learning disabilities are protected under the ADA. However, only those students with a disability who can benefit are integrated into the regular classroom setting. Some students may have disabilities so severe that inclusion in the regular classroom setting is not appropriate.

Given such a diverse group of students, an instructor may ask: "How will I evaluate this student?" "Shouldn't this student be expected to perform the same tasks as all other students and with the same degree of proficiency?" The fact is, all students perform some tasks better than other tasks; and few students perform a given task at the same level of proficiency. While research offers conflicting results on the impact of inclusion upon the academic and social development of students with disabilities, schools as well as places of employment must comply with the regulations of the ADA. Instructors who convey a positive attitude to students, parents, administrators, and other teachers and who remain flexible and sensitive to the special needs of students with disabilities have a greater chance of being successful. Instructors who are able to adapt instruction for students with a wide range of disabilities can create a positive learning environment and manage a successful inclusive classroom. Other aids to successful inclusion are developing specific criteria for inclusion so that all students know and obey class rules, assessing students frequently and giving constructive feedback, preparing students without disabilities to interact freely and positively with all students, and developing one's own professional expertise to better meet the needs of students with disabilities.

Aptitude, Ability, and Achievement

An individual's capacity to learn is of primary importance to the instructor. Students cannot learn material beyond their capacities regardless of the time or instructional method used. While educational processes tend to make a group of students seem alike, substantial differences in individual capacity continue to exist within the group.

In addition to differences in learner capacity, Piaget and others contend that certain types of learning are possible only after certain prior development has taken place. Instructors must recognize that students may not comprehend the subject matter or gain from a given learning experience unless they have certain prerequisite information. Even though the material to be learned is within the learner's capacity and may be understood later, it is quite possible that circumstances at the moment will not allow learning to occur. Learners clearly differ in their general patterns of strengths and weaknesses. Some are strong in verbal abilities but weak in quantitative or spatial abilities, while others have the opposite pattern of strengths and weaknesses.

Aptitude. *Aptitude* is an individual's potential to achieve in a given area. It is the potential, or "built-in" characteristics, that can be developed through training and experience. For example, a student may have aptitude for music, but not be able to play an instrument due to lack of training.

Aptitude tests attempt to measure or predict what the student can do after appropriate educational experiences. The specific aptitude that has the greatest impact on most cognitive learning in the school setting is intelligence (the potential to learn).

Ability. *Ability* is an individual's actual level of performance as contrasted to aptitude. It refers to what a student can do after education or experience. While a skilled carpenter with a sore hand may not perform well on a given day, the ability to perform still exists. A sick student may fail an examination, but the ability to demonstrate technical competency is only temporarily impaired due to the illness.

Achievement. *Achievement* is the attainment of specific goals based on given standards. When a student earns a high grade in a course, achievement is attained as measured by the instructor's standards. A good aptitude test, perhaps given years before the course, would have predicted such an outcome. When an aptitude test predicts success but achievement does not result during the educational process, it may be concluded that the student's interest in the subject, the instructor's methods, or other factors have affected learning.

If a student receives good grades in mathematics but not in English, a difference in aptitude for the two subjects may exist. Also, one teacher may be doing a better job or may have different standards than the other. Additionally, the student may simply work harder in mathematics than in English. Such factors (and many more) must be considered in understanding the achievement of a student.

Intelligence and Learning

Intelligence is the ability to learn. It is measured by assessing an individual's learning speed and ability to solve problems, understand relationships, and deal with abstract ideas.

Controversy continues regarding the amount of one's intelligence that is predetermined by genetic structure and the impact environment has on intellectual development and, especially, on measured intelligence. The most common position currently taken in the scientific community is that each individual's unique genetic pattern sets upper and lower limits on the possibilities for development. Very few individuals maximize their aptitudes. It is the instructor's responsibility to help learners achieve at increasingly higher levels.

IQ (intelligence quotient) is a means of relating general aptitude to age. The Stanford-Binet Intelligence Scale, originally developed in 1908 by Alfred Binet, is designed to be administered on an individual basis. The scales are standardized by mental age and compared to one's chronological age to provide an intelligence quotient.

The Wechsler scales (WISC & WAIS) measure several different verbal and performance abilities. The Wechsler scales are standardized by mental age and are compared with the individual's chronological age. Measures secured through use of these scales compare favorably with those from the Stanford-Binet.

The Lorge-Thorndike Intelligence Test was developed to test students in group settings. The test has five levels from kindergarten through the twelfth grade. Levels one and two use nonverbal tests and levels three, four, and five include both verbal and nonverbal tests.

The Davis-Eells Test places more emphasis on problem solving and less on verbal abilities. This test allows individuals to use several options to solve problems.

The California Test of Mental Maturity was constructed to measure intelligence as reflected in the individual's capacity to learn, solve problems, and respond to new situations. This test has five age levels and focuses on logical reasoning, spatial relationships, numerical reasoning, verbal concepts, and memory.

While IQ tests may yield a single score, they do not measure a single aptitude or ability. A large number of correlated yet different aptitudes are involved in intellectual functioning. No single aptitude or ability can be designated as intelligence. See Figure 3-1.

No simple, direct relationship exists between an IQ score and the size or functional efficiency of a particular area of the brain. Presently there is no common agreement concerning the number of human aptitudes that exist or how these aptitudes are related. Nevertheless, most of those who study this phenomenon accept the general developmental ideas of Piaget concerning the emergence of specific abilities as opportunities are provided for individuals to engage in specific developmental tasks.

INTELLIGENCE TESTS			
Name	**Author(s)**	**Developed or Revised**	**Form**
Stanford-Binet Intelligence Scale	Binet	1908	Individual
First Revision	Terman	1916	Individual
Second Revision	Terman	1937	Individual
Third Revision	Terman & Merrill	1973	Individual
Wechsler Intelligence Scale for Children (WISC)	Wechsler	1949	Individual
Wechsler Adult Intelligence Scale (WAIS)	Wechsler	1955	Individual
Lorge-Thorndike Intelligence Test	Lorge & Thorndike	1957	Group
Davis-Eells Test of General Intelligence or Problem Solving	Davis & Eells	1953	Group
California Test of Mental Maturity	Sullivan, Clark, & Tiegs	1963	Group

Figure 3-1. Intelligence tests are designed to be administered in individual and group settings.

Intelligence always refers to aptitude rather than achievement. An individual can be very intelligent yet accomplish very little in an educational setting. To compare one person with others of the same age, the person's score on a given intelligence test can be compared with the average score of hundreds of people of the same age. A person may score equal to, higher, or lower than the average of others of the same age. If the score of a 12-year-old student is the same as the average of thousands of other 12-year-olds from a given population for which the test was constructed, the student has an IQ of 100.

Traditionally, IQ was a ratio of mental age (MA) and chronological age (CA). The formula, IQ = (MA ÷ CA) × 100, was used to derive IQs. For instance, if a 10-year-old had a mental age of 12 years, the mental age (12) was divided by the chronological age (10) and multiplied by 100, giving an IQ of 120. A mental age of eight and a chronological age of 10 would result in an IQ of 80. The Stanford-Binet Intelligence Scale shows the distribution of intelligence quotients. See Figure 3-2.

DISTRIBUTION OF INTELLIGENCE QUOTIENTS		
Classification	**IQ**	**Percentages of all Persons**
Gifted	149 or above	.14
Very Superior	133 – 148	2.14
Superior	117 – 132	13.59
High Average	109 – 116	17.065
Normal or Average	92 – 108	34.13
Low Average	84 – 91	17.065
Dull or Borderline	68 – 83	13.59
Mild Retardation	52 – 67	2.14
Retarded	51 or below	.14

Terman, L. M., & Merrill, M. A. (1973). Stanford-Binet Intelligence Scale Manual (3rd ed.). Boston: Houghton Mifflin.

Figure 3-2. Intelligence is distributed across a wide range from high to low with the largest percentage of people in the middle.

The 1972 Stanford-Binet standardization testing program revealed that the average mental age in the United States had shifted upward, and, as a result, a child five years of age must have a mental age of five years and six months to be classified as average. As a result, IQ is now derived at each age level rather than calculated as a direct ratio of chronological age and mental age.

The growth of mental ability, like physical growth, is more rapid during the early years of life and then gradually levels off. For practical purposes, it can be assumed that full mental maturity is reached by most people between the ages of 20 and 25. The mental growth of a very intelligent person is faster and continues to a higher level than that of the person of average or below-average intelligence.

A true measure of intelligence can be expected *if* (1) the intelligence test is well-constructed, (2) the person being tested is from the same cultural background assumed by the test development team, and (3) the test is taken under ideal conditions when the individual is free from emotional or physical discomfort.

Under these conditions, the same test or similar forms of the test could be administered to an individual at different times during life, and the IQ would remain relatively stable, although the MA and CA would increase. The intelligence quotient is fairly constant for most individuals; however, the mental growth rate may fluctuate.

Factors such as intensity of interest, attitudes resulting from home conditions, and physical and emotional health may affect scores on a specific intelligence test. These same factors also affect success in learning.

Achievement is based on more than IQ. What a person does with intelligence depends on opportunity, general health, motivation, and other factors. Under the right conditions of education and environment, the individual with a measured intelligence of average or below can make contributions that are superior to those made by people of greater intelligence. Instructors must not limit an individual's performance level by low expectations any more than they should frustrate a learner by demanding a higher level of performance than aptitude and ability permit.

Physical Characteristics and Learning

Physical characteristics give little or no indication of intelligence, ability, or personality. An instructor's feelings and attitudes toward physical characteristics, however, may cause distortions in observation. Overgeneralizing from one or two examples can cause misjudgment. One may perceive differences that are not really there. An instructor who thinks high foreheads indicate high intelligence is more likely to think that students with high foreheads achieve better.

The professional instructor does not put all people of the same sex, age, or race into one classification. Very little can be determined about a person's ability or personality from physical characteristics.

While physical characteristics do not determine a person's aptitude for learning, they may influence the learner's self-concept, which does affect learning. Any negatively perceived physical characteristics may prevent students, especially those who are young or timid, from feeling accepted by fellow students or by their instructor. Unfortunate social experiences caused by the reactions of others to the student's physical characteristics or home background often lead to learning and behavior difficulties.

The effective instructor is alert to these possibilities and promptly takes whatever action is necessary to help the individual fit into the group in a normal way. Sensitivity to the feelings of students is part of the instructor's role, but even more important is the strategy used to help individuals overcome their hang-ups so that they can achieve their full potential.

Sex and Learning. In addition to the obvious physical differences between the sexes, adult males usually test higher on mechanical aptitude than adult females. Most of this test difference is due to early experience with mechanical things. In fact, most differences in the averages between men and women, except in physical strength and related characteristics, are probably a result of environment and educational experiences.

Age and Learning. The importance of age is easy to exaggerate. Often a difference in performance is attributed to age when other factors actually caused it. As a result, older persons may not get the chance to show their abilities. Compulsory retirement, regardless of the individual's level of competency, is being challenged by many competent psychologists and administrators.

In their ability to learn new mental skills, most individuals peak by age 25. From then on, during the person's working life, there is usually no significant decrease in the capacity to learn until physiological changes occur. These changes do influence the rate of learning. For example, physiological changes such as visual or hearing impairment often adversely affect learning.

Scientists, business leaders, and writers often reach their peak performance between the ages of 50 and 60. In skills of a physical nature, age is more significant. The average age of maximum performance in sports varies with the sport. For football, the age of maximum performance is between 20 and 30, but for less physically demanding sports like golf, peak performance age is estimated to be between 20 and 45.

Needs, Desires, and Interests

Needs, desires, and interests are significant instructional factors because they affect an individual's motivation to learn. A frequently cited way of classifying and describing human needs and desires is the structural hierarchy developed by Abraham Maslow, who theorized that experienced needs are the primary influences on an individual's behavior. According to Maslow's Hierarchy of Needs, an individual's behavior is determined to a large extent by a real or perceived need. In other words, individuals behave in certain ways in order to satisfy some need they perceive. According to Maslow's theory, an individual's unsatisfied needs become the prime source of motivation.

People's goals are a motivating force that can be channeled to help them learn more effectively. To gain insight into goal-related behavior, Maslow developed a hierarchical structure in which all human needs are categorized into five levels. These five levels of need relate to the natural process whereby individuals develop from an immature, primitive state to a more mature, civilized state. Individuals progress through these five levels of need as they would climb a ladder. They must experience security on the first rung in order to experience a need to step up to the next higher rung on the ladder. People's inability to fulfill a lower order need may cause them to maintain immature behavior patterns even though any one level of need may never be completely satisfied. There must be at least partial fulfillment of a given level of need before an individual can become aware of the next level of need and have the freedom and confidence to pursue it. Maslow's Hierarchy of Needs recognizes the five levels of need as (1) basic, (2) safety, (3) belongingness, (4) ego-status, and (5) self-actualization. See Figure 3-3.

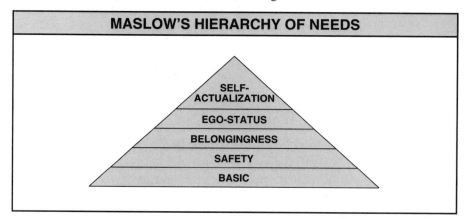

Figure 3-3. Human needs are classified in Maslow's Hierarchy of Needs. Needs at the lowest level must be met before an individual is motivated to pursue needs at higher levels.

The first level of the hierarchy represents *basic* needs of a physiological and survival nature. Needs at this level include shelter, clothing, sex, and food. In a culture where basic needs can be met by most people, there is little tension created concerning their fulfillment. Some individuals redefine this basic level upward to include such needs as physical comfort, a pleasant working environment, or money to provide for creature comforts.

The second level of the hierarchy relates to the individual's well-being or *safety* needs. As the individual at least partially fulfills basic needs, other desires will be created that relate to security, environmental orderliness, and the avoidance of risk. These needs are often satisfied through an adequate salary, insurance policies, fire and police departments, alarm systems, and door locks.

The third level of the hierarchy relates to *belongingness.* This is the need for belonging, acceptance, and appreciation by others. When one's needs for protection or safety have been met, there is less preoccupation with self and a need to form interpersonal relationships. This level of needs is met traditionally through the family, friendship, and group membership.

The fourth level of the hierarchy relates to the *ego-status.* This is the need to gain special status within the group as an individual begins to feel secure about relationships with others. This need-related tension is associated with ambition. These ego-status needs motivate the person to seek out opportunities to display competency that will secure social and professional rewards. Ego-status fulfillment is not within the individual's control because it depends on the appropriate response of others to the individual's efforts to perform in a superior way. However, if the person has gained satisfaction on level four, it is easier to move up to level five – self-actualization.

The fifth level of the hierarchy relates to *self-actualization* of an individual's personal growth. The individual may fulfill this need through internal motivation to become more creative, demand higher achievement, establish personal success criteria, and become more self-directed.

In formulating instructional strategy and dealing with individual learners, effective instructors are sensitive to the needs, desires, and interests of students. Students' needs for physical comfort and security must be met. Also, provisions must be made to accommodate student desires within the context of the class setting.

Need for Physical Comfort. The temperature level of the classroom or laboratory is significant. Students are easily distracted when they are either too warm or too cold. Substantial research evidence indicates that a higher level of achievement can be expected when students and instructors are comfortable. When feasible, the student should be seated for lectures, discussion sessions, and demonstrations.

Need for Security. Clean, well-lighted classrooms and laboratories as well as safe working conditions help meet student needs for security and provide a positive learning environment. Learning is not easily facilitated in an environment where a student is afraid or anxious. The instructor must provide a setting where students feel that they will not be injured or subjected to physical or emotional abuse.

Students need to feel that with reasonable effort there is a good possibility for success. A threatening environment in which failure is highly possible leads to insecurity. The instructor must be approachable so that a student's anxiety level can be minimized.

Need for Acceptance. Students should be treated as individuals. Encourage friendships and acceptance in the group. Showing respect for students, without becoming their pal, wins students' respect. The effective instructor is rewarded by the achievements of students and their respect through the years.

Instructors should learn the names of students as soon as possible. Knowing a student's name has numerous positive values. Initially it sends a message of individual worth to the student. Subsequently it reinforces that sense of worth. Recognizing individual differences in students and responding to those differences encourages learning. Students realize when an instructor has a genuine interest in them and will work hard to maintain that interest.

Need for Recognition and Approval. The effective instructor finds ways to provide recognition for achievement. Students must understand class standards and have opportunities to measure themselves against those standards. It is a sure sign of a poor learning environment when a student says, "I don't have any idea of how I am doing in this course." Students must know when they have done a good job. Grades are not the only way in which this recognition can be accomplished. Sometimes a few words or a pat on the back from the instructor meets a substantial need.

The instructor must be discreet in providing words of praise through private conversation or a note on the student's paper. An instructor's good intention may work to the disadvantage of students if those who are praised for good work become the scapegoats for poor achievement of others in the class. While it is appropriate to post examples of good student work, it is better to omit students' names. Likewise, when posting examination results, the students' identity should be masked. This practice saves much grief for both low and high achievers. Calling students by name and providing recognition for something well done pay dividends in terms of student motivation and higher levels of productivity.

Need for Self-Respect. Students' attitudes and feelings have great impact on the effectiveness of learning. All students desire to be respected. As indicated in Maslow's Hierarchy of Needs, the ego-status level represents a substantial set of needs. Society provides many examples of people who have sought recognition in both positive and negative ways in order to gain self-respect.

Effective teaching requires that individuals be helped to satisfy some of their ego-status needs. Effective managers are aware that good wages, steady employment, and physical comforts are not enough to develop high morale and productivity among employees. One of the most important needs is self-respect and the respect of others.

Need for Success. It has often been said in educational circles that "success begets success and failure begets failure." The need for success is important in terms of Maslow's Hierarchy of Needs. First individuals need to have others recognize their success. Then, at the level of self-actualization, the most important need is for individuals to consider themselves successful according to their own internally defined criteria.

In an educational setting, success is typically defined as the achievement of certain standards or objectives preestablished by the instructor. Students should understand the basis on which they are being judged so that they have a reasonable chance of being successful.

Projects, problems, and other learning activities should be consistent with the objectives of the course. The evaluation process should also be consistent with the objectives of the course and should be well-known. All assignments should be prepared carefully so that success is possible with reasonable effort. Assigned problems and tasks should increase in difficulty as the course progresses so students are challenged to do their best, continually working from one level of success to another. In some types of instruction, provision can be made for assigning tasks of varying complexity so that each student can achieve to a maximum level irrespective of the achievement level of others.

Time requirements can be varied so that slower or less able students can achieve success even though it may take longer. However, when occupational competency is required, all persons who are to be certified by the instructor as occupationally competent must reach some established standards, and time may be a variable that cannot be compromised.

Whenever possible, challenging experiences should be provided for the more able students in class so that they may exceed the standards and move on to higher levels of self-actualization if their ability permits. Supplemental materials and activities should be planned to challenge the most able students.

Student Interests. Students give greater attention to a learning task when they have a high level of interest and, as a result, they learn more effectively. Therefore, the instructor must find ways of relating the subject at hand to the interests of students. Instructors can often spark interest by relating the content to a current event, a personality, or to an interesting or humorous story. A few minutes taken to capture students' attention can pay valuable dividends in terms of increased learning. Instructors cannot depend on the internal interests and motivation of students. External stimuli must be utilized.

Variety in instructional methods also helps increase student interest. An audiotaped or videotaped interview with an individual who works in the area for which students are being prepared may help students perceive the relevance of a given lesson. The creative and resourceful instructor must explore and exploit students' interests to increase instructional effectiveness and student learning.

Learner Frustration

When one wishes to do something and cannot, a feeling of annoyance and tension results. This condition is often referred to as *frustration*. Frustration resulting from the complexities of a fast-paced technological society is frequent and unavoidable. It can come from rain when a picnic is planned, a telephone busy signal, or unsatisfactory progress in an occupation.

Frustration occurs whenever there is conflict between an individual's desires and level of achievement. The greater the number of tasks that must be accomplished in one's daily life, the more difficult it is to be in control. When a person is frustrated, strong emotions affect behavior in ways that make little sense to the casual observer. The person whose behavior is difficult to understand may be frustrated. Regardless of the cause, frustration can interfere with the individual's attention to the learning task. It should be acknowledged that some degree of tension may be desirable in a learning situation as it can cause an individual to pay attention and work harder at the task. Too much tension, however, leads to frustration and interferes with the learning process.

Instructors should know the causes and reactions to frustration in order to better understand their own behavior and the behavior of supervisors and students. Some common frustrations are:

1. frustration with impersonal problems;
2. frustration with people;
3. frustration with rules and regulations; and
4. frustration with limitations.

Frustration with Impersonal Problems. A stalled engine and a flat tire are examples of impersonal problems that cause frustration. It is not unusual for anyone in such situations to feel tension and become angry. Nevertheless, this tension and frustration must be controlled and kept in perspective. People who exert control may still reveal anger or frustration, but they keep the bad situation in perspective and do not allow it greater influence on their lives than the event merits.

Frustration with People. Although other people may help us obtain our goals in life, they may also stand in our way. Every person is a complex combination of needs, values, abilities, desires, and opinions. It is inevitable that people get in each other's way. Good human relationships satisfy many needs and desires; however, even the most perfect relationships are likely to be frustrating at times. The parent loves the child, but sometimes one frustrates the other because each wants something different at a given point in time.

Most adults learn to let others have their way at least temporarily and to at least partially hide their feelings. Frustrations in adults, therefore, may be less obvious than in children. For example, there are fewer fistfights among adults, but frustration shows up in other ways.

Frustration with Rules and Regulations. All organizations have rules and regulations. Most of these are recognized as necessary and beneficial to the organization in the long run. At the same time, these regulations interfere with one's freedom since they restrict an individual's actions from time to time. Those enforcing the regulation, whether they are instructors, police officers, or supervisors, often become the target of frustration caused by that regulation.

Frustration with Limitations. Individuals may become frustrated when they cannot perform a task due to mental or physical limitations. For example, not recalling the details of a particular event or not being able to explain one's point of view are mental limitations based on poor memory and articulation. Not being able to drive a nail without bending it or not being able to back into a parking place are physical limitations based on lack of skill.

Choices must often be made between two equally appealing goals. The skilled technician may have to choose between staying at the bench, where satisfaction is achieved from performing high-quality work, or moving to a supervisory position with greater responsibility and higher pay. Regardless of the choice made, there is likely to be frustration afterwards. It is common to hear a supervisor express the wish to be back in the production area where life is remembered as being simpler and less frustrating. Instructors who become school administrators frequently long for the good old days when they were teachers.

Reactions to Frustration. Many situations lead to frustration. Although the specific situation varies, frustration results from some type of barrier to the achievement of a goal. For a time, the individual may look for some way of getting around the barrier. If these alternate routes to goal achievement are unsuccessful, the person tends to become emotional, which may give some temporary relief, although the resulting behavior may seem strange to those who do not realize the source of frustration. One of the most common forms of emotional reaction is *aggression,* in which one becomes angry and attacks someone or something in an emotional rage. Kicking a door, hitting a wall, or swearing at the driver of a slow-moving car are examples of aggressive behavior.

A more complicated form of aggression is seen in a parent who returns home from work and takes out personal frustrations on other members of the family. It should be understood that the parent may not realize or admit the cause of the frustration. There is simply a need to release the pent-up emotions caused by frustration. Another form of aggression is seen when individuals blame their problems on a convenient scapegoat, such as their supervisor, a coworker, or a relative.

Another reaction to frustration is *regression,* in which a childlike or unquestioning dependence is placed on another person or group to solve the problem. Crying or a strong, continuous desire to return to simpler days are examples of regression. These behaviors are sometimes desirable because they may relieve frustration. While it is quite normal to exhibit occasional aggressive or regressive behavior in the face of frustration, repeated behavior of this type is not helpful or healthy.

Fixation is repetition of a negative behavior in the face of frustration long after it should be apparent that the behavior is not solving the problem. For example, a driver may continue to turn the car key after it should be clear that something else must be done to start the car. Likewise, people may develop very fixed beliefs and attitudes by dwelling on the meaning of life or complex problems of world affairs and insisting on answers that do not exist. Such individuals do not meet new problems with an open mind. Any information contrary to preconceived beliefs is rejected. New ideas and points of view that are in conflict with preconceived answers are painful. An individual with such a fixation may blindly follow and fight for some movement that fits a given pattern of thinking. Milder forms of fixation are observed in individuals who have very narrow topics of conversation.

Other reactions to frustration include apathy and negativism. Some individuals, when faced with many frustrations, simply quit trying. Those who have faced frustrations with little success may try to escape either physically or emotionally. Some may keep moving to another location, job, or friend. In the case of a soldier, going AWOL (absent without leave) may be seen as the answer. Others may escape emotionally by daydreaming, going to the movies or nearest bar, or by taking up a hobby such as fishing.

A certain amount of escape is normal. It may bring about a change of pace and provide helpful relaxation. Psychological escape is harmful only when carried to extreme, such as when one loses the ability to separate reality from fantasy. Milder forms of this behavior occur when one has an inflated sense of self-importance.

Learning to Live with Frustrations. Individuals differ in their ability to adjust to frustration. Some seem to have more ability than others to cope with frustrating situations. The ability to withstand frustration comes partly from early experiences with frustrations that were not too severe or too frequent. Parents, by necessity, frustrate their children because the child's demands cannot and should not always be met. This is a normal developmental process in which human beings learn that their needs cannot always be met. Sometimes the needs of others must come before the needs of self. Individuals need these developmental experiences as a normal part of living. Conversely, however, children who are consistently frustrated in all or most desires may develop habits of mental escape that will be harmful later when they must face reality in a positive, constructive way.

Individuals can learn to tolerate frustration when they understand its nature and attempt to make reasonable adjustments. Instructors must keep in mind that people learn and act as they do because of their own drives, frustrations, and attitudes. Frustration in instructional situations is recognizable by symptoms such as poor achievement, discipline problems, gossip, exaggerated complaints, absenteeism, and accidents in shops and laboratories.

Behavior is always the result of something. People are not born lazy, mean, aggressive, stubborn, or fearful. Consequently, the instructor must look for causes rather than trying to deal with symptoms. The instructor must remain open to new and objective information in judging the student's motivations, attitudes, and behaviors.

Most people become frustrated, if only to a relatively mild degree. No one is completely free of frustration. The effective instructor must recognize extreme cases of frustration and seek advice from the school counselor or psychologist, or other professional sources. To some extent, an instructor can help to reduce frustration by following accepted procedures.

Performance Differences

If everyone in a group receives the same instructions, differences in performance should be expected. The larger the group, the greater the range of differences will be. That range of differences is also greatest when aptitudes and levels of achievement vary within the group. A person with great aptitude for a given task is likely to perform it better at any stage of training and gain more from training than someone with little aptitude for the task. Instruction improves the performance of each student, but it usually has the greatest effect on those who have consistently demonstrated good achievement. For many reasons, success tends to beget success. The instructor should promote achievement by knowing the students, encouraging individual abilities, and providing group and individual instruction as needed.

Know the Student. In order to facilitate student learning, the instructor should gather basic facts about each student. A simple form will help to compile these facts in an orderly manner. See Figure 3-4. In designing such a form, avoid asking for unnecessary information. Interview each student to complete the information required on the form. The interview process provides an initial opportunity for the instructor to begin to know the student.

Encourage Individual Abilities. Talk with and observe students to determine their abilities. Allow the students to use their abilities to develop at their own pace. Do not keep all students on the same problem or assignment. Encourage fast learners by assigning more difficult and complex learning tasks. Encourage slow learners by assigning learning tasks consistent with their abilities. Expect students to work up to their individual potential, and be sure they are aware of this expectation. Encouraging fast learners to help slow learners is an excellent learning technique for both groups.

Provide Group and Individual Instruction. The typical classroom method of group instruction is well-known to anyone who has attended school. Its primary advantage is the time saved in preparation and presentation of the subject for a group, as opposed to the time required for individual instruction. Although group instruction is quicker, instructors generally prepare more thoroughly for a class than for an individual. Mass media, such as television and films, emphasize the advantage of more thorough preparations and presentations when promoting their product.

The primary disadvantage of group instruction versus individual instruction is that individuals in the group rarely need exactly the same instruction at the same time. Fast learners are held back to the rate of progress made by the group as a whole, and slow learners cannot keep up with the group. Another disadvantage of group instruction is that considerable time may elapse before some students have an opportunity to apply information or procedures presented, and instruction may be forgotten.

```
Name _____  Date _____
            Last           First    Initial

Address _____  Phone _____

Age     _____


Do You Have Any Health Problems? _____

With Whom Do You Live? _____


                                        Starting Date and Approximate
    Work Experience (Start with Present Job)        Time on Each Job

_____    _____   _____
_____    _____   _____
_____    _____   _____


Military Experience

_____    _____
_____    _____


Education
                        Length           Did you Graduate?
School                  of Time          Degree or Diploma

_____   _____   _____
_____   _____   _____
_____   _____   _____
_____   _____   _____


Hobbies and Special Interests

_____
_____


Do Not Fill in Space Below This Line.
- - - - - - - - - - - - - - - - - - - - - - - - - - - - - - - - - - - -
Notes on Interview _____
                   _____
                   _____
```

Figure 3-4. Instructors should use a form to gather basic information about a student.

The best plan in most instructional situations is a compromise between group and individual instruction. Group instruction on basic material should be followed by individual instruction. Written instruction sheets, short on-the-spot discussions and demonstrations, and coaching provide individual instruction for students.

The interplay of ideas and experiences as students interact with the group and with other students is a distinct advantage of group instruction. For example, in supervisory training, a major objective is the development of attitudes. The skilled instructor draws on the experiences and ideas of the group to influence the attitudes of individual students.

INSTRUCTOR'S PERSONAL INFLUENCE

Physical characteristics of the instructor, although very evident, have little influence on the instructor's effectiveness or student learning. The instructor's attitude, relationship with students, and professional competency have a substantial influence on learning.

Attitude

The unconscious influence of the instructor's attitude upon students is difficult to estimate, but evidence suggests that it is substantial. Enthusiasm and a positive attitude are two basic keys to effective instruction. Genuine enthusiasm displayed by the instructor motivates students as it tends to be contagious. An instructor's positive attitude also produces a pleasant atmosphere in the classroom and contributes to student interest. Instructors who believe in the importance of their work are well-prepared and devoted to the student's best interests. These instructors have a positive attitude that shows, and students tend to respond the same way. The instructor who continually looks for new, interesting material and better methods of presentation brings instruction alive. Enthusiasm and pride in the job of instructing lead to improved performance. These characteristics are transmitted to students and reflected in their attitudes.

Relationship and Behavior

By the time a person becomes an adult and chooses to teach, most personality traits that affect interpersonal skills have been developed. By being aware of the impact of certain instructor behaviors on student motivation and interests, the instructor can maximize instructional effectiveness. Research has not revealed one dominant personality type that ensures instructional effectiveness, but certain instructor traits enhance positive relationships with students, while other traits foster negative relationships.

Identification with the Learner. A common difficulty with the technical specialist who becomes an instructor is the lack of appreciation or understanding of the student as a novice. The specialist, with a high level of competency, has long passed the beginner's level and often has forgotten the difficulties faced by a beginner. To be an effective instructor, the specialist must learn the students' entering capabilities, how to communicate effectively with them, and how to pace the instruction.

Most adults who voluntarily enter an educational or training program want to learn. Yet many come with only a vague notion of the nature of the instructional program. Some come because they are sent by their employers. Others believe that going to school will result in a better career or a changed lifestyle, which will bring them increased prestige. Few recognize the self-discipline and time required to succeed. The universal desire to learn is not as prevalent at the secondary level as attendance is mandatory. Additionally, the benefits of employment and job advancement are often too far removed to provide day-to-day motivation for learning.

It has been said that an education is the only thing students will pay for and not try to get their money's worth. While students may want a diploma, they may care little for the learning experiences that are part of the educational process. Effective instructors must motivate students to want to learn. Most courses provide a start toward the goal of subject matter mastery. Students should be motivated in a way that inspires them to continue developing their abilities long after they complete a given course.

Instructor Behavior. An instructor's behavior conveys certain messages to the student. Because of the leadership role of the instructor and the impact of the instructor's behavior upon a learner, the instructor's behavior must be under control at all times. Often instructors express themselves or assume a physical posture out of habit that inadvertently sends the wrong message to the students. For example, the instructor's facial expression when concentrating may convey a frown of disapproval to a student who asks a question. The instructor who stands with crossed arms may strike a defensive posture as perceived by students. The instructor who seeks to be definite or very clear about a given standard of performance may be viewed as being inflexible.

Instructors should be considerate, cooperative, complimentary, friendly, and involved with their students. This type of instructor behavior conveys interest in the student and the subject while promoting learning.

Motivation. One seldom performs a task without a prior need that motivates the action. Sometimes the motivation is obvious. People have lifted tremendous amounts of weight to free a person in danger of being crushed. The immediate need to free the person provided the motivation to perform the superhuman task.

It is not always easy to develop the type of learning environment in which a student will be motivated to learn. The thoughtful instructor attempts to provide reasons for studying the content at hand and explains the importance of learning the content. All too frequently, the instructor has a difficult time relating the subject to immediate needs of students. Unfortunately, if an instructor can give no better reason for studying than "because I said so" or "because it will help you in the next course," this obviously will not provide much motivation. Much of the alienation of youth in today's schools comes from the conflict between the school curriculum and the student's perceived need or desire to learn. Effective instructors continually explain the relevance for their subject area in order to provide motivation for learning.

Motivation is not a separate and distinct step in teaching. Everything that happens in the instructional process affects the student's interest and motivation. For instruction to be meaningful, it must be initiated at the learner's level. If the learner does not understand the material, it is the instructor's responsibility to verify that the prerequisite level of knowledge is obtained before new content is introduced. This may require supplementary assignments for individual students. It may mean securing help from individualized instructional materials in the library or learning center. It may mean that the student will need to take a prerequisite course. When this situation occurs, some action must be taken. Students faced with continual failure cannot be motivated to extend their best efforts to learn.

Reward and Punishment. Reward and punishment are useful tools for the instructor. Reward, or *positive reinforcement*, is by far the most useful. When learners are rewarded for completing a task correctly, they are provided with positive reinforcement. Punishment, or *negative reinforcement*, focuses on mistakes. Negative reinforcement tends to make a learner concentrate on errors rather than on the correct procedure. Obviously errors must be corrected, but this should be done in a helpful, positive manner and mixed with the recognition of good performance.

While approval from the instructor is a common form of positive reinforcement, the highest level of reinforcement is the intrinsic reward that comes from the individual's competency as demonstrated through performance. The instructor should encourage students to develop the ability to judge and take pride in a job well done. In this way, the greater skill or accomplishment becomes its own reward.

Instructors often find it much easier to criticize than to praise. This is a matter of individual personality or orientation. Students seldom do perfect work, but the instructor should see the positive elements of even a mediocre performance rather than emphasizing errors that must be corrected. Even though honest praise can be given in almost every situation, praise loses its effect when it is given too frequently and when not deserved. The effective instructor knows the students and understands the type of recognition that works best for them.

Grades, properly used, can provide useful motivation. However, there is often too much emphasis on grades since a letter or numerical grade is, at best, only a partial indicator of competency. To be effective, grades must not become the major source of motivation for learning. Also, if grades are to motivate and not discourage, they must be determined by careful judgment of several factors. The instructor has a responsibility to grade in a manner that stimulates rather than discourages students.

Reprimand. Attempts to coerce or compel students into good habits of thought and action nearly always fail. The instructor who applies more "heat" than "light" is more likely to arouse resistance than compliance. However, when the instructor sparks students' interest through a fair, firm, and friendly relationship, students are compelled from within, and their achievements are often outstanding.

Too frequently, reprimands are carried out in a way that provokes resentment and a strong desire on the part of the student to retaliate. Reprimands do not pay dividends. When it is necessary to reprimand, instructors should use only those methods that will help the student progress to a higher level of achievement. If possible, the reprimand should be provided in a way that stimulates respect for the instructor and an increased desire to participate in the learning process. In most instances, the reprimand should be a private affair between the student and the instructor. Seldom does a public reprimand accomplish any positive ends. When a reprimand is necessary, the effective instructor:

1. remains calm;
2. considers the feelings of the student;
3. discusses the matter with the student alone;
4. knows and uses the facts;
5. criticizes the mistake or behavior, not the student;
6. includes encouragement and praise for work well done;
7. suggests a constructive course of action; and
8. ends the conversation on a positive note by acknowledging the student's past achievement and positive attributes.

INFLUENCE OF INSTRUCTION

In addition to the individual learner and the instructor, the teaching-learning equation includes other important variables. These variables include the learning environment, organization for instruction, knowledge of results, and repetition and skill development.

Learning Environment

The setting in which the teaching-learning process occurs has great influence on learning. Some types of learning require a substantial amount of physical performance, and in these cases a laboratory with appropriate equipment is essential. For example, computers and printers are required for learning word processing and data processing. Some types of learning require simulation, and authenticity of the environment is essential. For example, airline pilots are trained on simulators, which create take-off, flying, and landing conditions.

Regardless of the nature of the learning environment, physical comfort of learners is a primary factor in effective learning. Learners are easily distracted by glare, movement, poor air circulation, lack of visibility, or uncomfortable temperature. The classroom or laboratory, as a learning environment, must meet requirements for physical comfort.

Organization for Instruction

The manner in which an instructional program is organized has a substantial influence on learning. Whether the instructional program is a course, a unit within a course, a lesson, a workshop, or a seminar, instructional effectiveness begins with organization. Advanced planning is an essential component to the effective organization of instruction.

Clear Directions for Learning. The first step in providing clear direction for learning is for the instructor to have a carefully conceptualized instructional plan. The instructional plan must include specific objectives and an outline of the content to be covered. Only with a clear instructional plan can the teacher create clear directions for the students. The next step is to design a strategy for communicating the instructional plan to students. Students must know the objectives they are to achieve and understand the conceptual framework for the content being presented.

No two students can be expected to have the same map of associations. It is easier for learners to make meaningful associations when they are aware of the structural framework from which the instructor is proceeding. Unfortunately, some instructors have a mistaken view that the objectives and framework of the discipline must be discovered by the learner. The lack of a framework causes the learner to become frustrated. There is much wisdom in the old adage, "If you want someone to learn something, tell them what it is you want them to learn."

Meaningful Learning Activities. After the instructor develops specific objectives for the educational program and clearly identifies the content to be learned, appropriate learning activities must be designed to help the learner achieve those objectives. Designing or selecting appropriate learning activities requires an understanding of the principles of learning as well as mastery of the course content. For example, if a psychomotor skill such as welding a corner joint is to be developed, the instructor must demonstrate the physical movements and provide opportunity for the student to learn by doing through systematic practice and repetition. Provision must be made for positive reinforcement. The learner must perceive the need for engaging in learning activities in order to be motivated to give the activity the attention and time that it requires.

Consistent Evaluation. Consistency within the organizational framework is required for instruction to have the most positive influence on learning. After objectives have been specified and meaningful learning activities have been provided to help learners achieve those objectives, an evaluation plan must be developed in a manner consistent with the objectives, content, and learning activities. Not only must the evaluation be consistent with other elements of the educational program, but the learner must perceive and understand the relationships among the program's various components.

Evaluation should not be viewed as a guessing game between the instructor and the students. There should be no surprises when tests or other evaluation activities are conducted. Students should know what is expected of them even though they may not be able to answer questions or perform the task that they were expected to learn.

The structural framework for the course, unit, and lesson must be understood and organized by the instructor. The nature of this framework must be revealed to the learner in appropriate ways so that learning is not a series of isolated and unrelated events.

Knowledge of Results

Knowing how well one is doing helps improve performance. This is true whether the subject is metallurgy, mathematics, or printreading. Knowledge of results or one's progress toward a goal or level of skill can provide motivation to improve. For example, a class in health occupations might visit a nursing facility so students could compare their work with standards required in the field. The instructor should evaluate students' work at frequent intervals and let them know how well they are doing in comparison to a known standard. The instructor plays an important role in helping students establish appropriate standards and in evaluating their achievement in terms of those standards.

Competition among individuals and groups may motivate greater effort; however, intense rivalry may be counterproductive. Ruthless competition among students in an instructional program can be counterproductive when emphasis is shifted from learning to winning.

Repetition and Skill Development

Repetition and guided practice are essential in skill development. Practicing tile setting, tightening bolts, and driving nails involves repeating certain neuromuscular (mental and muscle) connections correctly without conscious thought. When this occurs, the learner has developed a skill, a thoroughly established habit of performing a task in an efficient manner.

Since drill takes instructional time, it is often necessary to provide this kind of repetition in a laboratory setting or outside the regular classroom. Large group instruction does not provide a good setting for individuals to receive the supervised practice essential for skill development. For drill or practice to be effective, a clear understanding of the process rather than mere imitation is necessary.

Empirical evidence supports the assumption that distributed practice in learning is more effective than long periods of continuous practice. For example, in learning freehand lettering as a part of a drafting course, five 15-minute periods per week are more effective than one concentrated practice of 75 minutes. Factors such as boredom and fatigue are critical to decisions regarding length of practice sessions. The periods of practice should not, however, be too brief nor necessarily of equal length.

The principle of distributed practice is important in the development of physical skills. There are times, however, when one reasonably long period of concentrated study is more effective than several shorter periods. A two-hour period of concentrated effort on a drafting assignment may be better than several shorter periods of instruction. Adults can generally profit from longer periods of study than children because of their longer attention spans.

The experienced instructor learns to judge the effectiveness of various lengths of concentrated study and practice for each level of student and type of subject matter. When the number of errors in a student's performance begins to increase, it may be time to stop the practice until the student is more rested or until more time can be given to thinking through the task to establish the procedures and principles more clearly.

Overlearning is the continued practice of a task after it is understood and remembered readily or performed with a high degree of accuracy. Subject matter that can be remembered without hesitation after a considerable period of time may be overlearned. Many facts and principles that are used for further learning must be learned beyond the point of mere understanding. Such skills as writing, spelling, speaking, or hand tool processes should be mastered to the point where they can be put to use without much thought.

Frequently, instructors must decide whether to teach each component part of a subject well before going on, or to teach the whole subject, to some extent, before drilling on the parts. This is often referred to as the "whole versus part" method. While it is possible to learn a five-minute speech all at once, a longer speech may be more easily learned in segments over several practice sessions. Complex tasks involving many identified skills and bits of information cannot be practiced as a whole from the beginning. In these situations, logical divisions must be made and learned separately.

Using Emphasis. The principle of repetition also applies to oral instruction. Emphasizing key points and repeating them in different ways has a positive influence on learning. An important element of effective instruction is the emphasis of key elements in a lesson to gain the learner's attention. The following techniques apply to the use of emphasis as an instructional method:

1. repeating the statement several times during the period;
2. writing the word, term, or phrase on the chalkboard or overhead projection transparency;
3. preceding the material with such words as "remember this," "make note of this," or "this is an important point";
4. pausing before and after a statement that has particular importance;
5. varying the speech pattern; and
6. using dramatic gestures.

The overuse of a given technique may decrease its effectiveness. The instructor's personality and teaching style as well as the nature of the subject may dictate which form of emphasis is most appropriate.

Learners are influenced not only by their assets and liabilities but also by the instructor. Just as learners vary, so do instructors. Physical differences among individuals have little or no impact, but variables related to personality and behavior have positive and negative influences on learning.

The instructional program is a major factor that impacts directly on the level of learning. The instructor has primary responsibility for the learning environment and the organization of the instructional program. Learning can be facilitated through the organizational structure of the course, unit, or lesson. The purpose of learning and the content to be learned must be communicated to the student. Learning is facilitated when students have a clear understanding of what they are learning and why they are learning it. The learners must receive feedback about their efforts. This involves frequent evaluation and prompt return of graded tests, papers, and reports. When the development of skills is desired, students must realize that correct procedures are essential and a high level of skill will not be possible without a substantial amount of practice.

Questions

1. To what extent do physical differences among individuals affect learning?
2. How does aptitude differ from ability?
3. What is the difference between intelligence and IQ?
4. Why is it desirable for an individual to take more than one standardized intelligence test?
5. What factors could result in a reduced ability to learn by individuals above the age of 60?
6. What impact does the principle of individual differences have on an instructor conducting group instruction?
7. What is the relationship between motivation and Maslow's Hierarchy of Needs?
8. What are the five levels of Maslow's Hierarchy of Needs?
9. To what extent can there be positive results from frustration?
10. To what extent is student learning affected by the instructor's behavior?
11. What is the fundamental difference between positive and negative reinforcement?
12. What major factors within the instructional process influence learning?
13. To what extent is practice necessary for skill development?
14. Under what circumstances does continued practice lead to limited improvement or even the possibility of decreased performance?
15. What is meant by the concept of overlearning?
16. How will diversity in the classroom impact the instructional process?
17. What is the difference between students with educational disadvantages and those with economic disadvantages?
18. In what ways can an instructor be responsive to inclusion?

Activities

1. Give specific examples of ability, aptitude, and achievement.
2. List three physiological effects of aging that might have negative effects on learning.
3. List three factors that give an older person an advantage in a learning situation.

4. Critique the following statement and identify its faulty premise: Everyone is created equal; therefore, if people try hard enough, they can accomplish anything.

5. Based on the principles of learning and individual differences, explain why it is sometimes necessary for an instructor to use a variety of techniques as well as individualized instruction.

6. Explain the relationship between Maslow's fifth level of need and the concept of the instructor as a facilitator of learning.

7. Explain the relationship between the planning and evaluation process in terms of Maslow's fifth level.

8. List three causes of frustration among learners.

9. Differentiate between aggression and regression.

10. Describe individual differences that have a substantial influence on learning that cannot be overcome by hard work and a positive attitude.

11. Describe the positive and negative impact on learners of an instructor's high level of skill and extensive experience.

12. Describe the negative influence grades may have upon student motivation to learn.

13. List four environmental factors that have an adverse impact on learning.

14. Describe the relationship that should exist between objectives, learning activities, and evaluation.

15. Explain the principle of distributed practice as it relates to such factors as the learner's attention span, fatigue, and interest.

16. List the kinds of diversity among students that you as an instructor might experience in your classroom.

17. Explain your concerns regarding teaching in an inclusive classroom.

Identifying Content and Specifying Behaviors

4

INTRODUCTION

An instructor's goal is to increase student competence in a predetermined subject area. Effective instructors know the objectives students should achieve by the end of the course. Certain behaviors are to be exhibited if the instructional program was a success. The student knows more, is able to do more, and/or exhibits different attitudes as a result of the instructional experience.

The knowledge, skills, and attitudes acquired are, in a real sense, the content of the curriculum. Depending on one's orientation, content may be synonymous with competencies to be acquired through a given educational experience. Many instructional design specialists, however, argue that individuals have acquired a competency only when they are able to perform a given task. This ability to perform typically requires that an individual has gained certain knowledge, skills, and/or attitudes. Therefore, competency depends on learning content in a manner that allows performance of tasks relevant to the field of endeavor.

Identification of content in vocational and technical education may be approached in several ways; however, the fundamental goal is careful investigation of occupational tasks. These tasks are often identified as the competencies required for workers to perform effectively in their occupation. Tasks or competencies are dissected to identify specific behaviors that competent workers exhibit. For the purpose of designing an instructional program, these behaviors (skills, knowledge, attitudes) must then be transformed into performance objectives that set parameters for instructional planning.

The fundamental reason for designing an instructional program in vocational and technical education is to enable learners to acquire occupational competency. The scope of the instructional program may be broad or specific. Regardless of the program's scope, the goals of the program, course, or lesson must be carefully defined and clearly communicated before an effective instructional program can be designed and conducted.

ANALYSIS

Analysis is the concept of reducing a complex whole into component parts. This concept is not unique to education; it has universal application. Anything that is composed of parts, or components, can be analyzed, such as a play, an automobile, an occupation, or a task within an occupation. Some individuals are more adept at analyzing than others; however, it is an essential competence for instructors to develop.

To illustrate the process of analysis, visualize a deck of playing cards. The deck is a complex whole made up of 52 individual cards. As the deck is analyzed, however, the first step is to subdivide the deck into 26 red cards and 26 black cards. Each set of cards can be subdivided into two additional sets based on the design (suits) of the cards. Each suit can then be divided into 10 numbered cards (ace = 1) and three face cards. Even further, each group of numbered cards can be identified by specific number, and each face card can be identified as either a jack, queen, or king. This illustration yields predictable results since decks of playing cards are uniform.

More variations result from an analysis of things that differ. For example, if one were to analyze a suit of clothes, the number of pieces would have to be agreed upon first. Is a suit just a jacket and a single pair of trousers, or does it include a vest and/or a second pair of trousers? After the nature of the complex whole has been ascertained, the first division is the parts of the suits, either two, three, or four items. Then each part is studied to identify the component parts (sleeves, lapels, pockets). As the analysis continues, one must decide which components are always present, or common, and which are sometimes present, or optional. For example, pocket flaps are clearly an optional part of a suit while pockets of some form are a commonality.

OCCUPATIONAL ANALYSIS AND CURRICULUM DEVELOPMENT

The analysis process is applied to curriculum development in vocational and technical education. *Occupational analysis* is the dissecting of selected jobs into their component skills, functions, and competencies for the purpose of tailoring instruction and training to meet specific job needs.

The application of specific occupational analysis techniques for the purpose of identifying content for a curriculum or even a course is typically not required of an instructor, especially a beginning instructor. Analysis, however, is practiced daily by instructors as they prepare demonstrations, lectures, laboratory assignments, and so forth.

Instructors must be familiar with the several means by which content for vocational and technical education programs are identified. Personal experience alone is an inadequate base upon which to identify the content for an educational program. Regardless of the strategy employed by a school district, an employer, a community college, or governmental agency to analyze an occupation for the purposes of developing an educational program, three major steps must be taken:

1. Job tasks must be identified.

2. Tasks must be analyzed to identify steps of procedures, knowledge, equipment, safety precautions, and worker traits.

3. Content must be translated into performance objectives.

The key element in occupational analysis is identification of job tasks. A *job task* is a complete unit of work performed on the job that results in a completed product or service that has value to a consumer. While the approach used to identify these tasks provides a measure of discord among curriculum specialists, the reality that the tasks must be identified, analyzed, and classified is well accepted.

Three primary approaches to the identification and verification of job tasks are:

1. Meeting with groups of workers in a given job or occupation.

2. Observing and interviewing individual workers on the job.

3. Submission of a tentative list of tasks to workers and/or supervisors.

After job tasks are identified and verified, they must be analyzed to determine (1) performance steps, (2) specific knowledge for effective performance, (3) specialized tools and equipment, (4) general related information, (5) safety information, and (6) critical attitudes essential for successful employment and advancement on the job. The third approach is most often used in mature occupational areas where a program is being brought up-to-date. For example, tentative tasks can be developed from a review of textbooks, handbooks, curriculum materials of other schools, or an analysis previously conducted by another organization or agency.

Developing a Curriculum (DACUM)

Developing a Curriculum (DACUM), an approach to occupational analysis, was imported from Canada in 1975 by Robert E. Norton and James B. Hamilton of The National Center for Research in Vocational Education. The process has been widely adopted throughout the United States and in a number of other countries.

Process Overview. The DACUM process is based on three assumptions:

1. Expert workers can define and describe their job more accurately than anyone else.
2. Jobs can be described in terms of tasks that successful workers in that occupation perform.
3. All tasks require certain knowledge and attitudes.

DACUM depends upon a panel of expert workers who analyze an occupation in terms of workers' duties and tasks. The process is efficient because it does not require the development of questionnaires or the use of surveys or interviews.

Under the guidance of a facilitator, the panel members perform a systematic analysis of their occupation. Steps involved in the analysis include:

1. Identification of the occupation's duties (general areas of competence).
2. Identification of tasks that comprise each duty in precise action terms (task statements).
3. Review of task statements for completeness and accuracy.
4. Structuring of task statements into a logical sequence.
5. Final review.

Standards. After more than two decades of experience with the DACUM process, the following set of conditions must be met if the process is to be maximized:

1. the coordinator/facilitator is qualified through training and practical experience,
2. committee members are expert workers,
3. committee members participate throughout the workshop,
4. task statements abide by all of the criteria for acceptable task statements,
5. there are 8 – 12 duty areas for most occupations,
6. there are six or more task statements in each duty area, and
7. the same task statement appears only once.

Job Tasks. The principal element of any occupational analysis process is the job task. It is the focal point of the performance objective that a learner is expected to meet. In an effort to standardize the efforts of DACUM panelists (expert workers), criteria were established to guide the process of task identification and description.

Job Tasks

1. Are the smallest unit of job activity that results in a meaningful outcome (product, service, or decision)
2. Represent a typical job assignment for which an employer or customer would pay
3. Have a definite beginning and ending point
4. Can be performed over a short period of time
5. Can be performed independent of other work
6. Consist of two or more steps
7. Can usually be observed/measured (Decisions are not often directly observable, but can be determined)

Task Statements

1. Concisely describe a task in performance terms
2. Contain an action verb and an object that receives the action
3. May contain one or more relevant qualifiers (but omit qualifiers such as effectively and efficiently)
4. Are explicit, precise, and stand alone
5. Avoid references to knowledge and attitudes needed
6. Avoid references to tools or equipment that merely support task performance

Results of DACUM. The outcome of the DACUM analysis is a profile chart of the tasks involved in the occupation studied. See Figure 4-1. Before curriculum development can proceed, additional information concerning the tasks of the occupation is needed. Subsequent task analysis and verification steps might include:

1. verifying task statements by expert workers and supervisors,
2. analyzing each task into procedural steps,
3. establishing acceptable performance standards,
4. identifying tools and materials used in each task, and
5. specifying related knowledge and worker trait requirements.

LEGAL ASSISTANT

DUTIES	TASKS						
Assist Clients	Establish Firm/Client Rapport	Record Interview Data					
Perform Communications Functions	Make Phone Calls	Arrange for Appointments and Meetings	Coordinate Meetings/Agenda	Write Memoranda	Employ Public Relations Techniques	Act as Inter-office Personnel Liaison	Keep Clients Informed
Implement Legal Procedures	Obtain Signatures	Perform Notary Services	File Pleadings and/or Documents				
Perform Investigative Functions	Obtain Reports	Conduct Non-legal Research	Gather Physical Evidence	Assist with Depositions	Digest Materials	Assemble and Transport Relevant Materials	Open Informal Court Proceedings for Estates
Perform Legal Research	Retrieve Previously Researched Information	Use Library and Other Relevant Resources	Locate Relevant Statutory Law	Locate Administrative Law	Classify Materials		
Prepare Instruments and Documents	Research Form Files	Compile and Compute Data	Draft Instruments	Prepare Instruments	Complete Prepared Forms	Proofread Written Materials	
				Draft Memoranda	Prepare Memoranda	Draft Briefs	Prepare Briefs
Assist with Judicial and Administrative Appearances	Prepare Trial Notebooks	Prepare Case Law Notebooks	Organize Files	Schedule Witnesses	Perform Emergency...	Acquaint Witnesses or Clients with Court Procedures	
Complete Client Projects	Conduct Real Estate Closings	Transfer Assets	Close Estates	Assist in Pursuit of Post-trial Remedies	Complete Post-trial Wrap-ups		
Continue Education	Participate in Educational Courses and Programs	Participate in Seminars, Conferences, and Workshops	Complete Required Readings	Read Current Publications	Interact with Other Professionals		
	Open Client Files	Maintain Office Equipment	Arrange for Maintenance of Office Equipment	Maintain Time Records	Update Library Materials	Maintain Office Accounting	Maintain Research Files
Coordinate Office Functions	Develop Legal Procedures Handbook	Monitor Legal Procedures Handbook	Prepare Interoffice Memos	Recruit Potential Employees	Interview Potential Employees	Orient ... to Office Procedures	

Adapted from *DACUM Analysis Conducted for*
CURRICULUM MATERIALS SERVICE
Department of Vocational Education
Colorado State University

Figure 4-1. The outcome of the DACUM analysis is a profile chart of the tasks involved in the occupation studied.

Surveys to collect additional information to supplement DACUM analysis and extend its usefulness for instructional development may also be conducted. For example, expert workers and supervisors may be asked to rate the relative importance of the various job tasks, the amount of time spent on job tasks, or the frequency of performance of job tasks.

If an occupation is undergoing rapid change, or is expected to do so, respondents may be asked to indicate how job tasks are expected to change with respect to importance, criticality, time spent, frequency, performance, and content. Such questions must be directed to persons employed in trend-setting organizations in the occupational area.

After the analysis has been verified and refined, the instructional design process is implemented. *Instructional design* is the process of building an instructional program based on task statements, related knowledge, and skill requirements of the occupation.

Traditional Occupational Analysis

The traditional occupational analysis process has evolved over a period of 60 years. The original work in occupational analysis was developed by Robert Selvidge, University of Missouri and Verne C. Fryklund, Stout Institute (now University of Wisconsin-Stout). In the purest form of traditional occupational analysis, skillful workers are observed as they perform job tasks. The observer lists work tasks (jobs) and subtasks (operations) being performed. Interviews with workers are then conducted to clarify procedures for performing tasks and identifying knowledge needed to perform and make job decisions. In the identification process, the individual making the occupational analysis typically draws upon literature related to the occupation. Results are often prepared as a survey instrument, which expert workers or supervisors use to verify skills, knowledge, and attitudes from which the instructional program is designed.

Literature related to occupational analysis refers to *doing* and *knowing* content. Recently, educators have done a more systematic job of classifying behaviors. The *Taxonomy of Educational Objectives*, edited by Benjamin Bloom, classifies all human behavior into the cognitive, psychomotor, and affective domains.

1. *Cognitive* – knowledge and information-related behavior;
2. *Psychomotor* – hand-eye, mental-muscle, or doing-related behavior; and
3. *Affective* – attitudes, feelings, and value-related behavior.

The teaching profession's emphasis upon competency is an integration of cognitive, psychomotor, and affective tasks. To complicate the process, the traditional occupational analysis approach tends to include these tasks in an instructional order. This manner of implementing the process might work reasonably well for a person already knowledgeable of an occupation, but it would be impossible for the analysis of a new or unfamiliar occupation.

Process Overview. Occupations and their major work segments are divided into *blocks*, which are major content areas. For example, three blocks of the secretarial occupation are shorthand, keyboarding, and filing. Each block is composed of at least two kinds of content, doing content and knowing content. *Doing content* refers to specific skills, operations, or procedures that occur repeatedly in daily work. For example, bolding text while typing on a personal computer (PC) is a specific operation. *Knowing content* consists of concepts and useful information directly related to performance. For example, knowledge of a word processing program is required to process words on an IBM personal computer.

Doing content is further analyzed into steps of procedure, listed in the order in which each step is performed. Knowing elements of content are further analyzed into specific items of information, and normally recorded in standard outline form.

Determining Blocks. The first step in completing an analysis is to identify and place the major segments, areas, or types of work in the occupation into blocks. Blocking identifies categories of content or required behaviors under which closely related elements of performance and elements of information can be listed. Determining blocks may be done in several ways, depending on the occupation being analyzed, amount of content, and type of instructional situation. For example, in machine shop, blocks may be listed according to major work processes or major pieces of equipment.

Processes	*Equipment*
BLOCK 1 – Printreading	
BLOCK 2 – Measurement and layout	Linear scale
BLOCK 3 – Drilling and boring	Drill press
BLOCK 4 – Shaping	Shaper
BLOCK 5 – Forming	
BLOCK 6 – Abrading	Grinder

Some instructors prefer to list measuring as a special block or combine it with printreading. There are many such choices the instructor must make. The important point is to list the blocks in such a way that all related content can be grouped in a given block. It would be ideal if each block contained approximately the same amount of content and be of similar importance; however, this seldom happens in practice.

Doing Content. The second step is to list specific skills, processes, and procedures found in each block. This doing content involves operations or skills that, regardless of the specific task to be done, remain basically the same and are used repeatedly by the worker. The skills of cutting, shaping, forming, and grinding in metalwork are examples. These doing units are performed in the same way regardless of the product being produced.

In the identification process, certain doing content is easy to classify because it is clearly psychomotor in nature. Other performance elements have a close tie to knowledge and are harder to classify. One key that helps in classification is to determine whether or not the content statement indicates action or performance requiring a degree of skill. In either case, the identification of all necessary content is more important than the classification.

Always list doing content in terms of action or doing behavior (for example, mix developer, fix negatives, test chemicals). Consistency in wording is strongly recommended. Examples of doing content from a block in Basic Photography entitled "Developing Black-and-White Film" could include the following elements:

1. Mix developer.
2. Mix short stop.
3. Mix fixer.
4. Place film in tank.
5. Develop negatives.
6. Short stop negatives.
7. Fix negatives.
8. Wash negatives.
9. Dry negatives.

When evaluating elements of doing content, the following questions should be asked:

1. Does the element contain steps to be performed in a given order?
2. Is the element of the appropriate length for a demonstration or lesson?
3. Is there only one recommended way to perform the element?
4. Is the wording specific enough to convey the behavior to be developed?

All elements should be listed in their order of occurrence. Longer elements should be broken down into shorter elements. If there is more than one recommended procedure, each is listed separately.

Wording should be specific. For example, "take measurements with micrometer" or "read micrometer." In an engine repair analysis, "take measurements of a cylinder" includes a definite procedure to follow and a definite behavior that can be observed. Note that some doing or manipulative content often becomes steps of procedures. See Figure 4-2.

DOING CONTENT		
Taught Early in the Course	**Taught at a Later Date**	**Taught at a Still Later Date**
Solder Metal 1. Lay out sheet metal to be soldered. Clean surfaces if necessary. 2. Heat soldering iron. 3. Tin soldering iron if necessary. 4. Apply flux. 5. Heat metal where solder is to be applied. 6. Tack seam. 7. Flow solder along entire seam. 8. Inspect joint.	Make a Lock Joint 1. Lay out joint. 2. Cut to layout lines. 3. Assemble pieces. 4. Lock seam. 5. Solder joints.	Make a 90° Elbow 1. Lay out elbow. 2. Cut to layout lines. 3. Form pieces. 4. Lock joints. 5. Assemble parts. 6. Tack parts. 7. Flow solder along entire seam. 8. Inspect and test elbow.

Figure 4-2. Manipulative or doing content may be cumulative in nature.

Knowing Content. The third step in completing an analysis is to identify concepts and information necessary for occupational competence. Many of the knowing elements of content are essential to performing a task with understanding and confidence. For example, while a patternmaker's chisel may be sharpened by simply honing the edge so that it produces a cut, knowledge of the cutting angle, clearance, and steel characteristics enables the patternmaker to produce a sharper edge on a consistent basis. Such knowledge of the knowing content pertaining to the sharpening procedure allows the worker to use judgment in situations that vary from routine procedures.

Several factors that may interfere with the logical identification of knowing content are prioritizing essential content, identifying basic concepts, determining student capabilities, and determining affective behaviors.

Prioritizing essential content. People tend to feel that whatever has been learned is useful and necessary. While all knowledge is useful in certain situations, some is more useful than others. Knowledge that is necessary or most useful must have priority in the establishment of an instructional program. The long-range objectives for the instructional program are helpful in deciding the extent to which content is essential.

Identifying basic concepts. Often, instructors overlook a great deal of content initially learned and minimize the importance of basic concepts and principles because they have been applied by habit over a long time span. Effective instructors realize the importance of basic concepts and use them as the cornerstone of instruction.

Determining student capabilities. Course content that is identified by an analysis process is likely to vary. Some students retain information that can be applied to the learning of specific skills. For example, a person with training in the physical sciences has an advantage over a person without such training. The difference in the general education background of students makes the analyzer's job more difficult. It is best to include more information during the analysis process.

Determining affective behaviors. There is much misunderstanding regarding the development of affective behaviors. Good attitudes and study habits have been considered to be natural by-products of well-organized and effective training programs. This is true to a degree. Educators are realizing, however, that the identification and development of behavior in the affective domain must be given greater attention. Appropriate affective behaviors must be identified and developed through careful analysis strategies just as done for doing and knowing forms of behavior.

Examples of knowing content from a block in Basic Photography entitled "Developing Black-and-White Film" could include the following:

1. Theory of film development.
2. Types and characteristics of film developers.
3. Time and temperature controls in the darkroom.
4. Types of developing tanks.
5. Contrast and development time.
6. Types of fixers.
7. Defects in negatives.
8. Care of chemicals.

Content Inventory. When the content inventory list is completed, some knowing elements appear to be related to only one doing element. Other knowing elements are related to several doing elements. Arrange the content so that closely-related doing and knowing elements are grouped logically. This content inventory list helps in planning the order in which content should be taught.

It is customary to list the doing and knowing content elements as an analysis chart or content inventory. See Figure 4-3. This chart illustrates a block of learning derived from an analysis of the plastics industry. Doing elements are identified with knowing elements through the use of codes. On Block 5, D stands for doing, and K for knowing. Thus, K 4 corresponds with D 6 and D 7 on Block 5.

BLOCK 5: ACRYLIC PLASTIC SHEET STOCK	
Doing (Skills to be Developed)	**Knowing (Information to be Learned)**
D 1. Handle and store acrylic plastics D 2. Cut acrylic plastics D 3. Drill acrylic plastics D 4. Tap and thread acrylic plastics D 5. Heat and form acrylic plastics D 6. Join acrylic plastics – soak method D 7. Join acrylic plastics – glue method D 8. Sand and buff acrylic plastics	K 1. Chemical characteristics of acrylic plastics (D 1-8) K 2. Working characteristics and use of acrylic plastics (D 1-8) K 3. Types of acrylic plastics (D 1-8) K 4. Types of adhesives for acrylic plastics (D 6-7) K 5. Types of metal fastening devices for acrylic plastics (D 3-4)

Figure 4-3. A block of learning should indicate skills to be developed and information to be learned.

The content in thorough application of the analysis process is always subdivided to detail the precise behavior to be learned and observed. The knowledge-related elements contain an outline of concepts and information, while the doing elements contain steps of procedures. Teaching without an outline of concepts and information and step of procedures increases the possibility of omitting essential information. For best results, steps must be listed carefully so that the instructor knows the exact procedure to be taught. The procedure for listing the steps in a doing element includes the following:

1. List specific steps of the given task in their normal order.

2. Perform the task and verify that each step is essential.

3. List key points and information essential to the performance of each step. Highlight points where safety must be emphasized. Emphasize these points during instruction.

4. Have the steps verified and corrected, if necessary, by specialists in the field.

Certain technical information is so closely related to the process of doing that it must be taught as an integral part of instruction. This includes basic concepts, characteristics of tools, equipment, materials, and safety precautions. These elements of content are typically presented during the lecture. Visual aids, samples of materials, and reading assignments reinforce instruction. The procedure for listing the steps in a knowing element includes the following:

1. List major headings under the title of the knowledge element. If the number of major headings is excessive, consider combining some of them.

2. List specific, detailed points of content to be learned under each major heading.

3. Have the outline checked by other instructors or specialists. An exchange of ideas on all units of instruction helps to prevent errors and omissions.

In most occupations, the analysis chart is never complete because of new developments and changes in procedures. It is, however, relatively easy to keep a well-developed content inventory up-to-date. Always start with a good content inventory as early as possible in the instructional planning process. See Figure 4-4.

TRANSLATING CONTENT INTO OBJECTIVES

Tasks and related knowledge are transformed into performance objectives. Educators who deal with secondary, postsecondary, and adult programs in vocational and technical education as well as trainers in the business, industrial, and military sectors have become outcome (performance) oriented.

Outcome-Based Instruction

Outcome-based instruction is referred to as

1. Competency-Based Instruction,

2. Criterion-Referenced Instruction,

3. Mastery Learning,

4. Individualized Instruction,

5. Performance-Based Instruction,

6. Objective-Referred Learning, and

7. Systems-Based Instruction.

These instructional approaches focus attention on the individual learner, and time as well as learning activities vary in order that the learner can perform at a predetermined level.

PHOTOGRAPHY – IMAGE CAPTURE AND MANIPULATION

BLOCKS
I. BASIC BLOCK
II. CAPTURING IMAGE
III. MANIPULATING IMAGE

I. BASIC BLOCK

Doing – The learner should be able to:	Knowing – The learner should know the:
1. Set up camera	1. History of photography
2. Focus camera with	2. Principles of the camera
(a) range finder	3. Camera parts and accessories
(b) ground glass	4. Elementary photographic optics
3. Load film in camera	5. Theory of image capture
4. Adjust shutter speed	6. Image resolution considerations
5. Adjust lens opening	7. Depth of focus and field
6. Test camera	8. Types of camera
7. Set up and adjust tripod	9. Properties of light
8. Read light meter	10. Filters and their use

II. CAPTURING IMAGE

1. Use artificial light	1. Film sensitivity and exposure of specific films
2. Use natural light	2. Factors of exposure
3. Calculate lens opening and shutter speed with exposure meter	3. Composition of picture
4. Mount filters and determine filter factor	4. Factors of good composition
5. Use tripod	5. Effects of lighting
6. Set up lights and camera for still objects	
7. Set up lights and camera for moving objects	
8. Set up lights and camera for portrait	
9. Set up lights and camera for copying	

III. MANIPULATING IMAGE

1. Turn on computer	1. Capabilities of image manipulation software
2. Launch photo manipulation software	2. Types and characteristics of image file formats
3. Download images from media card	3. Image resolution for print and web work
4. Adjust image exposure if needed	4. Types and characteristics of available output devices
5. Adjust image color balance if needed	5. Available print paper
6. Determine image usage (print or web)	6. Print defects
7. Crop image to proper size	7. Characteristics of materials used in mounting prints
8. Adjust image resolution for proper usage	
9. Save image to proper format for usage	
10. Send image to output device	
11. Mount prints	

Figure 4-4. Doing elements are stated in action terms. Knowing elements are topics that may be related to one or more doing elements.

Goals and Objectives

As educational programs are developed, there must be direction and boundaries for the developmental process. *Goals* are broad statements of desired end results. A primary goal of a vocational program is that the individual will become occupationally competent.

Objectives, clear statements of instructional intent, help ensure development of specific competencies. For vocational and technical education, objectives are drawn from the job tasks identified through an occupational analysis. Within a given course, there may be short-range or enabling objectives that specify behaviors the learner must exhibit while becoming occupationally competent. *Performance objectives* specify behaviors that students must exhibit at the end of a segment of learning. Performance objectives are derived from cognitive, psychomotor, and affective content.

Much time and effort are wasted in educational programs because of overlapping of course content, unintentional omissions of important content, and improper emphasis. The major problem in planning instruction is to identify, select, and teach elements of content most appropriate in terms of specified objectives. Therefore, carefully selected and properly stated objectives become the key to instruction. If objectives change, content will require modification.

Instructional objectives are

1. helpful in lesson planning,
2. useful in selecting learning aids,
3. beneficial in determining appropriate assignments for students,
4. valuable in planning and developing tests,
5. beneficial to the instructor in summarizing and reporting results of evaluation, and
6. beneficial in determining career goals for students.

Elements of Performance Objectives

The key to the performance objective is the job task identified through the occupational analysis process. Performance objectives are often called *behavioral objectives*. In the preparation of performance objectives, the instructor must be knowledgeable of and be able to apply the three basic components: performance, conditions, and criteria.

Performance. *Performance*, the first component, is a clear and concise statement of performance required of the learner. The task statement from an occupational analysis can often be used as the performance component of a performance objective. The instructor may rephrase the task statement to clarify what is expected of the learner. For example, the task statement may be written as "clean, gap, and test spark plugs" which might be altered as the performance component of an objective to read "remove, clean, gap, and test spark plugs, and replace in engine." The performance component does not have to include a repetitive statement such as "the student will be able to." This lead statement can be placed as the head of an entire group of objectives. The key word in the performance component is an action verb such as "remove," "clean," "measure," "list," "draw," "prepare," "fasten," or "describe." Performance can be related to knowing as well as doing content. A comprehensive list of appropriate terms is found in Bloom's *Taxonomy of Educational Objectives*.

Conditions. The second component of a performance objective is the *conditions* (the setting or set of circumstances) within which the learner is to perform or demonstrate competency. The conditions specify the necessary resources to be used as the learner performs. The following is a list of examples of necessary resource conditions:

1. an oxyacetylene torch and tanks of oxygen and acetylene,
2. appropriate handbooks, and
3. 18-gauge galvanized sheet metal.

Conditions may also describe situations or certain restrictions. The following is a list of examples of situation or restriction conditions:

1. results of a diagnostic test,
2. the use of a calculator, and
3. a detailed working drawing.

Avoid long lists of materials and equipment or items that can be logically assumed as necessary for performance. For example, the previously stated condition "given an oxyacetylene torch and tanks of oxygen and acetylene" would not be necessary if the course dealt only with oxyacetylene welding. This condition would, however, be necessary if the course included two or more types of welding. The conditions can make a difference in an individual's level of performance. *Input a manuscript* would be a different objective if the conditions varied, for example, "from a handwritten draft"; "from an audiotape"; or "from dictation transcribed from shorthand."

Criteria. The third component of a performance objective indicates the basis upon which the performance is judged. Criteria are used to assess how well the learner must perform to be judged competent. Examples of criteria are "with 90% accuracy," "with no errors," and "all steps performed in the specified sequence." The criteria may relate to either the process or the product; however, most of the time the bottom line for occupational competency is the extent to which a product or service would meet the employer's expectations. The instructor has the challenge of interpreting employer expectation in terms of the criteria to be met.

An example of a cognitive performance objective with all three components is as follows: with the aid of a sales tax chart, the student computes the sales tax for purchases of $.23, $1.25, $2.79, $51.50, and $103.92 with 100% accuracy.

Writing Performance Objectives

There are no shortcuts to well-written objectives. The instructor must communicate the performance, conditions, and criteria with sufficient clarity that students, employers, administrators, evaluators, and other teachers understand the instructional intent. The adage, "Objectives are not written, they are rewritten," emphasizes the necessity to revise objectives. An important consideration is that students are able to read and understand the performance objectives. In writing performance objectives, the choice of verbs is critical in identifying behavior desired by the student. Verbs used in the cognitive domain deal with intellectual learning and are identified according to six levels. See Figure 4-5. Verbs used in the psychomotor domain deal with physical skills. See Figure 4-6. Verbs used in the affective domain deal with attitudes, values, and feelings. See Figure 4-7.

The instructor must make numerous decisions as objectives are developed. It may be decided that the performance objective, based on the work task, is too broad to be used effectively. It is better to divide the task into several subparts with an objective for each part. The mastery of one objective should not be dependent upon the mastery of another. Instructors must be sensitive to the problems of timing, prerequisites, and sequencing if instruction is to be both effective and efficient.

A checklist for performance objectives includes:

1. *Performance* – describes the competency the learner is doing to attain the objective,

2. *Condition* – specifies the important circumstances under which the learner must demonstrate competence,

3. *Criterion* – describes the standard(s) by which the learner's proficiency can be judged,

4. *Precision and Clarity* – uses action words that preclude misinterpretation,

5. *Success Expectation* – includes sufficient detail to ensure that the expected performance outcome can be recognized, and

6. *Completeness, Relevance, and Achievable* – develops a separate statement for each performance objective to be achieved.

COGNITIVE VERBS		
Knowledge (Level 1) define list memorize name recall record relate repeat	**Comprehension (Level 2)** describe discuss explain express identify locate recognize report restate review tell	**Application (Level 3)** apply demonstrate dramatize employ illustrate interpret operate practice schedule sketch translate use
Analysis (Level 4) analyze appraise calculate compare contrast criticize debate diagram differentiate distinguish examine experiment inspect inventory question relate solve test	**Synthesis (Level 5)** arrange assemble collect compose construct create design formulate manage organize plan prepare propose set up	**Evaluation (Level 6)** appraise assess choose compare estimate evaluate inspect judge rate revise score select value

Figure 4-5. When writing objectives, instructors should use specific verbs to specify cognitive behaviors expected of students.

The identification of content and the specification of behaviors provide the foundation upon which educational planning efforts are built. In vocational and technical education, the goal of an educational program is to assist individuals to become occupationally competent or to increase their level of competence within an occupation. If competencies are not identified, the base upon which an educational program is built will be faulty. It would be of no value to do an excellent job of helping an individual develop a skill that is no longer needed by workers in the occupation for which the individual was being prepared. The identification of the work tasks and the translation of these work tasks into performance objectives is of vital importance in program development. Instructors should be involved in the identification of course content as well as participate in the translation of competencies into performance objectives.

PSYCHOMOTOR VERBS			
advance	enter	grind	perform
anchor	equip	heave	practice
assort	execute	inscribe	proceed
build	fabricate	inspect	rebuild
carry	fill	intersect	recast
climb	finish	juggle	remodel
converse	fix	make	straighten
convert	furnish	manipulate	transfer
demonstrate	gather	observe	transpose
enlarge	generate	operate	work

Figure 4-6. When writing objectives, instructors should use specific verbs to specify psychomotor behaviors expected of students.

AFFECTIVE VERBS			
accept	concur	enrich	induce
admit	confer	excel	invigorate
advocate	congratulate	exhibit	kindle
allow	correspond	express	motivate
aspire	dedicate	flatter	oblige
assist	deserve	fulfill	perceive
attain	engage	impart	ratify
belong	enhance	impel	reinforce
commend	enlighten	imply	stimulate
compliment	enliven	incite	urge
concern			

Figure 4-7. When writing objectives, instructors should use specific verbs to specify affective behaviors expected of students.

The concept of analysis involves a way of viewing complexity and reducing that complexity into components that are more readily understood. The role of the instructor is to organize and deliver subject matter in a manner that facilitates the development of competencies by learners. Instructors have a responsibility to examine subject matter in an analytical fashion in order that patterns or structures can be observed and communicated to learners. The instructor's goal is to facilitate learning and reduce complexity and ambiguity.

While many instructors are not involved directly in the process of occupational analysis, it is important that the general process is understood since it helps to provide instructors with an understanding of their profession. Performance objectives provide direction for the educational process and standards by which competency development can be judged. In an effective educational program, the learner has knowledge of the instructor's expectations as well as the criteria by which performance is judged.

REVIEW

Questions

1. What is the primary goal of vocational and technical education?
2. What is occupational analysis?
3. What is the DACUM process and how are experienced workers used to identify job tasks within an occupation?
4. What is the relationship between job tasks identified through occupational analysis and performance objectives?
5. How does an objective differ from a goal?
6. What are the three components of a performance objective?
7. How can a deck of playing cards be used to illustrate the process of analysis?
8. What is a job task?
9. Who developed the original work in occupational analysis?
10. How does Bloom classify human behavior?
11. How are objectives for vocational and technical education determined?
12. What do the conditions of a performance objective specify?
13. List several cognitive verbs that may be used at the knowledge level when writing objectives.
14. List several psychomotor verbs that may be used when writing objectives.
15. List several affective verbs that may be used when writing objectives.
16. What is the first step in completing an analysis?
17. What is instructional design?
18. What set of conditions must be met if the DACUM process is to be maximized?

Activities

1. Describe the relationship between course content and learner competency.
2. Describe the relationship between job tasks, task statements, and performance objectives.
3. Describe why it is desirable for instructors to be familiar with occupational analysis processes.
4. Describe the DACUM process of identifying work tasks.
5. List the blocks in your occupational subject area.

6. Differentiate between process-oriented evaluation and outcome-oriented evaluation.

7. Discuss how performance objectives are helpful to instructors, administrators, parents, and students.

8. Write six performance objectives in your occupational subject area. Identify the performance, conditions, and criteria of each objective by underlining or highlighting.

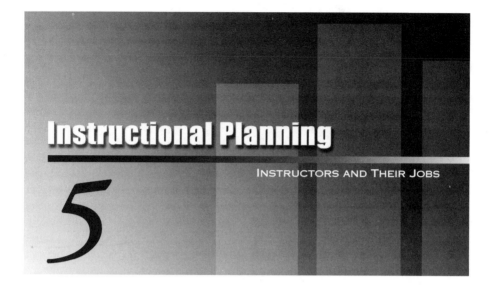

Instructional Planning

INTRODUCTION

When architects design a house or a commercial or industrial building, they must consider the owner's needs, building design, structural characteristics, and cost of suitable materials given the geographic area, site, and local and national codes. The architect draws the plans and develops the specifications for the structure. The plans give all sizes and dimensions and the specifications describe materials, fixtures, appliances, etc. The contractor may proceed with confidence once plans and specifications detailing all elements and their inter-relationships are complete.

An instructional plan is a document that reveals the logical organization of content and instructional processes designed to meet specific educational goals. Designing an educational program involves planning at all levels, from the total curriculum to the individual course, unit, or lesson.

In vocational and technical education, content is revealed through occupational and task analysis. After the content is identified, numerous decisions must be made regarding structure and sequence. The analysis is similar to the inventory of building materials used to construct a house. An occupational analysis provides an inventory of content that may be included in an instructional program. It may contain enough material for several courses; however, it does not indicate the best sequence or method for teaching the content. These decisions require strategic planning at the course, unit, and lesson levels.

PLANNING FOR INSTRUCTION

The essential elements of an effective educational program are instructional planning, execution, and evaluation. Instructional planning is the foundation on which the other two elements are built. Professional instructors know that time spent planning is a good investment. The dividends of planning are (1) increased learning, (2) more efficient use of class time, (3) fewer discipline problems, and (4) improved instruction.

Macro and Micro Planning

In vocational and technical education, whether at the secondary or postsecondary level, instructional planning begins with basic competencies required of workers in the occupation for which the educational program is designed. At the macro level, planning is typically referred to as curriculum design. After an occupational analysis is completed, course material is packaged and sequenced to enable learners to acquire the identified competencies. Curriculum design involves committees of instructors and administrators who jointly determine the required courses for a given program. *Curriculum* is a series of planned experiences designed to help learners achieve major goals. In vocational and technical education, the major goal is occupational competence.

At the micro level, instructors are responsible for planning courses, although the amount and type of planning varies. For example, the instructor may be given a course title, topical outline, and required textbook. In another situation, the course may be well-structured with performance objectives for several units, a topical outline for each unit, and lesson plans. The first example is more typical than the second and would involve more decision making and planning. Vocational educators and industrial trainers have long recognized the value of well-planned programs of instruction.

Conceptual Framework

Instructors must clearly understand the conceptual framework within which instructional planning takes place. This framework can be described and/or graphically illustrated in several ways. One example is provided by Richard Gebhart, teacher educator. See Figure 5-1. The illustration shows the relationship among the planning elements of competencies, programs and courses, objectives, lessons, and evaluation. Further, Gebhart emphasizes essential steps in the analysis of evaluation data used to improve the instructional program.

Another framework is provided by Gagné and Leslie J. Briggs, authors of *Principles of Instructional Design*, who describe a systematic process of instructional design. Gagné and Briggs view instructional design as an applied science that organizes the necessary elements for achieving all of the outcomes specified for a curriculum or course.

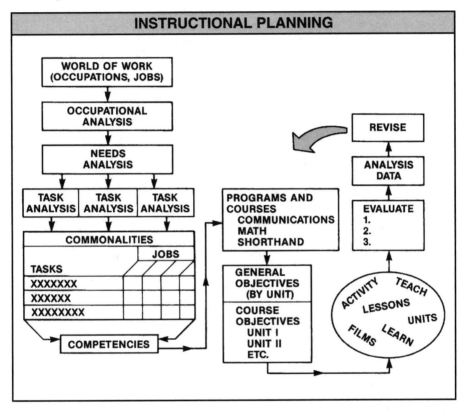

INSTRUCTIONAL PLANNING

Figure 5-1. Gebhart depicts a plan for developing and revising a vocational education program.

Gagné and Briggs specify four levels and 14 stages in the design of a complete instructional system. See Figure 5-2. The instructor is most directly involved at the course and lesson levels. Educational publishers, curriculum development laboratories, and others who design curriculum materials and learning systems should consider all 14 stages. This process could require recycling through several stages until each component of the instructional system enables learners to meet specified objectives. Instructors must understand basic principles of instructional design in order to identify flaws in learning systems. In addition, most instructors are expected to adapt curricula and instructional materials to meet students' needs. These activities require that an instructor execute the first nine stages described by Gagné and Briggs.

STAGES IN DESIGNING INSTRUCTIONAL SYSTEMS	
System Level	1. Analysis of needs, goals, and priorities 2. Analysis of resources, constraints, and alternative delivery systems 3. Determination of scope and sequence of curriculum and courses – delivery system design
Course Level	4. Determining course structure and sequence 5. Analysis of course objectives
Lesson Level	6. Definition of performance objectives 7. Preparing lesson plans for modules 8. Developing, selecting materials, media 9. Assessing student performance (performance measures)
Final System Level	10. Teacher preparation 11. Formative evaluation 12. Field testing revision 13. Summative evaluation 14. Installation and diffusion

Gagné, R. M., & Briggs, L. J. (1988). *Principles of instructional design*. New York: Holt, Rinehart & Winston.

Figure 5-2. Gagné and Briggs organize the instructional design process into four levels and 14 stages.

Systems Approach

The basic structure of a *system* includes the following elements: (1) input, (2) process (mechanisms, such as procedures, policies, materials, that convert input into output), (3) output, (4) feedback, and (5) environment (circumstances that can influence the input, process, output, or feedback). The instructional planner can use the general systems approach to depict the interrelationships of all elements involved in the teaching-learning enterprise. See Figure 5-3.

COURSE PLANNING

After macro level planning, with its focus on translating the results of an occupational analysis into educational curricula, educators must shift their focus to course planning. Course planning is used to achieve the desired goal of occupational competence.

Courses of Study

The document containing an instructor's plan for a course is a *course of study* (curriculum guide). A course of study should consider:

1. relationship of the course to the entire educational program,

2. objectives of the course,

3. needs of the student,

4. content to be taught,

5. equipment and facilities available,

6. appropriate methods of instruction,

7. student learning activities,

8. resource materials, and

9. procedures and instruments for evaluation.

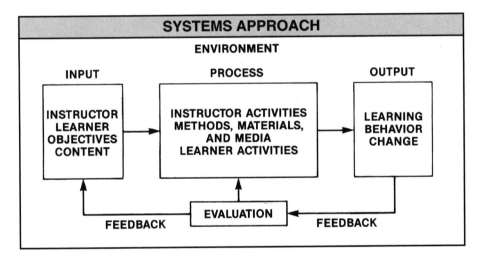

Figure 5-3. Application of general systems theory to instruction reveals the interrelationships among elements of the teaching-learning process.

This organizational framework, based on the course of study, units of instruction, and lesson plans, is helpful to most instructors. The length of a course of study may vary from several pages (10 – 15) outlining critical components of a course to a voluminous document, including materials such as transparency masters, printed supplementary materials, unit plans, lesson plans, and tests for the entire course. Regardless of its length and the types of materials included, the course of study is a planning document for the instructor's use and should be developed accordingly. The course of study serves as the basis from which units of instruction are developed. Keeping each course of study in one or more three-ring binders with a table of contents and page dividers to separate the sections facilitates the removal of dated materials and their replacement with state-of-the-art materials.

Basic components of a course of study are as follows:

1. Course Title
2. Course Description
3. Course Objectives
4. Course Content (Informational topics to be covered)
5. Instructional Materials
6. Learning Activities
7. Course Evaluation Activities

Course Title. The instructor should select an appropriate, descriptive course title, one that is as specific as possible. The course title should indicate content covered and type and level of instruction. Examples include

1. Basic Machine Shop Mathematics,
2. Radar Electronics,
3. Underwater Welding and Cutting,
4. Residential Roof Framing,
5. Sheet Metal Layout for Ventilating Systems,
6. Basic Nutrition,
7. Clerical Practice,
8. Computer Programming – Fortran,
9. Residential Landscape Design, and
10. Retail Sales Methods.

Course Description. After choosing an appropriate title, the instructor should prepare an introductory statement that defines the grade, age, or experience level at which the course is appropriate. Prerequisites and information about the length and nature of the course should also be specified. In addition, the course description may include general statements about the relationship of the course to further education or the world of work.

Course Objectives. Course objectives should be written in broad and general terms. The following general objectives might be written for a course in beginning photography. Note that the conditions and criteria components of the course objectives have been omitted.

The student should be able to:

1. understand the relationship between lens size and speed of exposure.
2. comprehend the measurement and control of light and the chemistry of development.
3. understand photographic chemicals and film development.

4. understand procedures to develop contact prints and enlargements.

5. appreciate good composition and technical quality in photography.

Objectives should be realistic. Always consider the facilities and amount of class time available, as well as the educational level and interests of the students. If objectives are realistic and instruction is effective, nearly every student should be able to exhibit the specified performance.

Course Content. With the course objectives in mind, instructors should select the knowing (cognitive), doing (psychomotor), and affective elements of content that they wish to teach. Instructors should select elements that best meet their objectives and can be included within the time limits of the course. After tentatively selecting knowing and doing elements consistent with course objectives and time limitations, instructors may find it beneficial to seek the opinions of other instructors and administrators.

Content identified through occupational analysis and behavioral objectives should be the same. Both should state desired student behavior. Through analysis, student behavior is identified, while in an instructional program, student behavior is specified as the desired end result of instruction.

When possible, the least complex content should be taught first. Also, knowledge-related content may be taught before doing, or performance, content. It is best to teach related knowledge and theory before the student needs it to solve practical problems. If possible, information should be taught in small segments throughout the course.

Instructional Materials. The selection or preparation of visual aids, textbooks, and other instructional materials should follow decisions about course content and teaching methods. Instructional materials must be consistent with student ability, emphasize key elements of the course, and effectively present information.

Good textbooks are essential for effective instruction. Textbooks are often written with general objectives in mind and are designed to be used in a variety of situations. As a result, supplemental materials are sometimes required for a specific course.

Selection of films may depend on availability from a film library. Therefore, films should be requested for a specific date as early as possible. Films from business, industry, and trade associations should be used if they clearly contribute to instructional objectives.

Other instructional aids, including charts, illustrations, and overhead transparencies, should be selected or prepared for each lesson. Special equipment and supplies should be ordered early.

Written examinations, performance tests, and assignment sheets should be prepared and reproduced as soon as the objectives, course content, and schedule have been determined. These materials should be ready well in advance of their use. The content of an assignment or test should not come as a surprise to the student.

Learning Activities. The purpose of planning instruction is to facilitate learning. Therefore, the selection of appropriate and effective learning activities is a critical factor in the planning process and the course of study. Learning activities may be as varied and creative as the instructor's imagination. Learning activities may include reading assignments, prepared notebooks, field trips, and other projects.

A *project* is a learning experience in which students apply skills and knowledge to create a product. A project may be a notebook in a class on cooperative education, a set of house plans in architectural drawing, a garden in agriculture, or a circuit board in electronics. The order of instruction is influenced by the practical nature of projects. For example, in a photography course, taking pictures would normally precede developing film and making prints.

The fundamental purpose of projects is to provide an opportunity for practical, meaningful application of specific skills as they are learned. When students are required to construct practice pieces that are thrown away, there is usually less motivation to succeed than when the same skills are developed through construction of useful projects. Projects must be designed so the right skills are emphasized. A common failure is to use projects without careful analysis of the skills and knowledge inherent in the activity, or to use projects in which a disproportionate amount of time is spent developing relatively unimportant skills.

In selecting or designing projects for instructional purposes, a number of objectives should be considered:

1. Projects should develop skills specified in the course objectives.

2. Projects should have intrinsic and/or extrinsic value.

3. Projects should use readily available materials where practical.

4. Projects should follow consistent principles and standard practices in the occupation.

Concepts in mathematics, physics, and chemistry lend themselves to various types of projects. Photography, printing, mechanical drawing, welding, cosmetology, and other subjects in which design is important are also taught effectively through the use of projects. A project is a meaningful product for the learner. Laboratory exercises that allow mastery of skills are beneficial for students. Since there is no finished project to grade, the preferred evaluation tool is a performance test.

Field trips are very important in allowing students to see beyond the classroom and understand the occupational world. Field trips also help the instructor keep course material up-to-date and interesting. Companies and industrial plants are usually pleased to have visitors. Arrangements should be made in advance, and students should be given a thorough briefing. A list of instructor-prepared questions for students to respond to or a guide for students to follow during the field trip will help to alleviate potential behavior problems and keep students focused on the important information. The instructor and students should discuss specific directions and expectations before the field trip begins. The host should know the students' backgrounds and the types of experiences that will be of particular value during the visit. If possible, a schedule of events for the visit should be prearranged.

Students should be given the opportunity to discuss the field trip. It is also appropriate for the teacher to send a letter of appreciation to the host after the visit. A letter from the students would be a nice touch.

Bringing outside speakers into the classroom often provides valuable experiences for students. Technical specialists, scientists, authors, designers, and hobbyists are frequently willing to demonstrate or lecture about their fields. These outside speakers can provide motivation for students and add variety and realism to the course. In making arrangements, be sure the demonstration or lecture is consistent with lesson objectives.

Since most potential speakers are busy, every effort should be made to facilitate their participation in the course. Transportation and a time schedule should be arranged carefully. A capable student may be assigned to assist the speaker with preparation details. The instructor and class should find appropriate means of showing their appreciation.

Outside reading assignments, in addition to regular assignments, are part of most technical courses of study. Instructors should make reading materials easily available. An occasional reference to a book, current article, or appropriate movie may urge alert students to expand their interest in the subject.

Course Evaluation Activities. Evaluation activities should be based on their relevance to course objectives. In developing the course of study, the instructor should make some general decisions regarding the methods and strategies to be used to collect and score student evaluation data. Methods and strategies for conducting evaluation activities may include a combination of quantitative data (scores on tests) and qualitative data (value judgments of the student's work). For example, course evaluation activities might include the student's final product or project, written examinations, and performance tests.

Effective instructors frequently change resource materials, teaching-learning aids, and student activities, even though course objectives and content may be relatively stable. A course of study may be prepared in advance of instruction, but it continually changes because the revision and updating process is never complete.

Teaching Plan. A teaching plan is a two- to three-page summary of the course of study. The teaching plan is usually an optional document in the instructional planning process; however, its utility outweighs the initial time, energy, and resources required to develop it. The teaching plan becomes the instructor's guide as it places instruction in sequence and provides a comprehensive overview of the entire course. A teaching plan permits the instructor to list

1. course objectives,
2. major units of instruction,
3. informational content covered in the unit, keyed to textbook or other resources,
4. demonstrations to be provided by the instructor,
5. supplementary aids or activities, such as field trips or films,
6. learning activities, and
7. evaluation activities.

The teaching plan should be filed in a separate section of the course of study. See Figure 5-4. The teaching plan provides general information for the course; however, it does not provide enough detail to successfully guide day-to-day instruction.

Unit of Instruction

A unit of instruction is different from the course of study and the teaching plan. Whereas a course of study presents information and materials for the entire course, and a teaching plan is an overview of the course of study, a unit of instruction includes specific and detailed information for a particular segment of the subject matter to be taught and serves as a guide for the instructional process. Unit plans help the instructor to stay organized and focused on the topic. Instructional units are based on the course of study. The number of instructional units varies from one course to another and from one instructor to another depending upon the type of course and the decisions made by the instructor. For example, six units may be sufficient for a beginning welding course; however, a beginning course in industrial electricity may require nine or more units. Some courses may require as many as 12 or 14 different units. If the instructor has prepared a teaching plan, each of the major units may be developed into a unit of instruction.

TEACHING PLAN

Fundamentals of Electricity

Course Objectives:
1. Understand uses and safety precautions related to electricity
2. Demonstrate knowledge of electrical testing meters and characteristics of AC circuits
3. Demonstrate knowledge of electronic schematic symbols and open and closed circuits

Major Units:
1. Wire a series circuit
2. Use a voltage tester
3. Wire a parallel circuit
4. Calculate electric power
5. Operate overcurrent protective devices

Informational Topics (Discussion, Lecture, Reading):
1. Increased use and decreasing cost of electricity
2. Nuclear structure and electron theory
3. Ohm's law
4. Construction use and precautions with meters
5. Characteristics of AC series circuits
6. Characteristics of AC parallel circuits
7. Electric power in AC circuits
8. Rate structures
9. Power unit conversion efficiency calculation
10. Overcurrent protective devices
11. Safety precautions and first aid
12. Grounding considerations
13. Open and closed circuits
14. Electrical and electronic schematic symbols

Demonstrations:
1. Safety precautions and first aid
2. Reading meters (ammeter, voltmeter, ohmmeter)
3. Solving problems with Ohm's law
4. Wiring meters in circuits

Supplementary Aids:
1. Film: "What is Electricity"
2. Film: "Series and Parallel Circuits"
3. List of power distributors
4. (a) File of newspaper clippings dealing with electric shock (b) Demonstration panel with various sizes and types of fuses (c) Film: "Electrical Safety in the Home" (d) Film: "How to Do Rescue Breathing"
5. (a) Chart of symbols (b) Architectural plans with wiring diagrams and schematic circuit drawings

Learning Activities:
1. Solve problems with Ohm's law
2. Read a voltmeter
3. Read an ohmmeter
4. Read a VOM
5. Wire meters in circuits
6. Take measurements with wattmeter, voltmeter, and ammeter
7. Overload a fuse

Evaluation Activities:
1. Written tests on knowledge of safety, first aid, electricity, meters, formulas, and circuits
2. Performance tests on safety precautions and first aid, wiring circuits, and reading meters

Figure 5-4. A teaching plan provides a skeletal framework for a course.

The length, depth, and breadth of a unit of instruction are influenced by the content to be covered, objectives to be achieved, time allotted for the unit, available resources, students' interests and needs, types of printed materials included in the unit (transparency masters, student handouts, student exercises, assignment sheets, lesson plans for the entire unit), and creativity of the instructor. For example, a unit of instruction on the identification, use, and care of hand tools may consist of 25 or fewer pages; whereas a unit on career choices may require 50 or more pages.

The format for a unit of instruction varies depending upon whether the school system requires a particular format or individual instructors develop their own. Regardless of the format selected, a unit of instruction should include the following basic components:

1. name of the course;

2. descriptive title of the unit;

3. duration of the unit written in terms of number and length of class meetings;

4. rationale or importance of the unit and its relationship to other units and the course;

5. topical outline of the subject matter content to be taught;

6. objectives written in terms of the students' knowledge, skills, and attitudes to be developed;

7. teaching and learning activities to include instructional strategies, demonstrations, and student applications;

8. instructional materials to include supplementary books, films, games, and computer programs;

9. facilities to include required classroom/laboratory space, furniture, tools, supplies, and equipment;

10. evaluation activities to include a description of special projects or products to be developed by the student, sample examination questions, brief descriptions of performance examinations, methods for assessing student outcomes, explanation of the scoring procedures; and

11. specialized information such as technical terminology, scientific symbols, or complex formulas.

A typical format for a unit of instruction is shown in Figure 5-5. A well-developed unit of instruction facilitates lesson planning, as individual lessons are necessary to help students realize the unit objectives. Instructors may wish to keep the units of instruction in the appropriate teaching order in separate sections of a three-ring binder with the corresponding course of study.

UNIT OF INSTRUCTION
Name Of Course:
Descriptive Title of Unit:
Duration of Unit (Number and length of class periods):
Rationale for Unit:
Topical Outline (Content to be covered):
Unit Objectives (Student outcomes):
Teaching-Learning Activities:
Instructional Materials:
Facilities:
Evaluation Activities:
Specialized Information:

Figure 5-5. A unit of instruction is developed for each major content area.

Course Syllabus

Students must know the direction of a given course. One systematic way to share the results of planning with students is through a well-designed course syllabus. See Figure 5-6. The format for a course syllabus varies from a one- or two-page topical outline, with test dates noted, to a comprehensive document including performance objectives and all supplementary materials for the course. The suggested format is between these two extremes and contains the following components:

Cover Page – Critical elements of this page relate to identification. It should provide the (1) name of the institution, (2) curriculum in which the course is included, (3) course title, (4) length of course, and (5) year.

Introduction – The introduction should place the course in context by indicating its place in the curricular sequence. The general nature of the course should be described. Include a catalog description for the course. Prerequisites or general expectations should be included in the introduction.

Course Organization – Include a section describing the format of the course and major units covered. Include the amount of time devoted to each unit so students can judge the amount of emphasis or depth of study expected in various areas. Also specify the selected instructional strategies of the course, such as lecture, group discussion, assigned reading, or research papers.

COURSE SYLLABUS

Circuit Analysis 101
5 Credit Hours

Circuit Analysis 101 (CA-101) covers basic DC electrical principles. Previous course experience in basic mathematics is prerequisite to success in CA-101.

I. Introduction

II. Course Organization
Content and Scope of the Course

Unit I	Current and Voltage	4 days
Unit II	Resistance	3 days
Unit III	Ohm's Law	2 days
Unit IV	Power and Energy	4 days
Unit V	DC Series Circuits	8 days
Unit VI	DC Parallel Circuits	8 days
Unit VII	DC Series/Parallel Circuits	8 days
Unit VIII	DC Methods of Analysis	18 days
Unit IX	DC Network Theorems	15 days
Review and Final Examination		5 days
		75 days

For each unit there are assignments, references, and study questions. Assignments specify learning activities. Chapters and/or pages of the text to be read are specified. Study questions are designed to present situational problems which call for acquaintance with and the interpretation of facts, understanding of concepts and principles, as well as formation of judgments.

III. Course Objectives
Through the content selected and the activities planned, students should be able to:
1. Explain the interrelationships between current, voltage, resistance, power, and energy.
2. Apply Ohm's law.
3. Analyze linear bilateral DC series, parallel, or series/parallel circuits with Ohm's law and the power formula when one or more quantities are unknown.

IV. Basis for Evaluation

A. Examinations	60%
B. Weekly quizzes	15%
C. Written reports	15%
D. Classroom participation	10%

Figure 5-6. A course syllabus indicates the results of course planning.

Course Objectives – Major performance outcomes expected of students upon completion of the course should be identified in the course syllabus. Course objectives are not as specific and complete, in terms of conditions and criteria, as performance objectives. Course objectives should focus on student performance rather than the instructor's actions and intent.

Basis for Evaluation – Students should know in advance the criteria and guidelines an instructor will use to evaluate students and assign grades. Student anxiety results from lack of information about the evaluation process. This evaluation information must be clearly and precisely communicated as early in the course as possible. Dates for examinations need to be set well in advance so students can prepare adequately.

Format for Papers and Reports – Format or style expectations need to be expressed to students. It is wise to include these detailed expectations, with examples, on the course syllabus. Providing examples of bibliographic citations or reference page format on the course syllabus will save class time and provide an information backup for students who are absent.

Assignment Sheets – An effective way to make assignments is with an assignment sheet that covers the unit. The nature of the assignment sheet can vary considerably depending on the type of course and the resourcefulness of the instructor. The basic elements of an assignment sheet include the introduction, assignment(s), references, and study questions. See Figure 5-7.

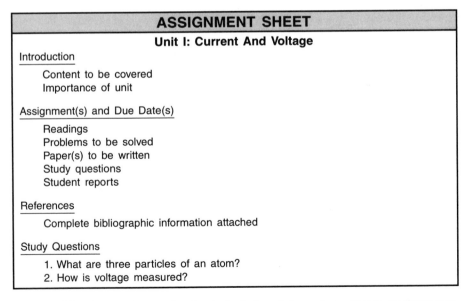

ASSIGNMENT SHEET

Unit I: Current And Voltage

Introduction

    Content to be covered
    Importance of unit

Assignment(s) and Due Date(s)

    Readings
    Problems to be solved
    Paper(s) to be written
    Study questions
    Student reports

References

    Complete bibliographic information attached

Study Questions

    1. What are three particles of an atom?
    2. How is voltage measured?

Figure 5-7. An assignment sheet includes information about assignments, references, and study questions.

Handouts and Organization

Handouts are printed materials distributed to students during a course. Handouts convey information that students need to achieve for certain course, unit, or lesson objectives. It is unreasonable to distribute all course handouts at the beginning of a course and expect students to retain and use them at the appropriate time.

Nevertheless, instructors need to teach organization and provide opportunities for students to practice organization. A notebook system can facilitate organization of prepunched handouts. All handouts, including the syllabus and assignment sheets, should be prepunched and distributed at appropriate times during the course.

DESIGNING LESSONS AND LEARNING PACKAGES

Instructors, like learners, bring unique backgrounds to the classroom, which cause them to view the structure of the subject in a certain way. Instructors develop the organizational structures that they believe are most beneficial to learners. As a result, no single organizational format or teaching method is universally adopted as a planning structure for instructors.

A lesson plan organizes the results of an instructor's planning and decision making and becomes a guide for teaching selected subject matter content. A learning package guides an individual's study of a given element of content. A *learning package* is a well-designed, carefully developed learning aid that provides students with necessary materials for mastering specific performance objectives. Learning packages include detailed instructions about the learning process. Learning packages vary from simple to complex in their composition and format. They may be categorized as direction sheets, learning guides, or modules.

Components

The format of lesson plans and learning packages varies greatly; however, key components are derived from the classic four-step method of teaching, which includes preparation, presentation, application, and evaluation.

Preparation. Whether one prepares a lesson plan for group instruction or a learning package for individualized instruction, it is always necessary to prepare students for the lesson. The introductory statement should emphasize the relevance of the lesson and motivate learners to spend time on the learning task. The importance of the lesson is best communicated to students through the performance objectives to be achieved in the class.

Presentation. The heart of a lesson or learning package is linking the learner to certain concepts, information, skills, or principles. This linking may be accomplished through lectures, demonstrations, reading assignments, or other various forms of media.

Application. Well-developed lesson plans and learning packages must provide opportunities for learners to apply newly acquired information, concepts, principles, or motor skills. This phase of the teaching-learning process should provide reinforcement, identify student weaknesses, and provide opportunities for practice.

Evaluation. Evaluation is the final step in all effective instruction. Evaluation may be completed in numerous ways: through oral questioning, observation of performance, or written tests. If objectives are properly written with a clear statement of (1) performance, (2) conditions, and (3) criteria, the evaluation step can be conducted.

Formats

Format is the manner in which the various instructional components are organized. The format may be relatively simple with printed directions guiding the learner through one or more activities to successful performance. On the other hand, it may be a mediated program that uses various types of instructional media.

Learning packages are often designed with instructional media and performance appraisals. Factors such as (1) volume of use, (2) cost, and (3) learning level of the students must be considered before a school district purchases a learning package.

A lesson plan is typically the instructor's plan for a given instructional session. Although there are notable exceptions, such as military, corporate, and private school systems with multiple locations, instructors are generally responsible for developing their own lesson plans.

Lesson Planning

A *lesson plan* provides detailed directions for teaching one or more class periods on a given topic or theme. Lessons may be as short as 30 minutes or as long as 5 hours. The content, age and maturity of the students, and nature of the instructional program (amount of student application) are some of the factors that determine a lesson's length.

It is possible, of course, for a lesson plan to be thought through and carried out without putting it on paper. For most instructors, however, a written plan is necessary if they are to do their best.

Purpose of the Lesson Plan. There are a number of reasons why a lesson plan is necessary. A lesson plan helps the instructor think through the lesson as it will be taught. The lesson plan assists in the organization of tools and materials needed to carry out the lesson plan. A good lesson plan helps the instructor to:

1. provide needed motivation;

2. properly emphasize various parts of the lesson, including those requiring student activity;

3. ensure that essential information is included:

4. provide for the use of instructional aids;

5. insert questions at the proper time; and

6. stay on schedule.

Skilled instructors may write a detailed lesson plan and reduce it to a few notes for use in the classroom. Other instructors may prefer to teach from a detailed outline. In any event, the plan should be designed to fit the instructor's needs for the lesson at hand.

Lesson plans prepared by someone else may be of value, but usually need modification. Each instructor needs a customized plan, which may be newly developed or modified from an existing plan.

Key Elements of Lesson Plan. A lesson plan may be prepared for a single class period, or it may be designed to cover two or more periods. Good lesson plans contain the following elements:

Title – The exact title of a lesson should be given. For example, the title "Micrometer" is not as good as the title "How to Read a Micrometer." The title of a lesson plan usually comes from knowing and doing content identified in the analysis. In addition to the title, a code consisting of course, unit, and lesson numbers may be used to assist in filing.

Objectives – A lesson plan should include objectives, for example, to list and describe types of house paints, or to apply exterior paint. Objectives should include the expected performance, conditions, and criteria.

Instructional Aids – As the lesson is planned, the instructor should list charts, models, films, and other aids that will facilitate learning. This list serves as an inventory when preparing to teach, and is of great help the next time the lesson is taught.

Texts and References – Be sure to identify specific knowing and doing content from the analysis to be included in the lesson. References to texts used to prepare the lesson plan should also be included. If the plan will be used for some time, space should be left to add new references as they become available. All instruction sheets and text material to be used by students should be listed. Care should be taken to include complete reference citations.

Introduction – A well-planned introduction will develop interest and motivate students to become involved in the subject. A good introduction may include:

1. what the lesson is about,
2. where and when students can use what they learn in the lesson,
3. how the lesson will be taught,
4. what will be expected from students during and after the class, and
5. a review of what was learned in previous lessons.

Repetition is always necessary for effective instruction. The procedure used, however, should not be repetitious. Essential information may be emphasized in many ways, one of which is reviewing the previous lesson as a part of the introduction to the current lesson.

It may be necessary to think through previous lessons and reinforce key points before the current lesson can proceed smoothly. The review should not be long and involved. The question and answer approach may be the most effective for certain lessons, or the instructor may simply remind students of key points previously discussed.

Presentation – This is the core of the lesson. It contains two interwoven elements: (1) a complete outline revealing exact content and the sequence in which it will be taught, and (2) notes about ways to teach various parts of the lesson. For example, the instructor might include the following notes:

1. "Ask the following questions . . ."
2. "Through discussion, develop the reason for . . ."
3. "Introduce the film and run first 11 minutes only."
4. "Discuss the following points before showing the remaining part of the film."

In planning the presentation, refer to the analysis for content to be taught, and consider lecturing, discussing, demonstrating, and questioning as ways to teach each part of the lesson. Make sure all parts of the presentation follow in logical order with no awkward gaps, and estimate the time required for each part of the lesson.

Interaction Items – Preplanned questions, both rhetorical ones and those answered by the instructor or students, provide stimulation and highlight a lesson. Questions appropriately interspersed in a presentation stimulate interest. Interaction items help instructors assess student understanding and focus student attention on a specific principle. Interaction items provide a basis for class discussion and communication between instructor and students. Appropriately phrased, these items can lead students to higher levels of analysis, synthesis, and evaluation.

Application and Activity – Application occurs mentally and physically as the student understands and applies learned content to a problem. Good questions, illustrations, problems, and examples cause the student to apply abstract concepts to specific, practical situations. This application is essential for full learning to transfer.

To make each lesson effective, an instructor will plan ahead and reserve part of class time for application activities. The instructor must be free to observe and guide individuals as they work through a learning activity. Well-planned activities serve many purposes, including offering variety and additional experience with the subject; however, their primary goal is to allow the learner to apply the information or skill.

Evaluation Items – As the instructor plans a lesson, it is appropriate to prepare evaluation items for use immediately following the lesson or later in the course. Evaluation items should be designed to measure student achievement related to lesson objectives. The objectives will suggest appropriate wording for evaluation items, which may ask students to recall, explain, describe, identify, perform, or draw.

Summary and Test – Lessons should be summarized by reviewing the main points. This is often followed by oral questions to ensure that students can apply the content of the lesson and to check on their understanding. Using a short test covering the main points in a lesson is a valuable teaching strategy because it gets students to analyze and synthesize content being learned. Tests can provide valuable feedback about parts of the lesson that have been taught well and parts needing clarification or more emphasis. Grades may be given if desired; however, it is more important to use the test as a teaching and learning device.

Assignments – When assigning work to be done outside the classroom, it is not enough to say, "For tomorrow, read chapter five." It pays to tell students what to look for, what to study, and what questions to answer. Written assignment sheets for large units might be prepared to facilitate lesson-by-lesson assignments. A good assignment:

1. is carefully planned in advance,

2. contains specific instructions about the method of approach and discusses anticipated problems or difficulties,

3. is given slowly (so notes may be taken) and is given at the beginning of the period (unless students need today's lesson to understand tomorrow's assignment), and

4. includes questions by the instructor and time for students to ask questions.

The instructor may allow time for students to start the assignment so misconceptions may be noted and corrected.

Sample Format and Plans

The lesson plan format provides a means for instructors to teach and evaluate students. A lesson plan format must be comprehensive, usable, reusable, and practical.

Page one of the lesson plan identifies the course and unit in which a particular lesson will be taught. The instructor may also record the type of lesson (informational or skill), the lesson title, objectives, and any supplementary items needed. The reverse side of page one is used to record assignments, reference data, and an introduction to the lesson.

Page two of the lesson plan is for recording an outline of the lesson. Page three of the lesson plan is for interaction items and to record classroom, laboratory, or other activities the instructor plans to use to facilitate student learning. The fourth page of the lesson plan is for recording evaluation items used to judge whether or not lesson objectives have been achieved.

Completed lesson plans accumulate to form an important part of a unit of instruction. The instructor should prepare lesson plans and file them under appropriate unit titles to conserve time and effort when preparing for a class presentation.

There is no universal format for lesson plans. It is typical, however, for a school system to adopt a common format in an effort to improve communication.

Instructional planning involves broader educational decisions than those related to a demonstration, lesson, or homework assignment. Although instructors are often uninvolved in macro level planning, it is important for them to be aware of the decision-making process that leads to specification of courses and course content in the curriculum. Instructors need to understand the conceptual framework involved in curriculum design as well as the more detailed planning for courses and lessons.

All subject areas have an inherent structure based on the organization of the discipline. It is important for instructors to be well-acquainted with the framework associated with their discipline.

Instructors are often involved in curriculum development decisions that affect the education of students preparing to enter a given occupation. Involvement at the macro level depends a great deal on the school setting and the instructor's experience. Instructors are directly involved in planning at the course and lesson level. Course planning involves many decisions regarding content, objectives, activities, assignments, evaluation, as well as the environment in which teaching and learning occur. Just as there is a structural framework in a discipline, there is also a logical framework for course planning. Developing a course of study and corresponding units of instruction in a systematic, organized manner has several benefits. First, writing objectives, specifying and arranging content, describing learning activities, and developing instructional materials provides a structured approach to teaching that facilitates learning. It is much easier for the learner to focus attention on the content to be learned if there is a discernable structure. Secondly, the planning effort can be drawn upon and improved as the instructor reteaches the course. Seldom does the instructor have the luxury of sufficient time to completely plan a course before it is taught the first time. In this context, a course of study documents the results of the decision making and planning process over time.

The primary reason for planning is to facilitate learning. This benefit of planning cannot be maximized unless key elements of the planning process are shared with students. When instructors have a clear-cut direction for teaching, students have a clear-cut direction for learning.

The course syllabus reveals the instructor's plan and directs students as it gives an overview of course content, organization, objectives, and evaluation. Effective instructors do not leave course organization up to students. Providing an organizational plan helps students keep course materials together and facilitates preparation of homework assignments and review for exams. Students have a collected body of material for the course.

At the micro level of planning, the instructor plans lessons and chooses the strategies and materials that will facilitate the explanation of a given body of content. The results of this decision-making process are recorded in the lesson plan. The effective instructor develops a standardized format for the sake of efficiency. The results of planning are retained and reviewed as the course is taught again. This allows the instructor to update and improve the lesson plan. Effective instructors are flexible and can adjust to changing classroom conditions, which may include students' questions, confusion, or lack of prerequisite knowledge. Instructional plans must sometimes be changed, but teaching without a plan can lead to a directionless class session.

Although there are no universal formats for lesson plans or learning packages, the classic four-step method of teaching does provide a framework for developing instructional materials. An instructor will not go too far astray if attention is given to the preparation of both self and the learner; the presentation of the content to be learned; opportunities for the learner to apply principles, concepts, and skills that are being learned; and evaluation activities that reveal, both to the instructor and learner, the extent to which objectives have been met.

REVIEW

Questions

1. What professional activity, related to course content, must precede instructional planning?
2. What is the foundation of instructional evaluation?
3. To what extent are instructors involved in curriculum design?
4. How is Gebhart's conceptual framework for instructional planning similar to that provided by Gagné and Briggs?
5. What are the five essential elements of a system that can be applied to instructional design?
6. What is a course of study?
7. What are the essential components of a course syllabus?
8. What is a lesson plan?
9. What is a learning package?
10. What are the essential components of a lesson plan?
11. What are the advantages of written assignments?
12. What is the relationship of course content to course objectives?
13. What is the purpose of projects?
14. What is the relationship of evaluation to course objectives?
15. How can a teaching plan help guide the instructional process?
16. What is the purpose of a unit of instruction?
17. In what ways can a course syllabus benefit students?
18. In what ways can handouts compliment instruction?
19. Why is a framework for curriculum design important?
20. What is the classic four-step method of teaching?

Activities

1. Distinguish between macro and micro planning related to (1) an educational program, (2) courses within the curriculum, (3) courses of study, (4) unit plans, and (5) lesson plans.
2. Describe the relationship between occupational analysis and instructional planning.
3. Depict an instructional system using general systems theory.

4. Prepare a course syllabus.
5. Describe the elements of a lesson plan.
6. Describe the essential components of learning.
7. Develop a course of study including the basic components.
8. Describe three projects that would enhance learning in your program area.
9. Develop a unit of instruction including the basic components.
10. Develop two handouts that are appropriate to supplement instruction in your program area.
11. Explain the purpose of a lesson plan.

Written Instructional Materials

INSTRUCTORS AND THEIR JOBS

6

INTRODUCTION

Written instructional materials are essential to the success of educational programs. Written materials must be carefully prepared or selected and skillfully used if their value is to be maximized.

Required textbooks are often used in courses, but they seldom eliminate the need for written instructional materials. Instructors often refer students to supplementary references or use laboratory handbooks for specialized segments of an educational program. Many books are available in most subject areas, and instructors must conduct a thorough review to select the best published materials for a given course. A carefully selected textbook reduces the amount of supplementary material that an instructor needs to prepare. The extra time it takes to make a good decision will be worthwhile for both instructor and students.

Most instructors prepare written instruction sheets, often referred to as student handouts. These written materials may be drawn from other reference materials and customized to fit the specific needs of a student or group of students. Instruction sheets sharpen the focus of instruction.

The instruction sheets most commonly used in technical subjects are those that illustrate professional practice. Instructors must be analytical in making decisions about written materials. Instructors should remember the importance of clarity and efficiency when writing or selecting written materials.

BOOKS AND HANDBOOKS

Professional instructors, acting as individuals or as members of selection committees, often need to choose appropriate books and handbooks for a given course. A good textbook is a basic requirement of most courses. Textbooks provide general or supplementary reading through which students develop a broad understanding of the subject being studied.

Textbooks used in vocational and technical instruction are often similar to a set of individual instruction sheets bound in one volume for convenience. Such textbooks can provide valuable step-by-step guidance as experiments are performed and skills are developed.

When planning a course of study, instructors can judge the potential value of a textbook by the extent to which it presents procedures and information consistent with the objectives and content of the course. An excellent textbook for one course may be inferior for another. For example, a beginning book on mechanical drawing might be ideal at a secondary school, but inappropriate at an adult level.

Textbook Selection

In selecting a textbook for a particular course, instructors should consider course objectives, equipment, student ability, and the type of student activity desired. Seldom are textbooks analyzed in the light of established selection criteria. Instructors, supervisors, and textbook selection committees often select textbooks on the basis of inadequate criteria. Textbook selection is basically subjective in nature; however, care must be taken in order to select the best textbooks for students.

Professional literature in the field of education contains a wealth of information regarding textbook selection. Whether textbooks are adopted by a state committee or a school system, the final choice of a specific textbook for a particular course depends largely on the needs of the teacher and the class involved. The reputation of the publisher and the qualifications of the author should also be carefully considered when making textbook selections.

Instructors can use rating scales established by professional associations, school systems, or at the state level where formalized textbook adoption procedures are employed.

Using a Rating Scale. Textbook selection is more systematic when a rating scale is used. A rating scale allows judgments to be made with a high degree of consistency. See Figure 6-1.

TEXTBOOK SELECTION RATING SHEET						
Part I						
Criteria	**Multiplication Factor**					**Remarks**
Cost	$X_1 =$					
Cover design	$X_1 =$					
Style of type	$X_4 =$					
Size of type	$X_4 =$					
Layout of page	$X_4 =$					
Content organization	$X_3 =$					
Page number placement	$X_1 =$					
Use of color	$X_2 =$					
Eye appeal of pictures, graphs, and illustrations	$X_4 =$					
Quality of paper (durable and glareproof)	$X_2 =$					
Binding (paper or hardback)	$X_4 =$					
Glossary	$X_3 =$					
Table of contents	$X_2 =$					
Index	$X_3 =$					
Appendix	$X_3 =$					
Appropriateness and accuracy of illustrations	$X_5 =$					
Unit or chapter summary	$X_1 =$					
Study, review, or discussion questions	$X_1 =$					
Suggested activities	$X_1 =$					
List of up-to-date resource material	$X_2 =$					
Current information covered	$X_5 =$					
Reference bibliography	$X_1 =$					
Teaching guide or handbook	$X_2 =$					
Laboratory handbook or workbook	$X_2 =$					
Total Part I						

Part II						
Main Topics of Course of Study	**Multiplication Factor**					**Remarks**
	$X_1 =$					
	$X_1 =$					
Sequence of content	$X_3 =$					
Total						
Total Part I						
Grand Total						
Rank						

Figure 6-1. Selection of a textbook for classroom use can be done in a systematic manner by using a rating sheet.

These steps will enable the instructor to make systematic comparisons:

1. At the top of the rating sheet, list the textbooks being considered.

2. Examine one textbook according to the criteria listed in the left-hand column of Part I. Evaluate according to the following rating scale: good, 3 points; average, 2 points; poor, 1 point. If a specific criterion (for example, "Appendix") is not included in the book being considered, this item can be omitted provided the other books do not contain this item.

3. After rating each criterion according to the 1, 2, or 3 scale, multiply by the factor listed for the specific criterion. For example, if "Layout of page" is given a rating of 3 and the multiplication factor is 4, a total of 12 points would be entered in the space provided opposite "Layout of page."

4. Total the points in Part I.

5. Repeat steps 2, 3, and 4 for each textbook being considered.

6. Refer to the section labeled Part II. List the main topics of the course for which the textbook is being considered.

7. Examine one textbook according to the main topics of the course, and rate each topic as a 1, 2, or 3. Use a factor 1 for all items except "Sequence of content," which has a factor of 3.

8. Total Part I and Part II in spaces provided.

9. Repeat steps 7 and 8 for each textbook being considered.

10. Rank the textbooks. The textbook with the highest total points would be best.

Professional and Technical Articles

In addition to books, there is a substantial body of literature available in professional and technical journals, magazines, and newsletters. Because of the time delay in the preparation and publication of books, an instructor may need to seek state-of-the-art technical materials in these other sources.

Articles are likely to be current, well illustrated, and valuable in most educational programs. Articles can provide additional facts and motivation for students, which can reinforce the value of knowledge and skills being taught in a program.

Copyright Revision Act of 1976

Professional instructors need to understand and follow federal legislation related to the use of copyrighted material. The 1976 copyright revision act is the fourth comprehensive revision of the copyright law "to promote the progress of Science and useful Arts by securing for limited times to Authors and Inventors the exclusive Right to their respective writings and discoveries."

Copyright is the cornerstone of the publishing industry. As such, it is crucial for the protection of authors and publishers, and for the public, which benefits from this protected creativity. When copyrighted works are duplicated beyond the bounds of fair use without permission, the author and publisher lose control over the use of the material. Such duplicating is illegal.

Guidelines for Classroom Copying. The purpose of the following guidelines, published by the Association of American Publishers, is to state the minimum and not the maximum standards of educational fair use under Section 107 of H.R. 2223.

I. SINGLE COPYING FOR TEACHERS:

A single copy may be made of any of the following by or for a teacher at his or her individual request for his or her scholarly research or use in teaching or preparation to teach a class:

A. A chapter from a book;

B. An article from a periodical or newspaper;

C. A short story, short essay, or short poem, whether or not from a collective work;

D. A chart, graph, diagram, drawing, cartoon, or picture from a book, periodical, or newspaper;

II. MULTIPLE COPIES FOR CLASSROOM USE:

Multiple copies (not to exceed in any event more than one copy per pupil in a course) may be made by or for the teacher giving the course for classroom use or discussion; provided that:

A. The copying meets the tests of brevity and spontaneity as defined below;

and,

B. Meets the cumulative effect test as defined below;

and,

C. Each copy includes a notice of copyright.

DEFINITIONS:

Brevity:

i. Prose: (a) Either a complete article, story or essay of less than 2500 words, or (b) an excerpt from any prose work of not more than 1000 words or 10% of the work, whichever is less, but in any event a minimum of 500 words.

ii. Illustration: One chart, graph, diagram, drawing, cartoon, or picture per book or per periodical issue.

Spontaneity:

i. The copying is at the instance and inspiration of the individual teacher, and

ii. The inspiration and decision to use the work and the moment of its use for maximum teaching effectiveness are so close in time that it would be unreasonable to expect a timely reply to a request for permission.

Cumulative Effect:

i. The copying of the material is for only one course in the school in which the copies are made.

ii. Not more than one short poem, article, story, essay or two excerpts may be copied from the same author, nor more than three from the same collective work or periodical volume during one class term.

iii. There shall not be more than nine instances of such multiple copying for one course during one class term.

INSTRUCTION SHEETS

Instruction sheets are written instructional units that are used by individual students. With the current increase in both the quality and quantity of textbooks, individual instruction sheets can be used in courses as supplements to required textbooks. Instruction sheets may be used for the following reasons:

1. Methods have been developed or materials marketed after the textbook was published.

2. Textbook material is too technical for the experience level of students.

3. Textbook material is too general for the instructor's purposes.

4. Textbook material requires considerable reading for only a few essential facts.

5. The instructor wants students to have tables and other important information in their notebooks.

Instruction sheets have greatest potential value in the following situations:

1. The instructor cannot spend time with each student because of class size.

2. Laboratory work is scheduled long after the related demonstration, and written materials are useful for individual review of the material previously taught.

3. Additional study is required of students outside of class.

4. Students must work on a variety of assignments at any one time because of the scheduling of limited equipment.

5. A wide range of ability and experience exists among individuals in the class.

Instruction sheets provide a practical means of supplementing and reinforcing instruction provided by demonstration, lecture, or printed material.

The five basic types of instruction sheets are operation, information, job, informational assignment, and job assignment sheets. These instruction sheets are consistent with the analysis process through which content areas are identified. See Figure 6-2.

INSTRUCTION SHEETS

Operation Sheet

Instruction on how to perform a standard operation. Based on doing content from the analysis.

Sample Titles

1. How to turn a taper with taper attachment.

2. How to harden and temper carbon tool steel.

3. How to prepare hardwood for finishing

4. How to input a footnote.

Information Sheet

Information related to an occupation or subject. Based on knowing content from the analysis.

Sample Titles

1. Types of tool steels.

2. Characteristics of American cabinet woods.

3. Opportunities in computer graphics.

4. Principles of the gyroscope.

Job Sheet

Instruction on how to do a task or job. Contains all details needed to complete the job. Based on a list of doing content from the analysis.

Sample Titles

1. Make a drift punch.

2. Construct a tripod.

3. Input a manuscript.

Informational Assignment Sheet

Specific instructions regarding the references to be read and studied. Includes study questions and problems.

Sample Titles

Titles must be same as those shown for Information Sheet. The Informational Assignment Sheet is not self-contained as it refers students to various resources.

Job Assignment Sheet

A modification of the Job Sheet. Most often used for production and service tasks. Usually contains drawings or diagrams as well as steps of procedure for completing a task or job. It differs primarily from the Job Sheet in that it is not self-contained. Steps of procedure are brief and refer students to a reference for performance details.

Sample Titles

Titles may be same as those indicated on the Job Sheet.

Figure 6-2. Instruction sheets provide a practical means for supplementing and reinforcing instruction provided by demonstration, lecture, and/or printed material.

Operation Sheets

Operation sheets are based on the performance element of an occupational analysis. An operation sheet should provide step-by-step instructions for performing a specific skill required to complete a job. The instructor's main concern is to identify and organize available materials in order to facilitate learning. See Figure 6-3.

Students using an operation sheet must perform each step before going on to the next. Operation sheets require the use of tools, equipment, and materials. Appropriate checks should be included so students know when performance is satisfactory. Normally, an operation sheet should contain:

1. a title that identifies the operation on which the sheet is based;
2. an introduction that describes the procedure and how it is used on the job;
3. a list of tools, equipment, and materials needed to perform the operation;
4. written procedures for performing each step;
5. performance standards that provide appropriate checks on student progress;
6. questions that direct students' attention to key points and basic concepts related to specific steps of procedure; and
7. a reference section that includes a list of sources for further information.

Information Sheets

An *information sheet* is directly related to the knowing content from the occupational analysis. The title of the information sheet is usually the same as the knowledge element on which it is based. On basic topics, it is most efficient to refer students to textbooks or other written material. Copyrighted material, however, should be used in its original form. An information sheet should contain the following:

1. a title that identifies content to be covered,
2. an introduction that provides a brief description of content to be learned,
3. text that identifies information students must know and provides illustrations where needed,
4. questions that direct students' attention to key information, and
5. a reference section that includes a list of sources for further information.

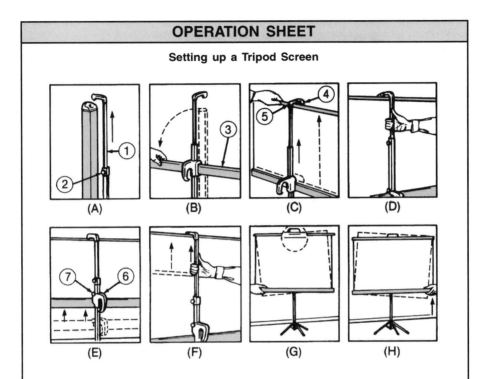

Figure 6-3. An operation sheet should provide step-by-step instructions.

A good information sheet:

1. does not duplicate material that is adequately covered in available texts;

2. is well organized;

3. uses common words and simple sentences to create easily-read paragraphs;

4. includes occasional questions to stimulate thought and check on understanding;

5. uses good analogies that tie new content to former experiences;

6. uses diagrams, drawings, and illustrations;

7. is technically correct;

8. highlights safety considerations; and

9. is as brief as possible.

Job Sheets

A *job sheet* is a list of doing elements required to complete a task. The job sheet can also be supplemented by drawings, bill of materials, and detailed procedural information needed by the student.

Job sheets are frequently prepared by the instructor for use in early stages of the instructional program. In later stages, students are required to plan their own job sheets. A job sheet contains:

1. a title that identifies the job or task on which the sheet is based;

2. an introduction that describes the job or task and why it is to be done;

3. a list of tools, equipment, and materials needed to complete the job or task;

4. drawings, photographs, and prints used to set standards for the completed job; and

5. a list of the doing elements in their proper sequence with sufficient detail to permit performance.

Assignment Sheets

An *assignment sheet* provides students with specific directions for completing an assignment. Assignment sheets often give learners secondary reading, problems to work, or questions to answer. Assignment sheets, frequently called informational assignment sheets, are used in the application of steps in a lesson. An assignment sheet should contain the following items:

1. a title that describes the assignment's scope, duration, and value to the student;

2. specific directions for completing the assignment, such as, "read pages 289 – 295 of *Fibers into Fabrics* by D. D. Martin"; and

3. a reference section that includes a list of sources for further information.

An assignment sheet may be used as a performance test. See Figure 6-4. Assignment sheets may also be used to develop students' problem solving and creative abilities. See Figure 6-5.

ASSIGNMENT SHEET

Measuring with the Architect's Scale

Directions: Read instructions carefully. Do step 1 first, then 2, and so on in succession. All lines are connected to form a continuous line. You will need a T-square, 45° triangle, scale, 2-H pencil, and one sheet of white paper.

Fasten paper to drawing board and then establish a point 1″ down and 1″ to the right of the upper left-hand corner of the paper. Draw a continuous line according to the following directions:

Step	Scale	Length	Direction
1	¼″ = 1′-0″	27′-6″	Horizontal (right)
2	1″ = 1″	6¹³⁄₁₆″	Vertical (down)
3	¾″ = 1′-0″	9′-6½″	Horizontal (left)
4	1½″ = 1′-0″	4′-3¼″	Vertical (up)
5	¼″ = 1′-0″	25′-10″	Horizontal (right)
6	¾″ = 1′-0″	6′-9″	Vertical (down)
7	1″ = 1″	5′-¾″	Horizontal (left)
8	⅛″ = 1′-0″	30′-8″	Vertical (up)
9	½″ = 1′-0″	7′-9½″	Horizontal (right)
10	³⁄₁₆″ = 1′-0″	15′-5″	Vertical (down)
11	3″ = 1′-0″	1′-1½″	Horizontal (left)
12	⅜″ = 1′-0″	6′-11″	Vertical (up)
13	½″ = 1′-0″	4′-9″	Horizontal (right)
14	1″ = 1′-0″	2′-¾″	Vertical (down)
15	³⁄₃₂″ = 1′-0″	60′-0″	At 45° slanting upward toward the starting point

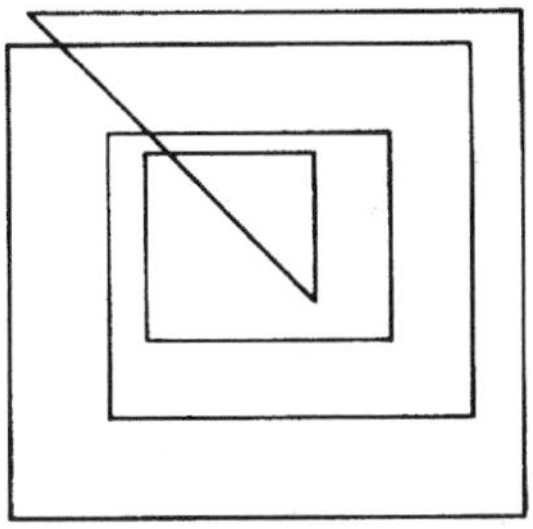

When completed, the last line should connect with the starting point; the series of lines should look like the drawing appearing at left, which has been reduced for reproduction.

Tech Directions

Figure 6-4. An assignment sheet may be used as a performance test.

ASSIGNMENT SHEET

Designing a Circle Scriber

The instrument must: (1) draw a 5′ circle, (2) hold a pencil, (3) be adjustable, and (4) have aesthetic appeal.

The solution to the problem must be on a 12″ × 18″ sheet of vellum. It must include (1) a detail drawing and dimensions of each part, (2) an isometric showing the assembled tool, (3) a title block and parts list, and (4) an area for notes describing special operations.

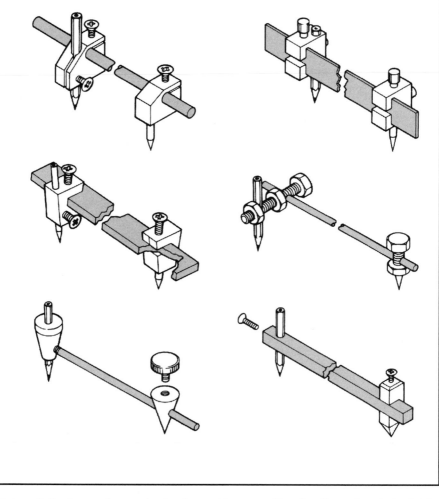

Figure 6-5. An assignment sheet provides specific directions to students for completing an assignment.

Information, operation, and assignment sheets are often combined. This is a practical approach when the information contained on the sheet is related to only one operation in the course. When material for an information sheet is related to several operations and assignments, a separate information sheet is more suitable.

Advantages of Instruction Sheets

1. Based on an occupational analysis and course objectives, instruction sheets provide for orderly, consistent arrangement of instructional content.
2. Instruction sheets are more concise and accurate than oral instruction.
3. Instruction sheets are available for review or independent study.
4. Instruction sheets reinforce learning.
5. Instruction sheets are based on major concepts of programmed instruction.
6. Students using instruction sheets may progress at their own rate; instruction sheets provide for individual differences within the group.
7. Students develop the ability to use written instructions.
8. Instruction sheets save valuable class time by eliminating the need for teachers to repeat instructions.

Limitations of Instruction Sheets

1. Ready-made sheets consistent with the content and organization of the course are frequently unavailable. This is especially true when the unit involves tools, materials, and equipment.
2. Preparation of effective written instructions, including graphic illustrations, is difficult for many instructors.
3. Creating instruction sheets is time-consuming for instructors.
4. Students with reading problems may have difficulty following written material.
5. Students may become too reliant on specific directions rather than developing analytical skills.
6. When used excessively, instruction sheets may reduce the opportunity for direct interaction between students and the instructor.

Instruction sheets are of great value; however, it is not always practical to use them extensively. In some situations, key areas of instruction should be covered by the instructor.

Written instructional materials are the backbone of all courses, even those with a large component of psychomotor learning. Instructors must present information in an organized, concise, and interesting manner to facilitate learning. Preparation of instructional materials requires several drafts, which are edited and refined. The instructor should review instruction sheets for technical accuracy, grammatical correctness, clarity, and relevance to course objectives. It is a good idea to solicit feedback from other instructors and to try out the instruction sheets before they are prepared in final form. If the instructor has adequate clerical support, one good way to develop instruction sheets is to outline the material and dictate the detailed information into a tape recorder. The transcription of the dictation may require editing to produce a high-quality instruction sheet.

Because of the limitations of instruction sheets, teachers should identify several good resources so that they will not spend time writing instruction sheets that are already available. It is much easier to modify instructional materials than to create them.

REVIEW

Questions

1. Distinguish between a textbook and a reference book.

2. How does federal copyright legislation limit the instructor's reproduction and distribution of instructional materials?

3. Under what circumstance would an instructor prepare an information sheet?

4. What is the purpose of an operation sheet?

5. Differentiate between a job sheet and an operation sheet.

6. What type of instruction sheet would be used to guide a student activity such as a term project?

7. What is the primary advantage of using an assignment sheet?

8. To what extent do instruction sheets accommodate individual differences?

9. What criteria should be considered when selecting a textbook?

10. What steps are taken when using a rating scale to select a textbook?

11. In addition to textbooks, what other types of printed material are available to instructors?

12. Under what conditions may an instructor make multiple copies of copyrighted material for classroom use?

13. Under what conditions may an instructor make single copies of copyrighted material for scholarly research or use in teaching?

14. Under what types of use do instruction sheets have the greatest potential value?

15. What are the five basic types of instruction sheets?

16. What are the essential elements of a job sheet?

17. What are some of the major advantages of an instruction sheet?

18. What are some of the limitations of an instruction sheet?

19. How does the cumulative effect enter into the copying of material?

20. What are the essential elements of an operation sheet?

Activities

1. Using the textbook rating form, rate two potential textbooks for a course you are planning to teach.

2. Develop an operation sheet using the format suggested in this chapter.

3. Identify a body of cognitive content for a course you plan to teach and prepare an assignment sheet.

4. Explain the rationale for developing an information sheet if the information to be taught is readily available in a textbook or resource book.

5. List three limitations of instruction sheets and describe how these limitations might be minimized.

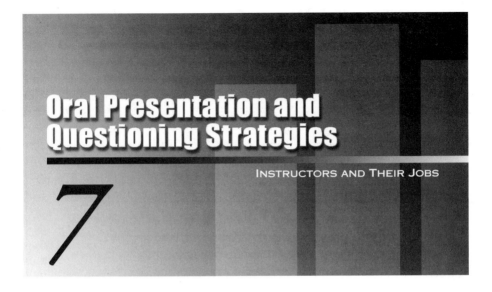

INTRODUCTION

Teaching requires numerous decisions. As the instructor plans a lesson, decisions must be made concerning the most appropriate methods and techniques whereby students will gain the expected competencies.

The lecture is frequently cited as the most maligned method of instruction. When properly used with other instructional strategies, oral presentations can contribute to effective teaching and learning.

Instructors know there is much more to teaching than telling. Effective instruction provides for two-way communication between the instructor and students. Direct lecture without some involvement by students should seldom exceed 10 minutes to 15 minutes. The lecture method is typically supplemented with written handouts, transparencies, chalkboard illustrations, student questions, student activities, instructor questions, or other means of interacting with the subject matter. A good lesson has several components, and the effective instructor seldom relies solely on a single instructional method.

PLANNING PRESENTATIONS

The lecture method is often criticized because it (1) involves too much lecturing, (2) forces the learner into a passive role, and (3) wastes time because students could gain the information through reading material. These criticisms are caused by overuse or inappropriate use of the lecture method, but these problems are not inherent in the method itself. The effectiveness of the lecture depends largely on the care and skill with which the instructor prepares and delivers the lecture.

Relationship to Lesson Plan

Planning for an oral presentation or lecture is not an isolated activity, as it must be viewed in the context of planning a lesson. The presentation is the key element in a lesson; however, there are components to be considered in the instructor's planning. For example, the objectives for a class session must be clearly identified in order that the substance of the presentation relates directly to the student's mastery of objectives. Likewise, appropriate resources must be identified that will enhance learning, and there must be an opportunity for student participation.

Lesson plan formats include an introduction. Effective teachers use a *set induction*, a method designed to put students in a receptive frame of mind, that will facilitate learning as the instructor seeks to (1) focus attention on objectives, (2) create an organizational framework for information presented, and (3) stimulate student interest.

Outline Preparation

The presentation or lecture must be prepared so that it contributes to instructional efficiency and effectiveness. The effective instructor prepares a topical outline of the oral presentation. The outline permits the instructor to consider all elements of the topic to be presented so a complete structural framework can be conceptualized. This organizational framework establishes major and minor points to be presented, as well as a chain of reasoning within the topic. Without a carefully developed outline, the instructor will have difficulty giving proper attention to the scope, sequence, and timing of the presentation.

The amount of detail included in an outline depends on many factors and can only be determined by the instructor. The instructor must consider the nature of the subject and students' level of development and personal knowledge of the topic. It should be assumed that an experienced instructor might require a less detailed outline than a beginning instructor.

Presentation Preparation

After outlining the content of the presentation, the instructor needs to prepare the lesson plan, which provides the context for the presentation and allows for other activities that will increase instructional effectiveness and learning. It is not necessary to prepare a complete manuscript for a lecture, nor is it necessary to memorize an entire oral presentation. However, it is desirable to have a thoroughly developed introduction that provides the set induction for the lesson.

A lesson plan should include appropriate questions that might be asked during or following a presentation. In the lesson plan format, questions are indicated as interaction items. Interaction items may be questions or alternatives to questions, such as the following:

1. Use declarative statements that reflect the instructor's thinking or rephrase student remarks. The instructor might begin with "So you think that . . ." or "I think you are saying that . . ."

2. Make declarative restatements that reflect students' thinking.

3. Pose indirect questions, for example, "I wonder why you think . . ."

4. Use imperatives, for example, "Show me the reason for that . . ." or "Tell us more about that . . ."

5. Use students to pose questions to fellow students.

6. Provide deliberate silence. When a student finishes speaking, the teacher maintains silence. It has been determined that when the teacher waits, the student will often resume speaking, or another student will speak up.

These techniques do not replace, but merely supplement, the skill a teacher might develop in questioning. Research has revealed that the more the teacher asks questions, the less the student participates. Questioning does not always stimulate student participation.

After the detailed introduction has been prepared and questions have been formulated, the instructor should prepare audiovisual aids. Handouts and other appropriate activities or assignments must be prepared in advance. In addition, notes should be made to remind the instructor of relevant examples, anecdotes, or analogies that will facilitate student understanding.

MAKING PRESENTATIONS

Success of an oral presentation is based on the planning process. Planning cannot, however, ensure a successful presentation. Environmental factors, such as room temperature and humidity as well as sudden shifts in the weather, can have a profound effect on the student's attention to the learning task. The instructor must capitalize on the results of planning by maximizing student interest and involvement and minimizing student distractions and apathy.

Audience Attention

Instructors often become so interested in the subject matter that they assume students are equally interested. This is not always the case. Instructors should give considerable attention to selling the lesson to all students, since a disinterested and unmotivated student will be a poor learner. Planning for the introduction should be substantial. An effective way to begin a presentation is to pose a provocative question, present a dramatic quotation, tell an interesting and related story, mention a puzzling or paradoxical set of facts from the content of the lesson, or use some other means of arousing student interest and curiosity.

An instructor's enthusiasm for a subject catches the student's interest. The more an instructor knows about a subject, the more potential applications can be perceived and the more interest and enthusiasm can be generated. Without knowledge, experience, and interest, it is difficult for an instructor to be enthusiastic. There is no substitute for firsthand experience about the subject matter. One cannot expect students to be interested in student material that is not of interest to an instructor.

Instructors can gain students' attention by knowing about their background and interests. When an instructor shows an interest by learning student names and by treating them as individuals, there is a reciprocal level of interest and attention generated toward the instructor.

It is important to maintain a high level of student attention throughout the lesson. The presentation must be varied by moving from one type of student activity to another and by limiting the amount of prolonged lecturing. A variety of stimuli must be used throughout the lesson. *Stimulus variation* refers to those teacher actions, which are sometimes planned and are sometimes spontaneous, that can develop and sustain student attention. Stimulus variation includes movements, sounds, or visual impressions that change or vary during the lesson.

Physical Behavior

The success of a lecture depends on the instructor's communication skills. The instructor's method of delivery affects the attention of the learner, which directly affects the extent to which learning occurs. An instructor's nonverbal behavior (e.g., vocal intonation, gestures, facial expression, body postures and movements, and use of space) contribute to or hinder instructional effectiveness.

No two individuals are exactly the same. As a result, behavior patterns of one effective instructor are not the same as those of another instructor who may be equally effective. Nevertheless, research and observation indicates the positive and negative behavior patterns of which instructors should be aware.

Movement. An effective instructor cannot be lectern-bound or seated motionless at a desk or table. Motion gets attention, although too much motion may be distracting. Body movements should be natural, not too rigid, rapid, or jerky. Research literature refers to an instructor's physical movements for the expressed purpose of maintaining attention and improving communications as *kinesic variation.* The physical movement from one part of the room to another focuses student attention directly on the instructor during the presentation. Movement needs to appear natural rather than mechanical. Moving freely represents changes in the instructor's physical position, which helps to maintain student attention.

Attending. An instructor should exhibit *attending* behavior when communicating with students in a manner that reveals interest, concern, and respect. It is not easy to make all students feel that they are receiving the instructor's personal attention. Instructors should make eye contact with each student in a class during the course of a presentation. Showing interest through attending behavior can affect how students feel about the instructor and the amount of attention and respect that will be given in return. For example, the instructor who responds in a manner that causes a student to feel foolish contributes to a negative learning environment. Smiling and moving toward a student who has asked a question often helps to provide the student with a positive learning environment.

Focusing. *Focusing* is the type of behavior used by a teacher to intentionally control the direction of student attention. This type of controlled attention is gained either through specific physical gestures or verbal statements or both. Gestures and facial expressions can provide animation. This type of directed movement can increase comprehension if it supplements oral communication and is not otherwise distracting. Gestures are used to reinforce ideas and to convey meaning. A shrug of the shoulders, a glance at the ceiling, or crossing one's arms may convey more meaning than words. It is important that key points are emphasized with gestures rather than using gestures continually. Gestures, such as using the hands expressively, motioning with the arms, pointing, clapping the hands, raising the eyebrows, smiling, or frowning can be used to direct the learner's attention to a particular thought, word, or concept.

Pacing and Pausing. *Pacing* is the rate of an instructor's speech pattern, physical movements, and the shift from one activity to another. The instructor's personality and habit patterns tend to influence the pace of class activity. The natural pace of an instructor may not be appropriate for the content being delivered or the learning style of the students. A pace too slow may induce boredom and cause students to lose interest; a pace too rapid may leave students frustrated and confused. Thus, relatively low level content may be taught with brisk pacing, while complex content may require slower pacing. Remember that the student is supposed to apply mentally as the instructor presents orally. If the learner has insufficient time to process information presented by the instructor, learning will not take place.

The concept of pausing is related to pacing. Recent research focuses on how pausing affects communication. A moment of silence is not only necessary for the learner to process information, but it can also be used to get attention. Professionals in speech and theater have long used dramatic pauses. Educational researchers have only recently become interested in evaluating frequency, duration, and the use of planned silence in the classroom. Instructors often overlook the value of pauses within the oral presentation. The insecure instructor may fear silence, as there is a compulsion to fill the silence with the sound of one's own voice.

As a stimulus variation technique, pausing enhances instruction by:

1. creating expectation or suspense,
2. providing a model of listening behavior,
3. emphasizing an important point,
4. providing an opportunity for students to process and mentally apply information,
5. capturing attention through the use of silence,
6. signaling that the teacher is moving to another point, and
7. showing disapproval of undesired student behaviors.

Mannerisms. Stimulus variation is important in maintaining learner attention. Behavior that is meaningless or repetitive can be distractive. Instructors often develop *mannerisms*, patterns of movement or speech that are distracting and interfere with the learning process. These movements and expressions are typically repeated without regard to the meaning that they might convey. Examples of distracting mannerisms include rattling pocket coins, repeating expressions such as "you know," or "okay," leaning over the lectern, tossing a piece of chalk in the air, or pacing back and forth. These behaviors are often so habitual that the instructor may be unaware of the adverse impact on learners. Instructors can use a video recording system to analyze personal behavior and speech patterns. Students can also provide feedback through anonymous instructor evaluations.

Clarity of Presentation

The extent to which a presentation is easily understood and free from confusion determines its *clarity*. A presentation that has clarity is clear, logical, and orderly. Educational researchers are giving an increased amount of attention to teaching clarity. Clarity of presentation has two dimensions. In the first dimension, clarity deals with the instructor's knowledge and ability to plan the presentation. The second dimension involves the manner in which the content of the presentation is delivered.

Thinking and Speaking. Before an instructor can express an idea clearly, the idea must first be thoroughly understood. Faulty choice of words is indicative of inadequate preparation. Some rules to remember include the following:

1. Use a vocabulary common to students. Consider the educational level of students. It is better to oversimplify instruction than to run the risk of talking over the students' heads.
2. Define technical terms the first time they are used.
3. Do not assume that acronyms are understood.
4. Use short sentences for emphasis.
5. Eliminate unnecessary words and phrases.
6. Be specific. Make statements exact and precise in meaning.

In order to make a transition from one phrase of a lesson to another, the instructor may introduce the new phrase with a statement explaining the nature of the concept and its relationship to the whole lesson. Use a variety of expressions for introducing new materials. Avoid the repetition of introductory remarks such as, "Next, we take up the . . .," or "Now, we go into the . . ."

Verbal descriptions of an object or process often cannot provide complete communication. Other means of communication including pictures, prints, tables, and charts are usually required.

Voice. Every student in the class should be able to hear what is being said by the instructor. The following suggestions may be useful to remember:

1. Relax.
2. Vary the volume of your voice. Consider the size of the class and the conditions under which instruction is given. Be particularly attentive to this when giving instruction in a room that has poor acoustics.
3. Watch students' reactions. The instructor can usually tell if students are having difficulty in hearing. If any possibility exists that the volume is not satisfactory, ask students at the back if they can hear.
4. Strive for vocal variety.

Articulation. The clarity of spoken words is more important than the production of sounds and syllables. The instructor should strive for good articulation in an oral presentation. Speak at a rate and with pronunciation that enables students to distinguish the words being used. One should

1. practice pronouncing each word distinctly and clearly;
2. be particularly careful in pronouncing words that may not be common to the vocabulary of students, and write unknown words on the board;

3. not slur or run words together;

4. not speak too rapidly; and

5. face the class when speaking.

Rate of Speaking. An average of 100 to 150 words per minute is considered satisfactory for oral instruction. Franklin D. Roosevelt spoke about 110 words per minute. Although many instructors can speak clearly at a faster than average rate, students ordinarily have insufficient time to understand the ideas expressed if the rate of speaking is increased. An instructor should consider the following rules concerning the rate of speaking:

1. Present easy materials at a fairly rapid rate.

2. Present difficult material at a slower rate.

3. Pause frequently to give students a chance to comprehend remarks and take notes.

4. If the time for a particular lesson is decreased, do not talk faster in an effort to cover the same material. Plan the lesson to fit the shorter schedule.

Correct English. Using poor English is a handicap few instructors can afford. Improper use of English also undermines the importance of effective communication skills, which should be a part of every educational program. Ask for help identifying errors and practice correct wording. Use a tape recorder. Listen carefully to those who have a reputation for speaking well. Consider seeking instruction in speech or communication. Review a good reference on oral communication.

Presentation Conclusion

Lectures should have a planned conclusion designed to accomplish certain objectives. *Closure* refers to actions or statements by the instructor that are designed to bring a lesson to an appropriate conclusion. Typically, the conclusion involves a review of the main points that the instructor wants students to remember. Closure helps students bring major points together and gain greater meaning from the presentation. Following this review, the instructor would ordinarily shift from lecture to some other mode of instructional interaction, such as questioning, applying, or evaluating.

It is important to recognize that closure helps to embed newly learned material into the learner's network of relationships, which facilitates storage into long-term memory and provides a number of possibilities as cues for the retrieval process. Closure is the compliment of set induction. Set induction is the initiating activity for the lesson, while closure is the culminating activity. Research indicates that learning increases when instructors help students organize information. In summary, closure is the teacher's way of (1) drawing attention to the end of a lesson, (2) providing assistance so students see relationships within the conceptual framework of the content to be learned, and (3) reinforcing major points to be learned.

Listening Skills. An instructor may present a carefully planned lesson, paying attention to all the rules of good oral delivery. However, it is a mistake for an instructor to assume that just because learners hear, they are listening. Hearing is the physical ability to receive sounds, while listening is interpreting the sounds and understanding the message. Instructors should never forget that communication is a two-way process and that their presentation is not complete without a receiver. In spite of the time instructors may have spent on the job or in the classroom and the time students spend in school, most people are not particularly effective or efficient listeners. Effective listening requires energy and conscious attention. Since most people assume that anyone who does not have a hearing impairment must be able to listen, there is little formal instruction in listening. In fact, ineffective listening is generally the result of poor listening habits or faulty assumptions about listening such as the most intelligent people listen well and the least intelligent people listen poorly and instruction in listening is unnecessary.

Successful instructors know that without instruction to improve listening skills, many students may develop poor listening habits that may carry over to the workplace and in other areas of their lives. Some of the most common bad listening habits are: (1) faking attention, (2) memorizing all the facts and losing the ideas, (3) avoiding difficult listening, (4) rejecting a subject as uninteresting, (5) finding fault with the speaker, and (6) concentrating on distractions. The instructor knows that students listen for a variety of reasons. Outside the classroom, students may listen carefully as a classmate tells a joke so that they do not miss the punch line. In class, they listen for information, to evaluate ideas, for entertainment, or to appreciate the worth of something they hear. The instructor should prepare students to listen by providing guidelines to good listening. For example, the instructor may present an overview of the importance of the lesson and the lesson objectives, telling students what to listen for and how to take notes on the main points of a lecture. Providing students with an outline of the lecture is an effective means to improve listening, particularly if space is allotted for students to take notes as they listen.

DEVELOPING ORAL QUESTIONING STRATEGIES

To be an effective instructor, one must be an effective questioner. Telling is not teaching. Good questioning strategies can be used to enhance the learning process. Questioning should be a part of the instructional strategy. Effective teachers ask questions to (1) check the student's understanding of key points, (2) check for mastery of basic concepts, (3) encourage critical thinking, and (4) stimulate interaction among students, as well as between instructor and student. The first step in effective questioning is to recognize that questions have distinctive characteristics, serve various functions, and provide opportunities to develop higher level thinking skills by applying, analyzing, synthesizing, or evaluating the content being learned.

Research in the area of questioning indicates that most questions asked by teachers demand nothing more than recall of facts. One way to avoid asking questions leading to the mere repetition of facts is to start each question with a word or phrase that calls for thought on the part of the students. Words such as *what, why, how, summarize, justify, trace, describe,* or *define* encourage thoughtful answers and meaningful interaction. Through the process of questioning, the instructor stimulates the learner to make use of information, to put together facts that may not have been thoroughly understood, and to draw logical conclusions.

The questioning technique is effective if it is carried out at the appropriate time, causes students to learn by thinking and doing, and changes students' roles from passive listening to thinking and applying. Skillful questioning can be learned through study, practice, and feedback. Instructors can improve their questioning techniques by learning to formulate more thought-provoking questions and encouraging critical thinking by students. Instructors can also learn to avoid practices that interfere with students' responses.

Types of Questions

Questions are typically categorized into two main groups: (1) factual or recall and (2) application or problem. A more meaningful classification system would be to relate questioning to Bloom's *Taxonomy of Educational Objectives* and differentiate questions by the six cognitive levels: (1) knowledge, (2) comprehension, (3) application, (4) analysis, (5) synthesis, and (6) evaluation.

Knowledge. At the knowledge level, the instructor's questions require students to recognize or recall information and to remember facts, observations, and definitions that have been learned previously. Although there is substantial criticism among educators of factual or knowledge level questions, this level of question does have its place in the instructional spectrum. The overuse or abuse of this level of questioning is the main reason for criticism. It is important for instructors to realize that the learner must function at the knowledge level before being expected to perform at higher levels. Memorization of information is also required in order to perform a variety of tasks. The meaning of words, correct spelling, multiplication facts, and rules of the road are examples of important information that must be committed to memory.

Comprehension. Questions at the comprehension level require students to interpret and translate information that is presented on charts, graphs, and tables as well as specific facts. It is important to realize that the student must have certain factual information in order to gain the understanding necessary to organize and arrange the material mentally. For questions of this type, the student must demonstrate a level of understanding by rephrasing, describing, or making comparisons.

Application. Questions at the application level require a student to apply previously learned information to solve a specific problem. At this level, it is not sufficient for the student to relate or even to paraphrase and interpret previously memorized information. Instead, students must use the information to answer questions or solve problems. For example, a student who has learned the definitions of latitude and longitude may be asked to locate a given point on a map.

Analysis. Questions at this level of cognition require students to look for hidden meaning or inferences of acquired information. As information is analyzed, one must reach sound conclusions or draw generalizations based on available information. Analysis questions ask students to (1) identify motives, reasons, and/or causes of specific occurrences or events; (2) reach certain conclusions, draw inferences, or make generalizations based on given information; or (3) identify evidence needed to support or refute conclusions, inferences, or generalizations. In many instances there are no absolute answers to the analysis question, as several answers are plausible. Furthermore, because it takes time to analyze these questions, they cannot be answered quickly or without careful thought.

Synthesis. Synthesis questions require higher order thinking processes. Students must make predictions, use creativity in developing original approaches, or solve problems that do not have single answers. Instructors can use synthesis questions to help develop and reinforce students' creative abilities. These questions demand a substantial amount of information and a thorough understanding of many factors as students consider possible responses.

Evaluation. Evaluation questions require students to judge the merit of an idea, to assess the plausibility of a solution, or to offer an opinion on an issue. These actions require that a student possess substantial information and be able to establish criteria for making a judgment.

Characteristics of Good Questions

In order to formulate and use appropriate questions, the instructor cannot rely on words and phrases that come to mind during a class presentation. Some questions, of course, will be spontaneous in response to a given set of circumstances. However, interaction items need to be developed in advance and keyed to specific sections of the presentation. When asking questions during a class period, it should not be necessary to read them. The instructor should state the questions with reasonable accuracy from memory after a glance at the lesson plan. The carefully prepared questions should provide a skeletal framework around which impromptu questions may be asked as the situation dictates.

Clearly Stated Questions. Questions should be stated in simple, straightforward language. The instructor should ask questions in a brief, yet sufficient manner to ensure understanding. The first word should be the action word, for example, explain, define, and compare. Questions ordinarily should be phrased in language adapted to the class level. If students do not understand the question, they will be unable to respond. See Figure 7-1.

KEY WORDS FOR QUESTIONS	
Key Word	**Student Response**
Explain	Requires clear evidence about the meaning of or reason for a subject.
Outline	Requires the listing of main or key points in a logical order.
Define	Requires an accurate description of the limits of a subject.
Compare	Requires the identification of similarities and differences.
Illustrate	Requires examples of principles or facts.

Figure 7-1. A well-worded question should use action verbs to ensure understanding.

Common Vocabulary. Questions should be designed to assess knowledge and understanding of the subject. An instructor's vocabulary must be understandable to students. In a teaching-learning environment, questions provide reinforcement, identify concepts that need to be retaught, and provide opportunities for students to gain greater understanding through verbal descriptions.

Thought-Provoking Questions. Questions should challenge students to go beyond the knowledge level whenever possible. Questions should be phrased to reach beyond the simple "yes or no" response. If the question is so easy that the answer is obvious, then it is probably not worth asking. Questions that are thought-provoking arouse the curiosity and interest of students and help them clarify their ideas as well as analyze and synthesize facts. This aspect of questioning is especially important to adult learners.

Value of Questions

For maximum effectiveness, the instructor should use questions to

1. stimulate interest in the lesson;
2. establish communication between the instructor and students;
3. focus students' attention on major points to be remembered;
4. stimulate learning by causing students to apply facts to analyze problems;
5. help students develop a feeling of confidence and success, which leads to greater motivation, further study, and experimentation;
6. help students develop ability to organize ideas and speak effectively;
7. build cooperation through group activity and responsibility;
8. provide for a democratic approach to learning; and
9. evaluate effectiveness of instruction.

Use of Effective Questions

Questioning has the potential for making a positive impact on students at several levels of cognition. It is important that the instructor develop techniques that enable questioning strategies to be used effectively. See Figure 7-2.

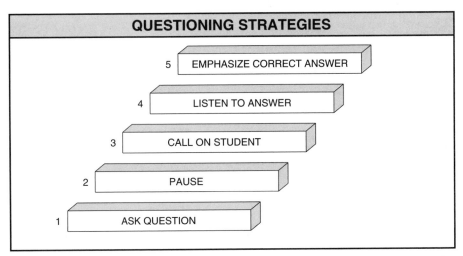

Figure 7-2. Instructors should develop techniques that enable questioning strategies to be used effectively.

To Whom is the Question Asked? Students should understand that questioning is a part of the teaching process, and that questions are asked for purposes of clarification, verification, implication, and evaluation.

The instructor should make sure the entire class is able to hear the question. A system should be used so that everyone is called upon to answer with reasonable frequency. Do not call an individual's name before posing the question. This practice encourages only one student, the one whose name is called, to listen. Posing the question and then waiting a few seconds before selecting a student is a better strategy. Choose individuals in a random fashion but record the number of questions that individuals answered.

Do You Provide Enough Time for a Response? Pacing is essential to effective questioning. Questions are intended to stimulate students to think about the content and formulate responses, rather than merely retrieve information from memory. It is important to provide adequate time for these processes to occur. This is especially true for complex questions where students may need time to process the question before formulating a response. The waiting period should be appropriate to the question being asked.

Often, the instructor feels uncomfortable with waiting. Classroom interaction is often characterized by an incredibly rapid rate of interaction as instructors fire one question after another without giving students sufficient time to think, formulate answers, and respond. When instructors can master the skill of waiting, particularly for questions at the higher levels of cognition, they will probably find positive changes in the quantity and quality of student responses. Both instructors and students need to realize it is okay to have a few seconds of silence. Research reveals that teachers tend to wait less than one second before asking someone to respond. Furthermore, even after selecting a student, instructors tended to wait less than one second for the student to answer. This behavior suggests that instructors are underestimating the value of questioning.

Does the Question Match the Individual? Effort should be made to match questions with specific individuals. Instructors should learn the names of students quickly and, even more importantly, become knowledgeable about intellectual abilities within a class.

Student responses should be evaluated carefully so class members can be made aware of the extent to which an answer may be correct or partially correct. The instructor may need to rephrase an answer in order to clarify meaning. In most instances, however, the exact wording of the student's response should not be repeated in parrot-like fashion by the instructor. The student responding should be encouraged to speak clearly and loudly enough for all to hear; the classroom should be quiet enough for the response to be heard. Students need to learn to listen to their peers. In fact, sometimes the wording chosen by a student has greater impact on other students than the phrasing that the instructor might use.

What is the Instructor's Reaction to the Student's Response? The instructor should provide appropriate reinforcement to students responding to a question. The most frequent types of reinforcement used by teachers are verbal reinforcers, which consist of a one word or brief phrase response. Examples include "good," "that's right," "excellent," "okay," or "nice job." A more powerful reward is to build on the student's response or elaborate on a point. A similar strategy can be used when a student does not give a complete or completely accurate response. The instructor can separate the correct part and then ask another student to provide additional information. It is important to provide verbal reinforcement to even partially correct responses in order to increase the student's desire to participate. Responses such as, "That's not right," "Where did you get that idea?" or "You should know better than that" are negative reinforcers that discourage student participation.

As powerful as verbal reinforcement is, nonverbal reinforcement may be even more powerful. *Nonverbal reinforcement* refers to physical messages sent by teachers through cues such as eye contact, facial expression, and body positioning. A teacher's smile or frown communicates to students. The way the instructor is standing may imply defensiveness or disapproval. Nonverbal cues may imply that the teacher is interested, disinterested, pleased, or displeased with the student's response. In subtle ways, nonverbal reinforcement encourages or inhibits student participation.

Are Questions Developed Sequentially to Lead to Higher Levels of Understanding? While increasing response time and reinforcement are two strategies that instructors can use to increase student participation, it is desirable to enhance the quality of student thinking through the questioning process. A questioning strategy leads the student from one level of thinking to higher levels by a careful series of questions. Probing questions should follow students' responses and attempt to stimulate thinking about their answers. This type of questioning may be used to prompt student thinking most effectively at the higher levels of analysis, synthesis, and evaluation.

In addition to questions, instructors must also be prepared to react to student-initiated comments and questions. Relevant student questions indicate a need for clarification or a desire to know more about the subject. Relevant comments suggest that students are actively thinking about the subject matter and relating it to past experiences. These questions and comments present unique opportunities that demand attention. Instructors should welcome such questions and comments and, when possible, should respond positively.

An effective presentation begins with a good plan. An instructor's presentation should be a vital component of the lesson. The presentation cannot be maximized unless the other elements of the lesson plan are carried out effectively.

Seldom is an oral presentation made in isolation. Typically, the instructor uses visual aids, involves students in an activity, or applies questioning techniques to check student learning.

Lesson planning involves the identification of interaction items that are used by the instructor to increase student participation. Interaction items are often questions, however, there are alternatives to questions that bring about interaction between instructor and students.

Planning alone cannot ensure a successful presentation. The effectiveness and the impact of the instructor's behavior depends on the instructor's personality and rapport with students. The effective instructor must be concerned about the structure and clarity of the presentation. The words used, the instructor's articulation, and the way sentences are constructed affect the manner in which ideas are transmitted. These techniques can be learned with practice, and instructors can become increasingly effective by giving careful attention to their stage presence, as well as the tone, volume, and pacing of the oral delivery.

It is important that student activities and interactions be anticipated and planned. A good way to stimulate student interaction is through effective questioning. Instructors should realize that there are several types of questions that assess learning at various levels of cognition. Although some questions occur spontaneously from the students or the instructor, instructors should plan several questions in advance so that the level of understanding resulting from the presentation can be systematically assessed.

In addition to the tendency to ask questions that require only recall, there is also a tendency for instructors not to wait for a student's react. Instructors are uneasy with a pause and feel a need to fill the void with the sound of their own voices. As the instructor focuses on higher levels of learning with questions that require the student to analyze, synthesize, or evaluate, more time must be given for the student to consider alternatives and provide a thoughtful response. Care must be taken by the instructor to react properly to student responses in order to encourage continued participation rather than to inadvertently discourage participation. Not only must instructors be careful of the words or phrases used in response to student questioning, but they must also be concerned with the nonverbal communication. The instructor's posture or facial expression may communicate more than words. The teaching-learning process requires careful planning and execution. The effective instructor gives attention to various elements of classroom interaction, maximizes the student's time, and helps them to achieve the objectives specified for the lesson.

REVIEW

Questions

1. What are the disadvantages of using lecture as the sole instructional method for a lesson?

2. What are the primary advantages and disadvantages of the lecture method?

3. What are several ways in which oral presentation is used as a methodology within a lesson?

4. What is the purpose of set induction?

5. Why is it desirable to prepare an outline for a presentation?

6. What are alternatives to questions used to stimulate interaction during a lesson?

7. What are environmental factors that influence the attention of students during an oral presentation?

8. How does the instructor's knowledge of students and interest in them affect student interest?

9. What is meant by stimulus variation?

10. What are the pros and cons of movement as it relates to the effectiveness of an oral presentation?

11. What is meant by attending behavior?

12. How can an instructor become aware of verbal and physical mannerisms that are distracting?

13. How does instructional planning affect instructional clarity?

14. If an instructor's voice has a relatively narrow range of tones, how can the instructor compensate for this in order to make the voice or speech pattern more interesting?

15. What is the meaning of closure, and how should it be used in an oral presentation?

16. How can student questions be used as feedback for instructional improvement?

17. What are the six levels of the cognitive domain?

18. What are three important characteristics of effective questions?

19. What is the primary advantage of asking a question and then selecting a specific student to respond?

20. What is the primary disadvantage of calling a student's name before posing a question?
21. What would be a reasonable amount of time to wait after asking a question before moving on to another individual or providing a verbal cue?
22. Why is it important to provide positive reinforcement to a student who did not provide a completely correct response?
23. What is the role of nonverbal communication in the teacher-student interaction?
24. Why is listening considered a skill?

Activities

1. Describe the interrelationships between the lecture method and questioning strategies.
2. Indicate the parts of a lesson plan that require oral presentation.
3. Develop several questions that would bring about instructor and student interaction in a lesson you plan to teach.
4. Develop a topical outline of a presentation and have it critiqued by your instructor.
5. Describe your instructor's physical behaviors that contribute to and detract from student interest, attention, and learning. Code the behaviors that involve movement, attending, focusing, as well as the use of pacing and pausing.
6. Audiotape and then critique a brief presentation covering a topic of your choice.
7. Develop a set of questions related to a topic you have presented or will present as an instructor. Deliberately structure questions at each of the six cognitive domain levels.
8. Critique a class session by noting the instructor's use of questions.
9. Describe your response to a student who asked a question that is not within the framework of your lesson.
10. Describe your response to a student's question that is not related to the topic of the lesson or even the course, although the question may have been stimulated by something the instructor or another student said.

Discussion and Group Participation Methods

8

INTRODUCTION

Lecture and demonstration, when properly applied in a classroom setting, provide for student interaction with the instructor. When class discussion is used, however, the instructor becomes a group leader who shares ideas, information, and opinions in order to (1) clarify issues, (2) relate new input to prior knowledge, or (3) attempt to resolve questions or problems that may have no correct solution.

Discussion is a participatory or learner-centered approach. During discussion, the instructor acts as a leader who structures the activity by setting boundaries and facilitating interaction. In this role, the instructor is less dominant and less judgmental. In groups containing adults, the instructor may be removed completely from the discussion to serve as a resource person. Learner-centered participatory methods take considerable planning by the instructor so groups have clearly defined objectives, know the process to be used, and understand expectations. When the group process is used, there is a shift of authority and responsibility. Involvement in setting goals and directing learning activities provide unusual growth opportunities for students. Participation methods also provide a change of pace and an opportunity for learner participation and application after a foundation has been provided through lecture, demonstration, and reading. The discussion process is not the most efficient means of providing new information; however, it is valuable when seeking to achieve high-level objectives.

Discussion encompasses learner-centered group procedures that provide for a substantial amount of learner participation and interaction. Specialized group procedures that use discussion methodology include cooperative learning, role-playing, brainstorming, the nominal group process, and quality circles.

INSTRUCTOR'S ROLE IN GROUP PARTICIPATION

Discussion is neither efficient nor effective for acquiring factual information or securing precise information of a procedural nature that leads to skill development. Discussion is an excellent methodology for the sharing of prior knowledge or experience, which can lead to a new or enhanced perspective by the participant. Instructors must identify points in a lesson where discussion or group participation would be appropriate. They must also determine the number and size of discussion groups, or whether the entire class can function effectively as a single discussion group.

Instructors should record ideas during discussion. Instructors must not place a value on student input as either good or bad, right or wrong. If someone else is leading the discussion, the instructor may wish to withdraw from the discussion and enter only to (1) make a connection between ideas, (2) point out similarities or contrasts, (3) request clarification or elaboration, (4) invite students to respond to one another, and (5) summarize the progress at various points in time. The fact that discussion requires less lecturing than other types of instruction does not suggest less preparation. Class preparation is necessary if the instructor is to develop a proper discussion atmosphere.

The instructor's or discussion leader's role is to involve students in an effective and constructive manner. The group leader must guide the discussion when necessary, without being too obvious, and bring the session to a close with an adequate summary. Above all, the instructor must be sensitive to individual responses and of all participants' feelings. A few suggestions are as follows:

1. Set the stage. Explain the method to be used and what will be discussed. Use questions to involve participants. Make sure students understand what is to be learned, and that no comment will be criticized.

2. Be prepared to ask questions during discussion. Avoid conflict or controversy that may cause students to withdraw from further participation. This can be accomplished by (1) giving credit where needed, (2) tactfully clarifying meaning, (3) suggesting a review of what has been said, or (4) asking a question to draw individuals back into the discussion.

3. Listen. Do not become emotionally involved in the discussion. The leader's job is to draw out the thoughts and feelings of individuals in the group.

4. Summarize the discussion and clear up misconceptions.

When using learner-centered methodology, the instructor is no longer viewed as the central source of authority. The effectiveness of the group process depends upon the instructor's willingness to lead the group without being the expert.

DIRECTED DISCUSSION

Directed discussion requires students, rather than the instructor, to provide most of the class information. In directed discussion, the instructor acts as a leader and directs or redirects ideas and information produced by class members. The term *directed* emphasizes the planned and purposeful nature of this method used by a skillful instructor. When using the directed discussion method, the instructor draws upon the group's experience, while in the lecture method, the instructor directly relates ideas and information to students. Directed discussion can be used effectively only when students have some knowledge of the subject. If learners lack prerequisite information and/or background experience, directed discussion may not be the most appropriate method to use.

The primary advantage of discussion is that it stimulates students' thinking. Discussion facilitates active participation by students and allows extra time for the instructor to provide individual attention.

The discussion method allows the instructor to identify misunderstandings and confusion on the part of one or more students. The instructor is able to judge when an explanation and/or review is necessary. The instructor can also discover which students are developing positive attitudes and making satisfactory progress and which students need additional instruction.

Directed discussion usually requires greater resourcefulness than the lecture method because the instructor must allow maximum student freedom and at the same time attempt to meet a predetermined goal. During discussion, attention must be given to individual comments as the instructor gains insight into each student's level of knowledge and understanding. Instructors must imagine themselves in the position of the learner and try to visualize problems from the student's point of view. Patience must be exercised with those who fail to grasp ideas. Instructors must, at all times, act with fairness and understanding.

Directed discussion consists of an orderly exchange of ideas in an attempt to meet a specific goal. Directed discussion should

1. arouse student interest,

2. draw points of view from all students,

3. provide the instructor with valuable ideas regarding the progress and ability of students, and

4. provide the instructor with an opportunity to correct misconceptions.

The discussion method is effective as an introduction to a lesson. The instructor may start a lesson by asking questions in an effort to focus attention on new content. Discussion may serve as a quick review with a gradual shift to the need for more information.

A discussion provides a good means of application. When new content is presented in a lesson, the instructor should provide ways for students to apply this material as soon as possible. One way to do this is to start a discussion that causes students to think through and use facts and principles presented in an earlier part of the lesson. This requires thoughtful preparation by the instructor, but it pays dividends through student progress.

Advantages and limitations of the directed discussion method need to be understood by the instructor so that this methodology is used at the right time and under appropriate conditions. Discussion is dependent on participation of group members. Participation among individuals within a group must be directed toward the achievement of desired ends. Directed discussion is an effective method for higher-order cognitive objectives. Discussion is also effective as a means of team building. Students should get to know each other and feel more comfortable in expressing opinions and sharing information. Directed discussion helps achieve this and can also be useful in the attaining of certain attitudinal changes, whereby students gain respect for the ideas of others and learn to disagree without becoming disagreeable.

When instructing large adult classes or groups, the instructor may divide the class into several small groups with a discussion leader and recorder. In these instances, the instructor serves as a resource person and coordinator of the group activity. To work effectively, there must be a considerable amount of planning so groups can stay on target and complete discussion in a systematic manner.

Discussion promotes cognitive development as it helps stimulate and clarify thinking. Directed discussion, however, has limitations. The instructor must recognize that discussion methodology is time-consuming and is not an efficient means for transmitting new information. Other limitations relate to inadequate or ineffective instructor planning. If the instructor (1) uses discussion methodology under appropriate conditions (for example, objectives to be achieved, maturity of learners, assurance of prerequisite information), (2) does an adequate job of planning for discussion, and (3) follows through, discussion can contribute substantially to the teaching-learning process.

Planning a Discussion

1. Decide on objectives to be met as a result of discussion. Is the purpose to find out the level of the student's knowledge and understanding, or to reinforce ideas and concepts through group interaction? Keep objectives clearly in mind when planning and when conducting the discussion process.

2. Plan the introduction carefully.

3. List the main headings of content to be covered.

4. Write challenging questions that focus attention on the content to be discussed.

5. Estimate the time for each step in the lesson. Set a time limit for each discussion segment and stay on schedule.

6. List the main parts of the discussion to be summarized.

Leading Discussion

Through research and experience, a number of suggestions have been identified that increase the effectiveness of the discussion process. Several of these are helpful to instructors who seek to be effective discussion leaders or who wish to help class members in that role. Effective discussion leaders must ensure that group members are willing to accept opinions from all group members. Student opinions should be recorded in order to be explored in depth at a later time. There must be a willingness to listen to each group member. A one-way or two-way dialogue is not acceptable in group discussion. After rules have been agreed upon, the leader should be sensitive to principles of group dynamics, whereby some individuals have to be drawn into discussion and others need to be prevented from dominating conversation. The following suggestions will permit discussion with a reasonable degree of effectiveness:

1. It is easier to create favorable attitudes toward an idea than to change negative attitudes.

2. Individuals are more inclined to accept new ideas from instructors they respect.

3. Policies, procedures, and practices are more acceptable when students are involved in their development.

4. Ideas are more likely to be accepted when immediate and personal rewards are offered. Individuals respond favorably to praise.

5. A new method is less likely to be accepted if a number of procedures must be mastered before the method can be put to use.

6. Students resent being manipulated by selling techniques.

7. The leader must have a target (objective), but must be flexible and not appear to be closed-minded or autocratic.

8. Students will participate more freely if a climate of openness exists, where all comments are valued and recorded. If students are embarrassed or ridiculed, they will cease to participate.

Teaching Through Discussion

The discussion method provides for individuals to share experiences and ideas related to a topic or problem. Discussion may be used in a variety of ways within a lesson. Discussion is often used at the beginning of a lesson to stimulate interest and gain attention. Student involvement in discussion helps stimulate subject interest. During the course of a lesson, discussion can be used to take advantage of the experiences of group members. At the end of a lesson, discussion techniques can be used to summarize or review major points.

Initiating Discussion. The physical setting affects student interaction. Whenever possible, arrange the group in a circle, square, or small rectangle so students can see each other. See Figure 8-1. The seating arrangement should be different for this method of instruction than for lecture or demonstration. When group discussion is used, it is especially helpful if individuals are positioned so they can see every member of the group and the instructor. Large groups may require several discussion groups that function simultaneously. Several geometric seating arrangements permit line of sight among the participants as well as between participants and the group leader. See Figure 8-2. To increase student participation, take time to (1) provide an introduction to the topic, (2) establish ground rules, and (3) define the task. The method used to initiate discussion will depend on the content and background of students. One of the most practical ways to begin discussion is to announce the topic and indicate that participants should feel free to express their ideas. Next, ask a challenging question and select an individual to respond. Finally, draw other students into the discussion by allowing them to express their opinions.

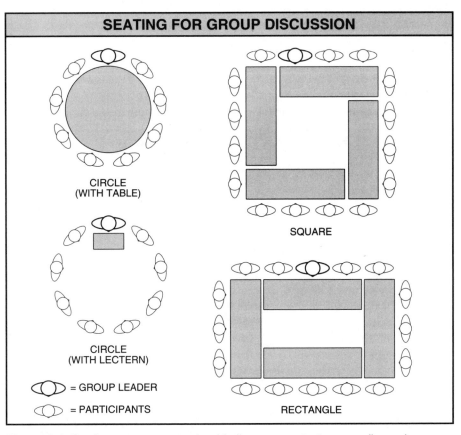

Figure 8-1. Seating arrangements should allow eye contact among discussion group members and their group leader.

Guiding Discussion. The instructor must guide students through the topic. The discussion must move toward meeting class objectives on a planned time schedule. Discussion can be guided by recording major points made by students. This technique allows students to establish the proper relationship between facts and ideas.

The most challenging task of the discussion leader is dealing with a loud, talkative, or disruptive student as well as a quiet, inhibited, or passive student. The leader must deal firmly and frankly with students who talk too much and prevent others from participating. For a discussion to be successful, no one student should be allowed to dominate the conversation. The discussion leader should provide opportunities for all students to participate. Techniques that can be used with shy or reserved students include:

1. establishing eye contact, especially with those who are quiet or reserved;
2. involving the quiet student by asking a low-risk question;
3. involving everyone in the discussion, including students who seem reluctant; and
4. providing positive feedback to those who participate in the discussion.

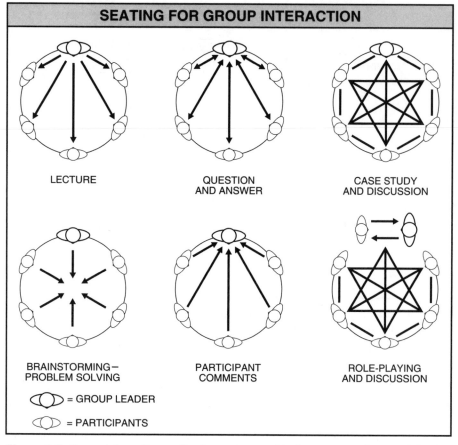

Figure 8-2. Group interaction methods can be used to increase student participation in the classroom.

Closing Discussion. During the discussion, individuals in the group interpret comments in their own way and in light of their past experiences. It is, therefore, necessary that the instructor summarize major ideas emphasized during the discussion.

GROUP PARTICIPATION METHODS

Direct student participation, *learning by doing*, is generally recognized as essential to effective learning. Student participation can be achieved through (1) discussion and questions, (2) application, or (3) techniques that involve individuals as members of groups. When objectives involve developing human relations, group participation methods are the most promising.

Learners should have experiences where they can be involved in the process of planning and conducting learning activities. Instructors are, in reality, most effective when they can help learners become independent. After individuals leave formal schooling and begin careers, they have opportunities to be involved in group activities, which involve participatory planning and decision making. Examples include cooperative learning, role-playing, brainstorming, the nominal group process, and quality circles.

Cooperative Learning

Cooperative learning is a method used to encourage students to work together as a team to complete some activity, project, or assignment. The teams usually consist of three to five students. Instructors and students favor cooperative learning over competitive learning and individualized learning. Competitive learning discourages sharing of information and students helping one another in the group. In individualized learning, the achievement of one student is unrelated to that of any other student. Cooperative learning promotes academic success through shared goals. Small groups help to enhance affective skills by encouraging mutual respect and understanding among students. The cooperative method reduces student isolation and increases opportunities for all students to experience success.

The way in which the instructor structures the learning environment is key to the success of the cooperative approach. Several criteria should be met if maximum benefits are to be received. When possible, it is desirable that the groups be formed to ensure the inclusion of males and females and students from special populations (disadvantaged, gifted, disabled, limited English proficiency, etc.). Group size should depend on the composition of the group as well as the group assignment. The instructor should communicate the lesson or activity objectives clearly so that all students understand their own role as well as their responsibility to the group. Some students may need more direction and assistance from the instructor than others. Arrangements for special materials, supplies, or tools and clean up, when necessary, should be specified by the instructor and understood by all group members. Further, it is important that the instructor structure the cooperative learning activity to ensure that students will be held accountable for their own achievement, as well as for the achievement of the group. Students should be aware of the method of evaluation before the activity begins.

The creative instructor can implement many different variations of cooperative learning. The most commonly used methods include:

Peer Tutoring. In peer tutoring, one student helps another to learn a skill, new information, or review a previous lesson. Peer tutoring is effective for grouping students at varying ability levels.

Student Teams-Achievement Divisions (STAD). Students work together to complete worksheets or other assignments after the instructor has presented a lesson. Upon completion of the activity, each student completes a quiz or test individually. The group earns points based on the extent to which each student improved over his or her past performance. Improvement over past performance could be based on each student's score on the last two quizzes or on some other basis.

Jigsaw. The jigsaw method requires that every student share information with the other group members to reach a common goal. The instructor should assign each student a task that is necessary and essential to achieving the goal of the group. The instructor may provide students with written materials and necessary information or students may be required to obtain the information through their own efforts. If more than one group is working on the same task or topic, students in different groups, but with the same assignment, can work together in sub-groups. After a predetermined amount of time, students are required to return to their original jigsaw group to share their results. Each student completes a quiz or test individually.

Group Project. The group project method requires students to work together to produce a single project representative of the efforts of all the group members. A project may be assigned by the instructor or individual groups may decide on a project and the responsibilities of individual group members. The instructor evaluates the project, and each member of the group receives the group grade.

Cooperative learning does not relieve students of their responsibility for learning, because each student must participate in the group process in order to improve his or her own grade and contribute to the group grade. Cooperative learning is adaptable to students in different age groups and flexible for diverse subject areas. Research shows that cooperative learning is a viable instructional method that helps develop and refine social skills, encourages understanding of individual differences, fosters peer acceptance, teaches responsibility, and enhances learning.

Role-Playing

Role-playing requires that participants act as though they are involved in a real-life situation. Role-playing is effective because it gives students a better understanding of others' emotions and behaviors in similar situations. This teaching method helps students to better understand their own behavior and to respond in positive ways to various human relationship situations.

Students often find it difficult to role-play and, consequently, gain little in the way of new insights from the experience. This is especially true when the roles played are artificial, or when the materials are hastily prepared. Many situations can, however, be acted out in a way that increases human relations skills.

In a typical role-playing session, each participant is given a description situation to be improvised. This may be achieved through a written assignment or by orally briefing each participant. With oral briefing, all students in the class should hear the directions. The role-players are then brought into contact with each other and play their parts.

Brainstorming

Brainstorming requires a group of students to suggest as many solutions to a problem as they can in a limited time period. No ideas are evaluated during the exercise and unusual ideas are welcomed. The objective of brainstorming is to stimulate imagination and to encourage creative approaches.

Nominal Group Process

The *nominal group process* involves structured group participation that seeks to tap the experience, skills, and feelings of group members. The primary objective of the process is to (1) increase the creative productivity of individuals, (2) enhance group decision making, (3) stimulate critical ideas, (4) provide guidance as individual judgments are gathered, and (5) provide participants with a sense of satisfaction. The technique is designed to be nonthreatening because it focuses on generating ideas.

An advantage of the nominal group process is that it can be used with any size group. The process requires a written format that enables unanimous participation and prevents domination by individuals. The process, however, is time-consuming, especially if the problem to be solved or the decision to be reached represents a real situation. The nominal group process involves the following steps:

1. Present the question or problem to the group in written form. Ask participants to write down their solutions separately and independently in brief statements or phrases.

2. Ask participants to present one solution from their list. The group leader records each and makes the list visible to all participants. Do not discuss individual items at this time. After the leader has recorded all responses, spend a few moments accepting additional solutions generated from the activity.

3. Ask each participant to explain their reasons for agreeing or disagreeing with generated solutions. This provides an opportunity for participants to explain their selection and allows refinement of the list.

4. Require each participant to prioritize (1 – 5) the solutions on separate cards. The leader should collect the cards and record the rankings in front of the group.

5. Ask participants to discuss any new concerns about the ranked items. This clarifying step may result in a slight alteration of wording of solutions.

6. Provide participants with a second opportunity to prioritize and then prepare a final list.

Quality Circles

Quality circles involve a group of individuals who meet on a regular basis to identify, analyze, and solve problems related to quality production or service in the workplace. Quality circles are typically voluntary. The ideal size of a quality circle is seven to ten members.

Vocational and technical education instructors should understand the nature of quality circles and recognize the educational implications of this form of group participation. Quality circles are a creation of business and industry that include many of the elements of discussion and brainstorming. Quality circles (1) bring about improvements in the quality of products or services, (2) increase productivity, and (3) increase employee motivation. Quality circles were conceived in Japan in the early 1960s under the leadership of Karou Ishikawa, professor of engineering at Tokyo University. In recent years, hundreds of western world companies have installed quality circle activities to improve quality and productivity through increased worker motivation.

The process by which a quality circle operates is based on the following four fundamental steps:

1. Group members identify problems.

2. Decisions are made concerning how problems are solved or minimized.

3. Problems are analyzed into component parts or subproblems.

4. Group members suggest possible solutions to the problem and formulate a recommendation to management.

The four steps in the quality circle process involve various techniques of discussion and other group participation methods. The quality circle leader must keep the discussion on track and summarize progress.

A company that engages in quality circles makes an investment in employee morale, which contributes to higher productivity and better quality products. It must be recognized that an investment is essential if the process is to be effective. Leaders must be trained and an organization must be committed to the quality circles process for it to be effective. Although participation by individual employees is voluntary, there are costs related to the (1) preparation of leaders, (2) coordination of the process, and (3) employee time to participate in meetings. The entire concept of quality is based upon trust, respect, and caring. These are important human characteristics essential to the development of self-reliance, confidence, and cooperation. Companies that are serious about human development must make an investment in their employees if they are to maximize both productivity and quality.

Again, it should be emphasized that quality circles is not an educational methodology. It is a process used by business and industry to improve quality and productivity through increased employee morale. The educational and human development implications are numerous, as the process uses discussion and other group participation techniques.

Discussion methodology has many applications through which individuals actively participate to gain greater insight, increase their level of understanding, and participate with others in decision making. The instructor should play a substantial role in the planning process and in actively leading the group participation process. Under certain circumstances, the instructor may use other individuals as discussion leaders. In most instances, however, the instructor will use discussion only for short periods of time in an effort to achieve a variety of objectives.

Discussion should be used under certain conditions and with specific groups of learners. Knowing the appropriate time to use a specific instructional method is as important as being able to carry out the method effectively.

The group discussion process must be planned and conducted with care. It is important to recognize that the instructor provides the direction in the discussion process. In fact, the term *directed discussion* is often used in education to indicate that there are planned outcomes that the leader is attempting to reach.

The specific use of discussion and group participation methods are identified in various ways through professional literature. Several variations include role-playing, brainstorming, the nominal group process, and quality circles. These specific forms of group participation, which typically involve elements of group discussion, have certain unique features that dictate their appropriateness under a given set of circumstances.

Instructors should recognize the value of discussion and group participation. Group participation techniques are valuable for achieving objectives, such as group decision making, application of knowledge, problem solving, increasing understanding, and interaction with others.

Instructors must learn to lead students in a variety of group participation processes. To become an effective discussion leader, the instructor must practice and develop the skills over a period of time.

Questions

1. What are three primary purposes of class discussion?
2. How effective is class discussion for acquiring factual information?
3. To what extent is the group leader viewed as an authority on a subject when using the discussion method?
4. How can an instructor use discussion to evaluate teaching and learning?
5. Under what conditions should an instructor serve as the discussion leader?
6. Under what circumstances should the instructor use students as discussion leaders?
7. How can discussion promote a learner's cognitive development?
8. How can a discussion leader keep one individual from dominating the discussion?
9. What is the principal difference between group discussion and the nominal group process?
10. What is the principal advantage of role-playing as a process to learn?
11. What are the steps in the nominal group process?
12. What are the primary purposes of quality circles?
13. What steps should an instructor follow when planning a discussion?
14. How can conflict or controversy that may cause students to withdraw from discussion be avoided?
15. What are the key elements of directed discussion?
16. How is discussion used at the beginning, during, and after a lesson?
17. What are several seating arrangements that may be used to promote effective discussion?
18. What is the most challenging task of a discussion leader?
19. When are instructors most effective?
20. What are four methods an instructor may use to facilitate cooperative learning?

Activities

1. Describe the advantages and limitations of the discussion method.
2. Describe how discussion can be used to introduce a lesson.

3. Describe a strategy that a group leader could use to encourage a shy or reluctant group participant to become involved in class discussion.

4. Describe how brainstorming is used to facilitate learning.

5. Contrast the nominal group process with the discussion method.

6. What relationship do quality circles have to discussion methodology used in an educational setting?

7. Describe the relationship between brainstorming and quality circles.

8. Discuss the advantages of cooperative learning.

9. Discuss two cooperative learning methods that could enhance student learning in your teaching area.

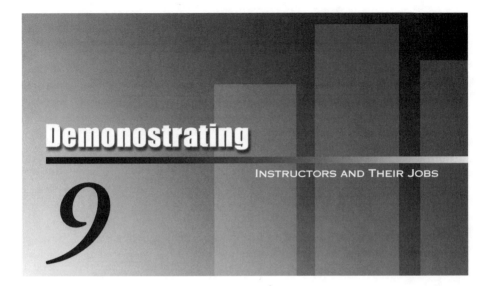

Demonostrating

9

INTRODUCTION

Effective instruction requires a competent instructor who can design effective instructional procedures and activities and who can choose and execute appropriate methodology at the right time and under appropriate conditions. Instructional effectiveness requires a high degree of decision making skill and judgment by the instructor. To be effective, the instructor must be well-informed regarding the various methods and conditions of instruction.

The demonstration is an instructional method used to show and explain the procedures involved in completing a series of steps necessary to accomplish a task. If the objectives call for students to be able to develop a skill, the demonstration method is an appropriate strategy. This method may also be used to explain a scientific principle or a mathematical formula.

The demonstration method includes telling, showing, questioning, testing, and applying. The method involves several key elements when learning a skill. The learner must:

1. know the steps to be followed and understand the purpose of each step, as well as the interrelationship among the steps that determines the sequence;

2. be guided through an initial performance correctly; and

3. apply and practice the skill.

DEMONSTRATION METHOD

The demonstration method is the primary means by which students receive instruction related to psychomotor objectives. Through the process of task analysis, psychomotor tasks completed in an occupation are identified and course content is developed for instructional purposes. These psychomotor tasks are also used to identify performance steps used by the instructor in the demonstration.

The demonstration method can also be used effectively to help learners gain a better understanding of cognitive content. For example, a demonstration of the principle of leverage would be an effective strategy. With a model, the instructor could demonstrate the factors of force, fulcrum, and resistance which would enhance the explanations of several scientific principles.

There is more to the demonstration method than showing. When skill development is the desired outcome, practice must also be included as a major demonstration component.

Appropriateness

Instructors must consider the best instructional method to use for a group of students under specific conditions. The objectives and content of a lesson must be considered before determining an appropriate instructional method. If students need specific information to solve a problem, a chalkboard demonstration of the procedure may be necessary in addition to the lecture. If the instructor merely intends to provide a lesson overview to advanced students, a brief lecture without a demonstration may be appropriate.

Textbooks on the teaching of technical subjects often emphasize demonstration as a teaching method. Demonstration is generally effective in teaching science and mathematics, as well as subject areas within practical arts and vocational-technical education. These fields of study include agriculture, business and office, marketing and distributive, home economics, health, technical, and trade and industrial education.

The instructor may use models or audiovisual aids to supplement the demonstration. The showing and application phases provide an effective means for student learning. Many psychomotor skills, such as shooting a basketball or hammering a nail, require the use of demonstration. In general, the demonstration is most effective for teaching:

1. scientific principles and theories,

2. movement or relationship of parts,

3. proper use of tools and equipment, and

4. manipulative operations or hand skills.

Effective instructors should use demonstration when teaching principles, procedural steps, and ideas and relationships.

Timing

A demonstration is most successful when given at a time when students feel a need to learn content. It is difficult to have all students in a class ready to view a demonstration. To apply the principle of timing, these alternatives are suggested:

1. The demonstration may be given to the entire class whenever advanced students need to perform the operation or task. Later, individual or small group demonstrations may be given. Written instruction sheets can be used by individual students to perform the previously demonstrated operation.

2. Students may be divided into groups based on the instructor's judgment of anticipated needs for a demonstration. Therefore, the demonstration can be given to each group at a time when individuals are ready for the instruction. This strategy is also useful in situations where a number of different student activities are going on simultaneously, or where a limited amount of equipment is available.

As a general rule, the knowledge content related to the task to be demonstrated should be taught prior to the showing phase.

Skill Development

The demonstration method should be the major delivery system used when a high degree of manipulative skill is required. The instructor should consider these points when planning demonstration lessons to facilitate skill development:

1. Learners must know the procedural steps to follow and the physical motions necessary to perform.

2. Learners should understand the purpose of each step and the relationship among steps that determine the sequence.

3. Learners should be guided through an initial performance correctly and successfully.

4. Learners must practice the physical-mental steps until the process becomes automatic.

Skill is performing a task in an efficient and effective manner. When skill development is an instructional objective, a substantial amount of practice under supervision is necessary. Practice without supervision may be detrimental to proper skill development.

Some skills can be learned best by practice, with emphasis on accuracy and the gradual development of speed. Other skills can be learned best by performance at a required speed with the gradual development of accuracy. When learning to throw a ball, one must concentrate on the proper arm and leg movements and, from the beginning, use proper speed. Accuracy comes with practice. When batting skills are being learned, however, the ball should not be thrown so hard that the batter cannot make contact. The speed must be adapted to the batter's hand-eye coordination and then gradually increased. In keyboarding, emphasis is placed on proper hand position and stroking techniques so speed and accuracy are developed simultaneously. In learning basic skills such as spelling and arithmetic, the emphasis is first on accuracy and then on speed.

PLANNING A DEMONSTRATION

Careful planning is essential to effective instruction. Some instructors, however, make the mistake of preparing less for a demonstration than they do for instruction by other methods. This may be true of instructors who possess a high degree of skill. This pitfall should be avoided, especially by the competent technician who becomes an instructor.

Analyzing Tasks

Instructors must complete a task analysis of operations to be demonstrated. The doing or performance elements identified through analysis are used as course content and taught through the demonstration method since they are composed of procedural steps that must be seen to be understood. Instructors must identify the procedural steps and the physical movements involved in the operation to be demonstrated. Procedural steps should be written. This forces the instructor to think through the process from beginning to end and also provides the basis for an instruction sheet, which could be used to assist students during or after the demonstration.

The skillful instructor may demonstrate many of the operational steps or procedures in such an efficient and automatic manner that the identification of detailed steps may be difficult for students. The instructor should recognize that students must understand all steps and movements if learning is to take place. There may be times when the task to be performed will require two separate demonstrations. The decision to use one or more demonstrations to cover content depends on the (1) background of the learner, (2) content, (3) time available, and (4) learner's level of readiness. Generally, a demonstration should not exceed 15 to 20 minutes. The instructor must consider variables when determining the appropriate length of time for a demonstration.

Tools, Materials, and Equipment

Tools, materials, and equipment needed for a demonstration must be identified and assembled in advance. Instructors should not have to send a student for a tool or a piece of equipment. Such distracting interruptions diminish the effectiveness of a demonstration. A list of items needed should be part of the written lesson plan.

Performance Standards

The instructor should rehearse the demonstration to ensure that awkward gaps or mistakes do not exist. The demonstration should not be used as a showcase for the instructor's speed of performance. The instructor must be careful and deliberate so that students understand the steps and physical motions involved in the operations.

CONDUCTING A DEMONSTRATION

A properly conducted demonstration has positive influences on learning. While there are several ways to perform an operation, it is advisable to use one method in demonstrating. Changing from one method to another causes confusion.

Physical Setting

Students must be seated or standing so they can see and hear a demonstration. When demonstrating around stationary machines or equipment, students in the front should not obscure the view of others. The instructor should be sensitive to the physical arrangement of students since the demonstration method depends upon the sense of sight to transmit movement and relationships.

Telling, Showing, and Questioning

The central focus of the demonstration is on the process of telling and showing each step. The telling portion should be kept to a minimum. Elements of informational content that make the steps meaningful and/or contribute to the students' understanding should also be included.

Safety instructions may be part of special demonstrations, lectures, or discussions. Key points of safety should be included whenever possible and should be emphasized at the point where they are most applicable.

Technical information that takes a considerable amount of teaching time should be presented as separate lessons. Information should be essential and closely related to the procedures being demonstrated.

Although demonstrating an operation requires attention to tools, materials, and equipment, the instructor must stop periodically and look at students. Maintaining good eye contact is essential to judge reactions, provide an opportunity for questions, repeat parts of the demonstration, and ensure understanding. A periodic pause also keeps the instructor from pacing the demonstration too rapidly for students.

After each procedural step, the instructor should provide the opportunity for student questions. Students often hesitate to ask questions because they fear peer reaction. To encourage participation, the instructor might suggest questions to students. Instructors should anticipate questions that students might ask during the lesson. The instructor should also ask questions to be sure the demonstration is understood. Use good questioning techniques and allow appropriate intervals for student response. Always ask questions about key points and safety procedures.

Instructional Aids

Demonstrations are often more effective when actual equipment and/or instructional aids are used. Instructional aids might be used to show hidden parts of the equipment, enlarge very small parts, or emphasize graphically the effect of an incorrect procedure.

It is often practical to use inexpensive materials in demonstrations. For example, a clothing instructor will frequently demonstrate cutting and fitting using paper instead of cloth. Drafting and sheet metal instructors often use cardboard when demonstrating sheet metal layout and construction. If an object is to be made of brass, copper, stainless steel, or any other expensive metal, a sample may first be made using a less expensive material. These inexpensive materials provide valuable learning experiences without the high cost.

Assistants

Depending on the type of equipment being demonstrated and the nature of the subject matter, it may be wise to consider using student assistants. Variety may be added to a demonstration by having a skilled student present that part of the lesson. Demonstration assistants allow the instructor time to observe others and emphasize key factors as they occur.

FOLLOWING UP A DEMONSTRATION

The application step that occurs after each demonstration provides learners with an opportunity to test their understanding and ability to perform. Without application, a demonstration fails to have impact on student learning. Instructor application consists of (1) assigning work to students, (2) allowing students to begin working, (3) supervising, (4) correcting errors, and (5) providing individual supplemental instruction. No student should practice incorrect methods that lead to bad habits. It is also more psychologically sound for students to succeed from the beginning.

When providing individual instruction, care should be taken not to take the work away from the student. It is a better strategy to direct attention to an error while leaving the tools and equipment in the student's hands. The student then can apply the new or altered information while experiencing satisfaction for completing the task.

Consistent high-level performance requires a substantial amount of practice. When the objective to be achieved is a high level of skill, the student must be willing to repeat the performance numerous times to make the mental-muscle association.

In technical subjects, the demonstration method is a predominant means of teaching procedures and concepts. This method is characterized by instructors showing and by students observing.

The demonstration method, in addition to showing, involves several other elements. The instructor must explain the procedural steps in an order that can be identified clearly. Instructors must use questions and responses during and following the showing step to clarify and reinforce key elements of the process. The application stage allows students an opportunity to perform procedures shown by the instructor.

Students can often better understand a concept through demonstration than through words alone. Principles such as magnetism, gravity, deflection, and elasticity may be difficult for students to understand using abstract wording. Clarity may be enhanced through demonstration of a principle.

REVIEW

Questions

1. What are the primary applications of the demonstration method?

2. What are the major components of a demonstration?

3. What is the primary factor to be considered as the instructor chooses an instructional method?

4. Under what conditions would it be essential to supplement a demonstration with instructional aids?

5. What type of informational content is best taught prior to a demonstration?

6. What type of informational content is best taught during a demonstration?

7. How does an instructor use the analysis process in planning for a demonstration?

8. Should speed or accuracy be emphasized when skill development is a lesson objective? Explain your response.

9. Why is it necessary for an experienced instructor to write out steps of a procedure prior to demonstrating an operation?

10. Although there may be several methods through which a given task can be accomplished, why is it important to limit a demonstration to one method?

11. What is the purpose of questioning as a component of the demonstration method?

12. To what extent and under what circumstances would it be desirable for the instructor to use an assistant in a demonstration?

13. Under what circumstances would it be appropriate to perform an operation or complete a task for a student?

14. Under what circumstances would it be appropriate to use substitute materials during a demonstration?

15. How and when should safety precautions be taught in conjunction with the demonstration method?

16. What factors must an instructor consider when deciding on the number of demonstrations to cover content?

17. What are the major steps of application that follow a demonstration?

Activities

1. Select an operation or set of procedures to be learned and prepare a lesson plan using the demonstration method.

2. Explain several elements that must be accommodated by an instructor when the lesson includes the development of a manipulative skill.

3. Describe when it would be desirable to use instructional aids in a demonstration.

4. List the types of content that are most effectively taught through the demonstration method.

5. Explain how timing relates to teaching and learning.

6. Describe a situation where practice may be counterproductive.

7. Select an operation and use the analysis concept to identify procedures necessary to accomplish the operation.

8. Prepare a demonstration of a procedure you have mastered.

Instructional Media and Devices

10

INTRODUCTION

The phrase "a picture is worth a thousand words" indicates the power of communication techniques to go beyond human language to convey thoughts and ideas. Primitive people drew pictures in the sand and on the walls of caves. Illustrations have always helped to convey ideas and describe people, events, and objects.

Effective instruction requires a variety of media to help convey meaning and increase learning. Media is the graphic, photographic, electronic, or mechanical means for enhancing the transmission and reception of visual or verbal information. Instructional media is the hardware and software used to assist learners in acquiring knowledge, skills, and attitudes.

Adults and children are surrounded by auditory and visual impressions, which are created by a combination of pictures, words, and sounds that evoke emotions, change attitudes, communicate information, and motivate action. The power of the media can be observed by viewing television commercials and print materials that motivate people to buy products, vote for candidates, or donate to charities. Impressions created through media are retained by people significantly longer than when the same messages are only written or orally communicated.

Instructional media must be viewed as aids to teaching and learning. An inappropriately chosen medium or one used at the wrong time may contribute little or nothing to student learning. The effective instructor uses all instructional media in an effective manner, and when it can best facilitate learning.

175

INSTRUCTIONAL MEDIA

Instructional media improves the communication of information, ideas, concepts, or relationships so individuals can learn more efficiently and effectively. Instructional media makes use of the power of pictures, words, and sounds to stimulate interest, compel attention, and enhance the understanding of ideas that may be too complex for verbal explanation alone.

Media Impact on Learning

The selection and/or development of instructional media is based on its potential for facilitating the achievement of an objective. Instructors must choose the medium that best establishes conditions that enhance the learning of content at a precise point in time under specific circumstances. Media selection is a part of instructional planning and should be reflected in the lesson plan.

Need for Instructional Media

The actual object (equipment, device, or tool) is usually the best instructional aid for learning. There are times, however, when instructional media may be more appropriate than using an actual object. Instructional media may be necessary under these conditions:

1. Actual objects are either too big, too small, or not sufficiently compact to be viewed effectively.

2. Objects are unavailable to students except through media. For example, newly developed and unavailable products or places that are too distant to be visited may be brought into the classroom through instructional media.

3. The actual object or process is too expensive, dangerous, or delicate for students to manipulate.

4. The process is too slow moving. For example, plant growth or chemical changes, motion picture animation, or time-lapse photography can be effectively shown with media.

5. Rapid human or mechanical movement prohibits perception of detail. Slow-motion photography or videotape may be an excellent aid in such cases.

6. The process or phenomenon is invisible. The flow of electricity and the action of many gases are invisible to the learner. In such cases, media may be used to illustrate the process.

Classification of Media

Instructional media can be classified by the (1) characteristics of each medium, for example, color, motion, and sound; (2) manner in which each medium is presented, for example, a still picture can be projected, displayed, or incorporated in a book; and (3) use of each medium. An orderly classification of media may enable the prospective instructor to systematically review materials that are available.

In instructional media, *hardware* is equipment (for example, projectors, videocassette recorders, printers, central processing units, monitors) that stores and/or transmits instructional content. *Software* used in instructional media is the medium (for example, slides, videotapes, transparencies, computer programs) that stores and transmits content. Instructional media is often classified as:

1. *graphic materials*, which include flat pictures, posters, graphs, charts, diagrams, and chalkboard illustrations;
2. *projected materials*, which include motion pictures, transparencies for overhead projection, slides, and filmstrips; and
3. *mechanical and electrical materials*, which include reduced or enlarged models, actual objects, cutaways, computer-controlled stimuli, electronic trainers, and other types of teaching machines.

Types of Media

Once content has been identified and objectives specified, the instructor should begin the process of designing instructional strategies for students. Instructors should be knowledgeable about the various media available, their unique or special characteristics, and the variety of ways in which each medium may be presented. For example, a still picture may be presented as a slide, a filmstrip frame, an overhead transparency, or in a textbook.

People, Events, and Objects. When people, events, or objects are readily and economically available, they should be used instead of media. The actual object is more meaningful than a re-creation in some other media form. However, an actual object is often unavailable or is too small, too dangerous, too expensive, or too time-consuming to use in the instructional setting.

Verbal Representations. Printed materials preserve spoken messages. For the visually impaired, the words may be placed into tactile context through braille. Printed words may also be represented through use of an overhead or a filmstrip projector. These media increase learning potential.

Graphics. *Graphics* are information placed into a two-dimensional context for the purpose of communicating relationships. Typical graphics include charts, graphs, maps, diagrams, and drawings. These graphics are often used directly in textbooks, self-instructional programs, or as handouts. Graphics may also be combined with other media and appear as overhead transparencies, slides, or filmstrips.

Still Pictures. A *still picture* is a reproduction of a person, event, or object that may be enlarged or reduced and appears in color or black-and-white. Photographs or textbook illustrations may be projected through slides, filmstrips, or transparencies.

Videos. A *video* is a moving image produced from live action or graphics. Video can be saved or videotaped as electronic files (video clips) that can be accessed using a personal computer. Video clips provide better flexibility during instruction.

People, events, or objects may be photographed in normal motion, slow motion, time-lapse motion, or stop motion. The film can be edited for purposes of highlighting or abbreviating the presentation. The motion picture may be combined with sound and narration can be added.

Audio Recordings. *Audio recordings* are recordings made on CD-ROM magnetic tape, disc, or on a soundtrack for motion pictures. Audio recordings allow the reproduction of actual events, or may be used to provide sound effects for other presentations. Sound provides reality to instruction. Audio recordings permit oral presentations to be captured for later listening or repeated listening, which helps reinforce or clarify information.

Simulations. *Simulations* are replications of real situations that are designed to represent an actual process or set of conditions. Many forms of media, including the computer, can be used to enhance simulation. Computer technology is often used to provide simulated settings for learners.

Models. *Models* are replications of an original. A model may be the exact size, although often it is a reduction or an enlargement of the original. Models can be made to illustrate the atom, which could not be viewed without the aid of visual representation, or a building, allowing a detailed study of various features.

Television. *Television* is the presentation of an image on a monitor. The source of the image may be live from a studio, from a videotape, or from a motion picture film. The source may be directly from a camera, central transmitter, cable distribution center, or satellite. Satellites can be utilized in presenting instructional programs for correspondence schools to learners in remote areas throughout the world.

Programmed and Computer-Assisted Instruction. *Programmed instruction* is prepackaged sequences of information that are designed to lead a student through a learning process in which there are predetermined and predictable responses. This type of instruction may take the form of programmed textbooks or instructional programs prepared for computers. The information may be presented through one medium or a combination of media. For example, the learner may be presented with information through text, audio clips, or video clips. The learner may be required to respond to information that activates the presentation of additional information. The learner's response is typically reinforced immediately in terms of success or failure. Programs also have built-in remedial units for incorrect responses.

MEDIA MATERIALS AND DEVICES

Instructors should be knowledgeable about the various media materials and devices available so that appropriate materials and devices can be selected to increase the effectiveness of teaching and learning. After the instructor has identified the content to be taught and the objectives to be achieved by learners, consideration must be given to media materials and devices that will maximize instructional effectiveness.

Multimedia Projector

A multimedia projector is a projection device that projects images from a personal computer on to a flat surface. A multimedia projector and computer have become a standard for instructional media used in the field. Multimedia projectors evolved from liquid crystal display (LCD) technology in projection pads used with overhead projectors. The first portable LCD projectors were limited in usage because of the low light output and visible pixels. Improved technology has allowed the creation of lighter, smaller, and more powerful multimedia projectors that produce high-quality images, video, data, and sound.

Presentation software used with a multimedia projector can be used to develop an organized collection of text, photographs, illustrations, video clips, audio clips, and other elements for enhancing instruction. See Figure 10-1. Revisions and presentations customized for specific classes are easily accomplished using presentation software. In addition, presentations created by the instructor allow for photos and video clips of the specific instructional program to be depicted, which provide greater topical relevance.

Different presentation software products are available for purchase such as Adobe® Acrobat® and Microsoft® PowerPoint®. The navigational functions of these software products allow the instructor the ability to select and enlarge images for greater clarity and emphasis during instruction. If necessary, a laser pointer can be used to identify specific elements displayed.

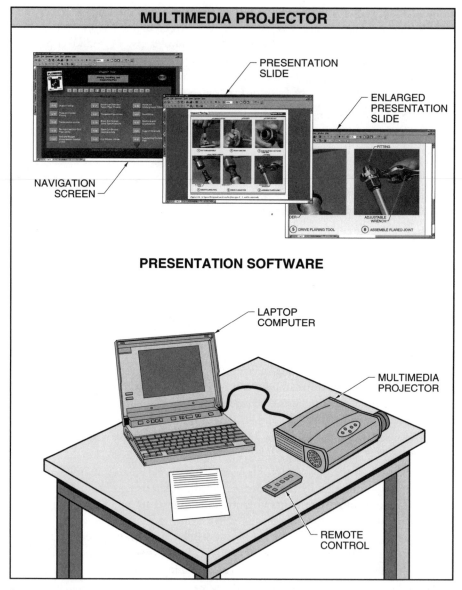

Figure 10-1. A multimedia projector and computer have become a standard for instructional media used in the field.

Whiteboard

A whiteboard is a bright smooth surface panel that uses markers for sketches and notes. Like traditional chalkboards, whiteboards are used to display key points or for creating quick sketches to coincide with other instructional material. Whiteboards offer better clarity and contrast than chalkboards and do not produce chalk dust. Different colored markers can be used to enhance sketches and emphasize important elements. Special markers are designed for use on whiteboards. Using a permanent-type marker can result in damage to a whiteboard surface.

Electronic Whiteboards. An electronic whiteboard is a whiteboard with electronic circuitry that allows direct interface to a personal computer. The circuitry can be embedded in the whiteboard panel or as an attachment mounted on the surface. With an electronic whiteboard, notes and sketches on a whiteboard can be captured by a computer. The captured image can then be saved, uploaded to a web site, or displayed to learners at a remote location. The captured image may also be edited and/or used as part of another electronic document.

When used with a multimedia projector, an electronic whiteboard can also serve as a large touch-sensitive screen. The computer screen image is projected on the electronic whiteboard. The navigational buttons projected can be activated by touching the whiteboard surface with a finger. Other mouse functions can be performed by moving a finger or stylus along the surface.

Overhead Projector

The overhead projector is one of the most versatile projection devices for general classroom use. See Figure 10-2. When using an overhead projector, the room need not be darkened. It can be operated from the front of the room so the instructor can maintain eye contact with students. Transparent overlays can be used to show (1) steps of procedures, (2) stages of construction, or (3) the internal assembly of equipment.

Overhead projectors can be equipped with a roll of transparency film, which is wound across the machine and makes it possible to project a considerable amount of material that has been prepared in advance or that is developed through discussion in the class.

Instructors often prefer to use the overhead projector as they would use a whiteboard, by writing directly on the transparency at the same time that it is projected. Transparencies can be used in conjunction with a whiteboard. Diagrams and equations may be projected on the board and then enhanced with colored markers. This allows greater flexibility when explaining a process using a diagram.

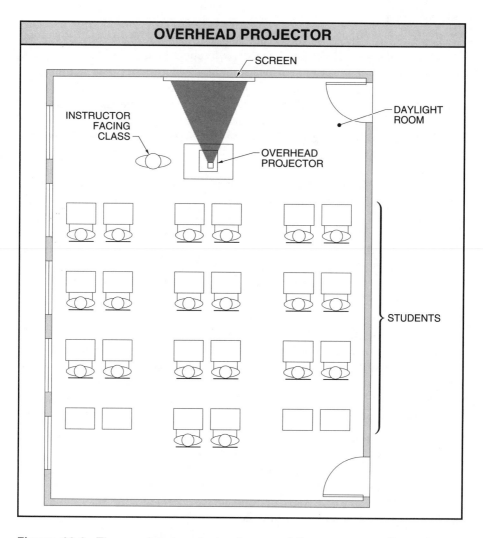

Figure 10-2. The overhead projector is one of the most versatile projection devices for general classroom use.

Thermal and plain paper copier transparencies can be made quickly. The process requires no chemicals. Material is edited by blanking out unwanted items with a sheet of plain paper while the transparency is being made. Transparency stock is available in several colors.

The suggested procedure for using the overhead projector is:

1. Arrange transparencies in the proper order for showing.
2. Prepare an outline of commentary for each transparency.
3. Plan additional comments or symbols that are to be added.
4. Indicate on the lesson plan when each transparency is to be used.
5. Set up and focus the projection on the screen. See Figure 10-3.
6. Show each transparency at the proper time and with appropriate comment.
7. Be prepared to show transparencies again for review and emphasis.

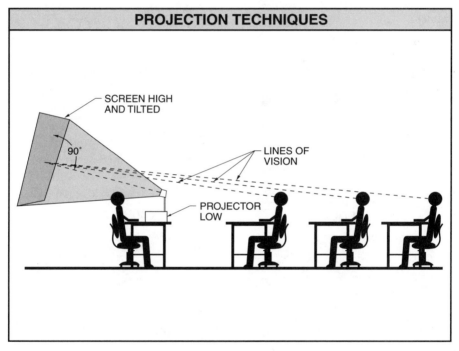

Figure 10-3. Proper projection techniques enhance the effectiveness of using an overhead projector.

Overlays. A distinct advantage of the overhead projector comes through the use of a static transparency with one or more overlays. A *static transparency* is one transparency sheet displaying graphics and/or data. Successive overlays present additional information one step at a time. Successive overlays may be used when the instructor wishes to develop a complex idea in a series of steps. The following shadow compass technique for finding directions when lost in the woods was developed by Robert Owendoff, a boy scout from Falls Church, Virginia. See Figure 10-4.

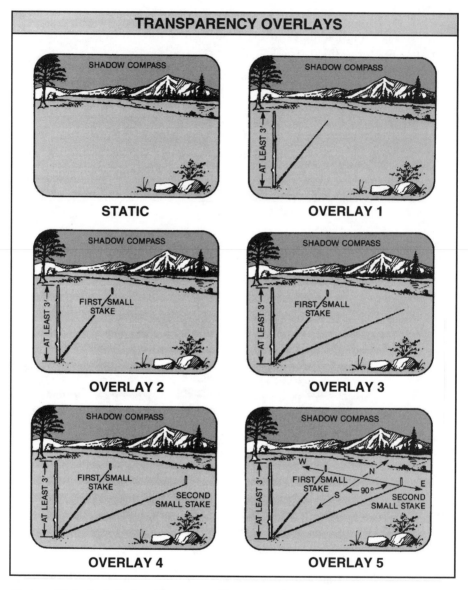

Figure 10-4. A static transparency with successive overlays is used to develop complex ideas in a series of steps.

1. In an open area (static frame) a stake is driven into the ground with at least 3′ of its length above the ground (overlay 1). The tip of the shadow cast by this stake is marked with the first small stake (overlay 2).

2. After a wait of not less than 10 minutes a second shadow is cast and is marked with the second small stake (overlays 3 and 4).

3. A line is drawn to join the two small stakes (overlay 5). This line always points east and west, regardless of the time of day or year. A line drawn at 90° to the first line will point north and south. Under some conditions, this method of finding directions is more accurate than a compass. The average error is 8°.

Projection Pad. An overhead projector can be used with a projection pad to project a computer screen image onto a large surface. The overhead projector provides the light source to project the image. The image on the computer screen is displayed on the LCD panel of the projection pad. Light passes through the LCD panel similar to a transparency, and an image is projected. See Figure 10-5. A projection pad offers flexibility to the instructor by allowing overhead transparencies or computer screen images to be shown during instruction using the same overhead projector.

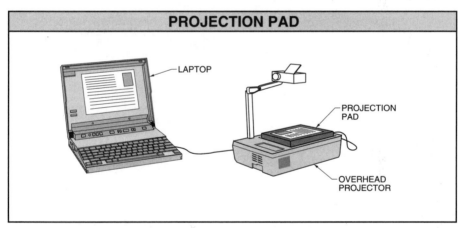

Figure 10-5. A projection pad used in conjunction with an overhead projector enables an instructor to project computer-generated images onto a screen without a video projection system.

Slide Projector

A *slide projector* is instructional hardware used to project an image from a slide to a screen. See Figure 10-6. Slides have an advantage over filmstrips in that the order in which the pictures are used can be changed, and slides can be removed or added. The instructor, or a student, can take pictures of operations, demonstrations, etc. and have them developed as four-color slides. An instructor proficient with a camera can develop a substantial inventory of slides for instructional use.

The flexibility of slides provides relatively low-cost individualized instruction. Frequently, a set of slides is prepared with an accompanying audiocassette tape, which can be used by a student as a self-instructional package. This means of packaging instruction brings together both a visual and audio stimulus.

The technology involved in bringing the learner in contact with the message through a variety of media materials ranges from a slide projector and an audio recording to a device having the capability of electronically controlling the visual and audio message as the learner presses the appropriate button. Many slide/cassette presentations are easily converted for interactive use on a personal computer.

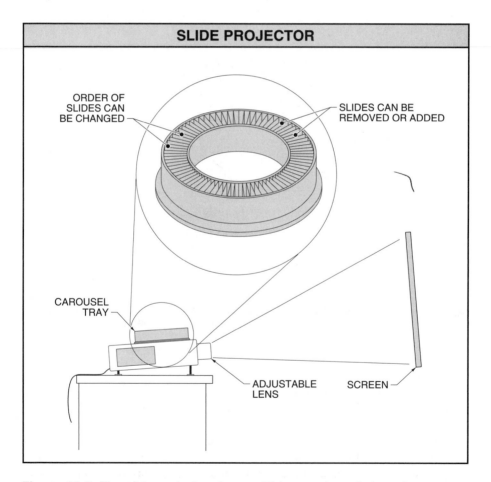

Figure 10-6. The slide projector shows still images in a darkened room.

Opaque Projector

An *opaque projector* is instructional hardware that projects an image of a printed picture, photograph, or flat illustration. The room must be dark when the opaque projector is used. Some opaque projectors are equipped with electronic pointers, which are useful in placing an arrow of light at any point on the projected image. Small illustrations should be mounted on uniform paper or cardboard. Suggested procedures for using the opaque projector include the following:

1. Arrange illustrations in the proper order for showing.
2. Plan comments to be made for each illustration.
3. Set up equipment (if pictures vary in size, move the projector to change the size of the projected image) and arrange student seating.
4. Use a pointer to illustrate key ideas.

Television and Video Monitors

Television is a powerful means of mass communication. Educational television stations broadcast hundreds of cultural and educational programs. Technical training programs are being added to the programming on several stations. Television can be used to present instruction about a variety of subject areas. As an educational aid, television has demonstrated its usefulness for mass delivery to remote locations.

A major disadvantage of television is that the instructor cannot see or hear a student. The instructor has no way of observing the student's reaction.

Closed-Circuit Television. Closed-circuit television can be used in a number of situations, including medical and military service schools. The image is sent to receiving monitors in one or more classrooms. The following are advantages of closed-circuit television:

1. One demonstration can be sent to several classrooms at the same time.
2. Magnification of small and hard-to-see demonstrations is possible.
3. Dangerous, distant, or current phenomena can be transmitted back to viewers by the television camera.
4. A complex procedure may be shown repeatedly when required. For example, medical students may repeatedly watch a skilled surgeon perform an operation.

Video Playback. Immediate video playback can be used for instruction. For example, human resource development (HRD) specialists can practice interviewing techniques and self-critique performance. The instant replay makes it possible to go back over important phases of the interviewing process immediately following first-time observation. Videotapes of such sessions can also be used for more intensive study of staff behavior. HRD departments often videotape new instructors as a means of providing immediate feedback on performance.

Within a training facility, television can be used to magnify people, events, or objects. For example, a television camera can be mounted on equipment in motion, which makes it possible for students as a group to see the action. A television camera can also be mounted on a microscope, thereby making it possible for a large group to see individual slides.

Video Cameras. Advancements in the capabilities and lower cost of videos has increased their use for instructional purposes. See Figure 10-7. This has allowed customizing video footage, which used to require specialized studios, large capital investments, and technical specialists.

Video, like other instructional media, has limitations, strengths, and weaknesses. An instructor must decide which materials, methods, and aids contribute most to the teaching-learning process.

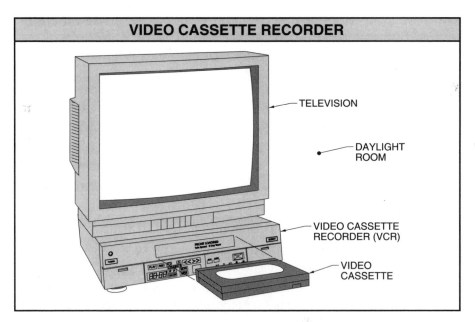

Figure 10-7. VCRs have increased the use of television for instructional purposes.

Audio Recordings

Audio recordings are used in schools, particularly in music, language, and speech training. Sound can be recorded on CD-ROMs or magnetic tape.

The electronics industry has succeeded in making recording equipment compact, lighter in weight, and less complex to operate while increasing sound quality. The audiocassette player/recorder uses a self-contained tape cartridge that is easy to load or remove. The audiocassettes are relatively inexpensive and can be erased and reused indefinitely.

Recording equipment can be most useful for individual or self-instruction or for practice in speech, language, or music training. Recordings can also be used to aid students in the recognition of sounds, such as the sounds of an improperly operating cutting tool, a worn bearing, or an overloaded motor.

Simulators

A *simulator* is a device that is similar to, but not identical with, the real equipment in operation. The degree of similarity required depends on the way the device is to be used in an instructional program. A simulator may be created using a personal computer and software.

Simulators are designed to provide instruction on critical skills, which are required on the actual equipment. Simulators are often superior to actual equipment during the initial phases of instruction.

The need for simulators in educational programs increases as complex human-machine relationships are involved. High fidelity simulation is common in military training and on critical skills required to operate complex equipment. Simulators are also useful in less complex instructional programs.

A simulator provides systematic practice of critical skills that may not be feasible when the actual equipment is in operation. For example, a portion of a complex machine can be simulated so that the student can gain experience under the most favorable conditions. This is important with such skills as engine troubleshooting, production line work, and work to be done under hazardous conditions. The simulator need not duplicate the whole task, but it must truly simulate whatever the student must transfer to the operating situation.

Simulator training that produces habits that are not the same as those required in the operating situation may result in negative transfer and can be dangerous. For example, a target simulator used to train military personnel to fire on a moving target must represent an authentically real situation.

The last phase of simulation instruction usually consists of training on the actual equipment. This instructional phase bridges the gap between the simulator and the actual equipment under true operating conditions. Generally, this live operation is provided on the job by the supervisor responsible for the work or by a highly skilled employee who reports to the supervisor. Simulators have their greatest value in the following situations:

1. The actual equipment is so complex that the trainee cannot be given adequate experience and practice on specific procedures before total integrated performance is required.
2. The actual equipment is dangerous in the hands of a trainee until the ability to adjust quickly to emergency conditions has been developed.
3. The emergency situation does not occur often enough on operating equipment to maintain the degree of skill required for such situations.
4. The actual equipment is too expensive to be used exclusively for instructional purposes.

In making decisions regarding the selection and use of simulators, it is important to:

1. determine the critical skills for which instruction is required,
2. compare costs of simulator and actual equipment,
3. analyze the degree of positive transfer required, and
4. consider the possibility and danger of negative transfer.

Nonprojected Graphics

Graphics in the form of large pictures, diagrams, posters, and charts are practical for instructional use. Graphics can be drawn or constructed by the instructor to fit a specific teaching situation. The characteristics of a good graphic are:

1. all unnecessary details are omitted;
2. lettering is simple and easy to read from any seat in the room;
3. color is used to identify related parts and to direct attention toward main ideas; and
4. technical details and symbols are correct.

Graphics may be placed on the bulletin board or wall for further examination by students. Graphics must be changed frequently. The following is a suggested procedure for using posters and charts:

1. Select and prepare graphics that help emphasize or illustrate points in a lesson. Many ideas can be illustrated by sketches drawn on paper using grease pencils, colored chalk, or crayons.
2. Mount illustrations where they will be seen and used by students.
3. Plan how and when the graphics will be used in a lesson.

Chalkboard

The chalkboard is still one of the most flexible and practical aids used by instructors. The chalkboard can be used to list important points in a lesson, solve problems, and illustrate ideas. The chalkboard should never be used as a means of conveying large amounts of written information that can be provided to each student on a handout. Suggested procedures for using the chalkboard include the following:

1. Plan all chalkboard illustrations before class.

2. Prepare complicated drawings before class by reproducing light lines on the chalkboard, clearly visible to the instructor but not to the class. By tracing over these lines with chalk, a neat and accurate drawing may be made quickly while the class observes.

3. When the same basic outline of a drawing is needed several times, it may be transferred to the board by using a stencil.

4. When the outline of an object such as a tool, chemistry flask, map outline, or machine is needed repeatedly, it may be desirable to construct a template.

5. Illustrations may be placed on the board by projecting an image with the opaque or overhead projector, and then tracing the important parts of the image. This is also an excellent technique for increasing the size of an illustration. A large sheet of paper may be taped to the wall or chalkboard if a permanent illustration is desired.

Models

Models may be examined and handled by students, and they show relationships and shapes better than any other instructional aid. Mock-ups, cutaway models, and exploded models are used chiefly to show location and movement of internal parts and unique equipment features. Working models are valuable when demonstrating the operation of tools or machines. The following is a suggested procedure for using models:

1. Select or construct the models needed. Many models are made from common construction materials.

2. Display models to be seen and used continuously.

3. Plan to use models in instructional lessons.

4. Allow students the opportunity to examine the model.

Programmed Instruction

Programmed instruction is a systematic approach to individualized instruction. While many instructional materials and methods can be individualized, programmed instruction is designed specifically for use with the individual learner.

One step at a time is the way people learn to walk, read, drive an automobile, and solve mathematical problems. In learning, students must proceed from simple acts to more complex acts as they gain confidence and increase judgment on the way.

Generally, programmed instruction must have the following characteristics:

1. Material to be learned is presented in relatively small steps, or frames. A *frame* is instruction that consists of information plus questions.

2. Material is carefully sequenced so that the student is led from one frame to the next by questions, illustrations, or clues.

3. The student responds to the information contained in each frame by writing a response, manipulating equipment, or making a computation.

4. Immediate feedback is provided to the student to indicate whether or not the response is satisfactory.

5. The rate of progress in a course is determined by the individual's ability to master the materials. The learner sets the pace of learning.

6. Each unit of material is prepared so students may proceed with little or no help from an instructor.

The history of programmed instruction and teaching machines dates back to the 1920s and the work of Sidney Pressey at The Ohio State University. Pressey invented several devices intended to provide a mechanical grading method for testing students.

Renewed interest in what is now called programmed instruction came from the work of B. F. Skinner at Harvard University Psychological Laboratories. Skinner's 1958 article, "Teaching Machines," generated a renewed interest in programmed instruction.

Although there are many variations and combinations of programming, there are two distinct types used with written materials. These are linear and branching.

Linear Program. In a linear program, the content of the program is arranged from simple to complex. The information is presented in brief statements through which a single idea is emphasized. In preparing the program, the idea is presented in a direct and complete written statement. The statement is then rewritten and a key word or other information is left out and indicated by a blank space. The student fills in the blank. The response is checked by uncovering the correct answer as supplied in the program. After observing the correct response, the learner proceeds to the next step.

Linear programs present information and require responses that provide meaningful practice. Linear programs may also use illustrations and diagrams to convey concepts. See Figure 10-8.

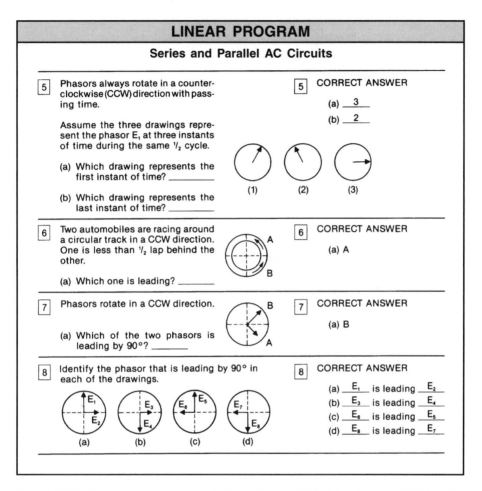

Figure 10-8. Linear programs present information and require responses that provide meaningful practice.

Branching Program. A branching program is characterized by presenting several paragraphs of information at a time. Each unit of information is followed by a multiple choice question. The student must select an answer. This is done in machine programs by pressing a button. In a programmed text, the student's selected answer then refers to another page in the text. Such pages tell the student whether or not the answer is correct. If correct, the student is referred to the next unit in the program. If incorrect, reasons are provided as to why the response was wrong, and additional information is provided. The learner is then referred to the next appropriate unit in the program. See Figure 10-9.

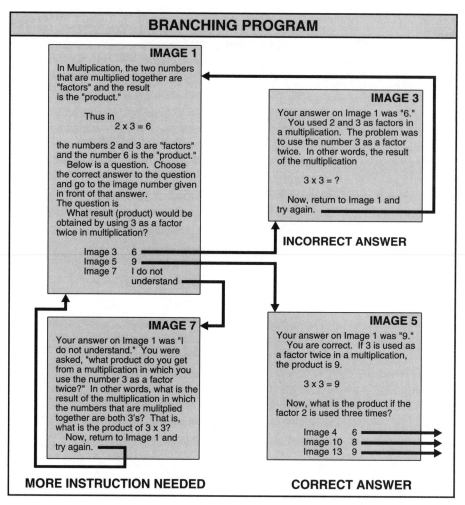

Figure 10-9. A branching program is characterized by presenting information followed by a multiple choice question.

Adjunct Programmed Material. A practical approach to programming is to use available material such as a well-written textbook and programmed questions. Several advantages to this approach include:

1. The text material may be used for programmed learning and also for review and reference. Adjunct programs have a distinct advantage over programmed materials, which are self-contained. Adjunct programmed materials allow an overall view of the content for review and serve as a ready source of specific information.

2. An adjunct program is relatively easy to prepare and to modify.

3. The student has all the advantages of the textbook, including the table of contents and an index that provide for quick review and the location of specific information.

4. The rapid and experienced learner is not held back by having to read and respond to a large number of small and relatively simple steps as found in linear programs.

Dividends From Programmed Instruction. Programmed instruction has helped to improve instruction by requiring objectives that specify outcomes in terms of behavior. Programmed instruction emphasizes the need for an analysis of what the student must know and be able to do. With a thorough and accurate occupational analysis, the job of programming a course of instruction is half complete.

Programmed instruction should be built on sound principles of learning, such as:

1. students should work and learn at their own rate;

2. one-student-to-one-instructor learning is ideal;

3. students should be informed of progress; and

4. programmed texts may be used advantageously for out-of-class study so class time can be used for creative thinking and the use of tools and equipment.

An appropriate and skillfully designed unit of programmed instruction may provide for individual student practice and drill, thus saving the instructor's time for more creative work. Programmed instruction is often highly effective in those instructional programs that have precise standards of performance specified as an objective. Instruction of this type has been used successfully for training that has exact and standardized procedures.

Educational specialists who use programmed instruction have always:

1. required specific objectives for each course and lesson;

2. analyzed jobs as a basis for designing instructional programs;

3. taught through a series of properly sequenced steps;

4. provided for practice and drill on key elements of the program; and

5. evaluated instruction in terms of the student's performance as defined by the objectives.

Instructional technology provides a means for translating instructional materials into visual and/or audio formats, which can be presented to the learner on an individualized basis through the use of a variety of devices. At this time, no one device has proven to be most effective for individualized instruction. Increasingly, computer technology is being used to deliver and control programmed instruction. The effectiveness of the instructional equipment is closely linked with the quality of instructional materials being presented to the learner, as well as the nature of the content being presented.

EFFECTIVE MEDIA USE

Selection and use of instructional media must be viewed within the total context of instructional planning, execution, and evaluation. Instructional media should be carefully selected or produced. Well-developed media materials not only communicate information, but also impact students' interest, attention, and motivation.

Characteristics of Effective Media Materials

Instructional media materials should appeal to the senses, attract and hold attention, and highlight or focus on key elements to be learned. Instructors recognize that no single medium is best for all purposes. Instructors should not select classroom media only on the basis of familiarity and convenience. The process of selecting media materials is subjective and depends on the instructor's knowledge, insight, and experience. A review of the factors involved in the instructor's decision may be helpful in this selection process. Media should be judged on the following criteria: appropriateness, technical quality, cost, availability, simplicity, flexibility, and level of sophistication.

Appropriateness. The instructor should select a medium that helps students acquire the specified behavior called for in the objectives. If a picture of an actual object is desirable, decisions must be made regarding the size of the photograph, whether it should be in color or black-and-white, and whether the photograph should be of an actual object or a facsimile. If the objectives require detailed information about a manufacturing process, should the instructor show a film that describes the process, take a field trip to see the product being manufactured, or listen to an audiotape from a production line supervisor? In the process of selecting media, the instructor often finds that different forms of media are available and that several are appropriate.

Technical Quality. Physical characteristics of a specific medium may impact significantly on the effectiveness of a lesson. An overhead transparency is usually an appropriate medium to facilitate learning; however, if the lettering used is too small, appears too crowded, includes too much prose, or contains errors, it may have an adverse effect on student learning. Unless the technical quality of an instructional aid is relatively good, it probably should not be used. Poor quality media materials may be more detrimental to effective learning than supportive.

Cost. Instructors must give consideration to the monetary as well as the time costs involved in the acquisition or development of media for a lesson. The instructor must ask, "Is the cost in either time or money worth the potential learning gain or efficiency that can be derived from a particular media?" For example, a chart that depicts items in enlarged form so they can be viewed by students in the back of the classroom may not be necessary if the same chart is available in students' textbooks. Cost should not be the sole criterion when selecting the optimum medium to accomplish an educational objective. Decisions about media selection may not always be clear, and compromises may need to be made on the basis of cost.

Availability. On occasion, an instructor might identify a specific medium that would be appropriate to use in a lesson but not available when needed for instruction. In other instances, the media may not be usable in its present format. For example, the media's form may be a videocassette that is incompatible with available instructional hardware. Acquiring materials that cannot be used or that cannot be used at the appropriate time is pointless. Media materials not used at the appropriate time lose their effectiveness. Films shown when the films or the auditorium is available are often useless in terms of achieving specified educational objectives.

Simplicity. Instructors often use complex media materials that overload learners. Students cannot assimilate too many facts presented at one time, and a variety of ideas presented simultaneously also tend to confuse the student. Many instructional films are prepared with no specific objectives in mind and, as a result, interfere with the achievement of specific objectives. Short films on specific subjects are more effective learning tools.

Flexibility. Media materials should be used at the appropriate time and for the proper length of time. The medium should not control the lesson, but should be chosen to facilitate the achievement of specified lesson objectives. Overhead transparencies are very flexible, whereas educational films are not. The effective instructor seldom teaches the same lesson twice in exactly the same way. No two groups of students have precisely the same needs; therefore, media may need to be used at different times or in different contexts. Flexibility is a key factor to consider when selecting appropriate media for classroom use.

Level of Sophistication. The level of media sophistication is determined by the vocabulary used, rate at which content is presented, type of visualization, and subject approach. Commercially prepared material is often aimed at a wide age level of audience in order to increase the product's marketing potential. The instructor should determine the level of media sophistication to be used.

To illustrate this point, consider the medium of programmed instruction that is designed so the learner moves through the process learning concepts or principles in a step-by-step progression. Frequently, the steps are minute, and advanced learners are bored because they could move more rapidly. In this case, the level of sophistication is too low for these learners and leads to disinterest. When this occurs, another medium, such as a well-selected textbook or reference materials, might provide a better learning experience than the programmed material.

Factors Affecting Media Use

The effective instructor reviews lesson content to identify areas that need illustration, amplification, or clarification. No instructional media takes the place of an instructor, nor does it necessarily make the instructor's job easier. Media materials may assist an instructor to teach more effectively, save time, and facilitate student learning. After objectives have been determined, the following guidelines may be helpful in selecting instructional media:

1. To the extent that content and procedures within the medium bring about responses that are similar to the desired behavior, a high degree of transfer from the situation to actual practice will occur.

2. When facts and concepts are presented with visual cues, the potential for learning is enhanced.

3. The process of learning is facilitated when media present examples of the concept to be learned.

4. Media typically provide the learner with an opportunity to identify relationships that may not be as easily discovered when presented in written form.

5. The use of media helps the instructor change the pace within the classroom, and this factor, in and of itself, attracts attention and focuses student learning.

Effective instruction requires the management of time, people, ideas, materials, and equipment. Instructors are called upon to make hundreds of decisions each day as they plan, execute, and evaluate instruction. These decisions include the selection or development and use of instructional media to facilitate learning.

Media materials contain the essence of the content to be taught or the stimuli to be presented, for example, words in audio or print form and visual images in photographic or illustration format. The primary criterion for selecting media materials relates directly to the impact of a given medium upon the achievement of an objective by a learner. It is also important for the instructor to consider other criteria such as appropriateness, technical quality, cost, availability, simplicity, flexibility, and the level of sophistication of the media. The use of media materials must be consistent with the content, objectives, background, and experience of learners, as well as the instructor's level of knowledge and skill. Not every technique can be used with equal effectiveness in all settings and by all instructors. Effective decision making results when an instructor is knowledgeable about media materials and their potential for influencing learning in the instructional planning process.

REVIEW

Questions

1. What is the primary purpose for using instructional media?
2. What is instructional software and hardware?
3. What is the difference between an actual situation and simulation?
4. What criteria should be used to select appropriate media materials?
5. What is the purpose of transparency overlays?
6. What is the primary advantage of slides over a filmstrip?
7. What is a disadvantage of the opaque projector?
8. What is the primary disadvantage of an instructional film?
9. What projection technique can be used to make a large illustration from a small one?
10. What are the primary reasons for using simulation as part of the instructional process?
11. When might instructional media be more appropriate than actual objects?
12. What are four major advantages of using an overhead projector in the classroom?
13. Under what conditions do simulators provide the greatest value?
14. What are the characteristics of a good graphic?
15. What are the general characteristics of programmed instruction?
16. How are linear programming and branching programming different?
17. What is a simulator?
18. What are some of the advantages of closed-circuit television?
19. What determines the level of media sophistication?
20. What are some of the suggested procedures for using a chalkboard?

Activities

1. Explain how instructional media can help overcome the limitations of time, space, and size in an instructional setting.
2. Explain the difference between instructional software and hardware.
3. Describe the degree of flexibility inherent in the following media: (1) films, (2) overhead transparencies, (3) slides, and (4) filmstrips.

4. Gather information on instructional media showing the influence of technology.

5. Load slides in a tray. Mount the tray in a slide projector and adjust the focus and image for correct projection.

6. Load a filmstrip projector. Display the film on the screen so each frame is centered.

7. Make an audiotape of an oral presentation. Play back the presentation and pay special attention to the tone and volume of the recording.

8. Use a video camera to record an instructor's demonstration. Play back the demonstration using the pause, fast forward, rewind, and slow-motion features.

Computers in Instruction

11

INTRODUCTION

Earth has entered the information age. The explosion of knowledge and the means by which that knowledge is processed, stored, retrieved, and communicated has been revolutionized by the microprocessor. Microprocessors are found in microwave ovens, hand-held calculators, cameras, robots, appliances, automobiles, and electronic games. The application of the microprocessor in the development of the computer has brought about a revolutionary change in information processing. Not since the invention of the printing press has a technological device held such implications for the learning process.

PERSONAL COMPUTERS

Although computers have been commonplace in business and research for many years, the significant breakthrough in computers for education developed in the late 1970s with the introduction of affordable personal computers (PCs). *PCs* are used to transmit, process, store, and retrieve data. The PC, however, is not a magical panacea; it is a tool requiring the same careful use as any other educational device. See Figure 11-1.

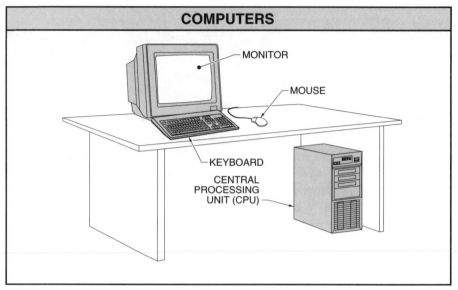

Figure 11-1. Computers are an integral part of education and training.

Computer Hardware

Computer hardware consists of the physical units of a computer, which include the keyboard, monitor, and disk drive. The control center of the computer system is the *central processing unit (CPU)*. See Figure 11-2. The CPU controls all the computer's functions. It is made of electronic circuits that carry out instructions written into the computer software. Components of the CPU are the memory, the control unit, and the *arithmetic-logic unit (ALU)*. The ALU performs mathematical calculations required for data processing applications. This component performs these calculations with greater speed and accuracy than is possible for the human mind.

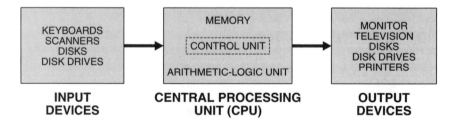

Figure 11-2. The central processing unit (CPU) is the electronic control center that translates input into output.

Computer Software

Computer software is the program that runs the computer system. Computer software transmits information to all areas of the computer system to carry out its basic operations. Software programs can be retrieved from a floppy disk or a hard disk. *Windows* is a software package that displays icons for various computer programs. Windows software is user-friendly and very popular. With Windows, one no longer has to memorize the names of specific programs as is necessary when using a Disk Operating System (DOS). The latest version of Windows software for PC and small network use can run DOS programs as well as Windows programs. Software programs allow the operator to input information through the keyboard console, move the information in predetermined ways, and save the information for storage and retrieval. Software programs include wordprocessing, database, spreadsheet, and specialty programs (for example, computer-aided design programs and computer-aided manufacturing programs).

COMPUTER USE IN EDUCATION

Computers are becoming commonplace tools in most educational settings. In order for students to be prepared for future jobs, instructors must include computer instruction and use in their curriculums.

Computer-Assisted Instruction

Computer-assisted instruction (CAI) presents instructional material on a monitor. Typically, the student scans the presentation and indicates readiness to proceed. The computer may give further information, or may present questions to be answered and stored in the computer's memory. CAI includes several forms of instruction, each with unique features and formats. *Drill and practice* is the simplest form of CAI and involves the practice of skills already learned. *Tutorial* CAI provides information in small segments and tests students' mastery of the information. Some tutorial programs provide additional information when students respond incorrectly. Other forms of CAI are simulation and problem solving. Simulations allow students to assume roles in situations where several options are provided, and they can experience the results of those options.

Another application of computer instruction is *computer-managed instruction (CMI)*. CMI manages instruction in a classroom through computer-assisted testing and recordkeeping, and it monitors student mastery or the absence of mastery of specified objectives. *Industrial management systems (IMS)* must rely on computers to handle the recordkeeping required for competency-based programs where large numbers of behavioral objectives are involved for each student. Each CMI program has its own design and capabilities. Some systems provide reports for teachers and parents that list objectives mastered by each learner over a period of time. The CMI software automates the recordkeeping process and is a computerized version of a criterion-referenced system for instructional management. It is possible to customize a CMI program for the unique needs of a school district or for the learning objectives of a particular subject area. While the computer can manage certain elements of instruction, such a system should never be used as a complete instructional plan for all students. Many other instructional strategies and learning experiences, such as discussions, experiments, discovery, and peer learning, play important roles in the educational process. The computer is a tool to use in the process, but it does not absolve the instructor of the responsibility for planning, executing, and evaluating instruction.

Drill and Practice Programs

Many computer programs are commercially available that provide the learner with a series of questions or exercises similar to those that might be found in a workbook. Drill and practice computer programs begin by posing a problem and soliciting a response. The response is judged and feedback is provided before the next problem is posed. Elaborate programs may begin with questions or a pretest to assess the prerequisite knowledge of the learner and then use that information to provide practice at the most appropriate level of complexity. Some programs maintain a record of student responses that are reported to the student and instructor at the end of the program. This performance record serves as a basis for prescribing additional instruction.

For as long as there have been educational programs, there have been procedures for memorizing. For many years teachers have used exercises, flash cards, and memorization rituals that are difficult to individualize and provide in the proper amounts necessary to meet the students' needs. Computer-based instruction, however, provides an opportunity to identify through pretesting the areas in which students need practice.

The best drill and practice computer programs have formats that encourage student reuse. Reuse ensures mastery of the skill or the establishment of the stimulus-response association required for effective memorization. When selecting or developing drill and practice programs, the instructor should judge their appropriateness in terms of ease of use, adaptability to a variety of learner levels, level of interest for learners, and educational validity.

Tutorial CAI Programs

Tutorial CAI programs provide written explanations, descriptions, questions, problems, and graphics. Tutorial CAI programs resemble a dialogue between an experienced teacher and a student. The program accomplishes the learning goals by guiding a student from one concept to another until that student grasps the meaning of the lesson.

In the tutorial CAI program, a question or problem is posed for the learner. The computer provides the next learning experience based on the nature of the student's response. If the response is correct, the computer moves to the next block of instruction. If the response is incorrect, the computer selects one of several remedial sets of instruction depending on the nature of the student's error.

Tutorial CAI programs require complicated instructional design and programming techniques because they must anticipate all possible student responses. Programs must also react to incorrect responses and offer tailored explanations and learning experiences for the most common incorrect responses. Many tutorial CAI programs resemble programmed instruction with a frame-to-frame approach that breaks down material into small segments of information. See Figure 11-3.

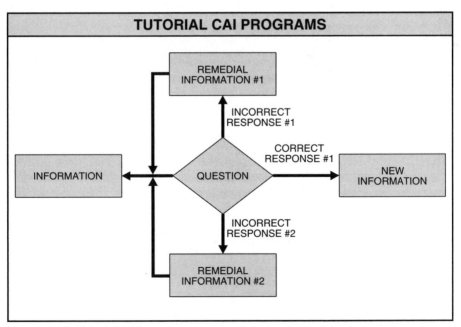

Figure 11-3. Tutorial CAI programs must anticipate all possible student responses.

Tutorial programs are aids rather than teacher replacements. The instructor should identify those situations in which tutorial programs can be most effective for learners to achieve desired objectives. Other factors to be considered when selecting tutorial programs are student interest, cost, efficiency, and appropriateness for learners of differing abilities.

Simulation Programs

Simulation programs allow students to experience situations that would be difficult or impossible to duplicate in a classroom setting. Specially designed simulators for flight training and for driver education have been available for years. Computers provide a quick and economical means of providing students with variable sets of data from which the student may select certain options and then witness the result of a decision.

Computer simulations for technical and vocational subjects can be valuable learning devices when properly integrated into the curriculum at appropriate times. Computer simulations are most effective when used to illustrate skills, ideas, and experiences that may have been first explored through other delivery methods such as lectures, questioning, discussion, or reading.

Computer simulation programs offer the opportunity to experience realistic problems without the associated risks. In addition, a well-designed computer simulation can radically reduce the cost of instruction as well as compress the time needed for learning. Computer simulation aids transfer of learning as students who acquire a skill through simulation find it easier to transfer that skill to the real world than when training consists only of traditional lecture and demonstration.

Simulations are one of the most powerful instructional applications of computers, but the programming is complex and time-consuming, and a limited amount of effective simulation software is available. To be effective for instructional purposes, computer simulation programs must reflect accurately the processes they are to simulate. As with any other type of instructional aid, the advantages and limitations that must be considered are student interest, economy, safety, realism, development costs, learning time, and learner anxiety.

Classroom Management Programs

A substantial part of an instructor's job is the management of information. Instructors should be able to use the computer to help with administrative and managerial functions such as testing and grading; filing, retrieving, and reporting; and recordkeeping. The instructor can also use the computer for graphics and wordprocessing.

Tests. Developing tests is a difficult and time-consuming task. Computer programs are available that allow an instructor to create a bank of test items classified under specified objectives within various units of the course. Directions for different types of test items can also be stored in the bank. This ability to manipulate items and directions can save the instructor several hours each time a new test is developed. The computer can also facilitate the assessment of test items and record information relative to each item's strengths and limitations.

Most testing procedures require the test to be in a paper format. Properly prepared response sheets, however, can be scored by the computer. In addition, the test items can be analyzed and information regarding the difficulty and discrimination power of each item can be recorded for future use. Computer programs can also calculate the percentage of correct responses and assign letter grades.

Grades. One of the more popular uses of computers by instructors is in the management of grades assigned to students in each class. Programs are available that provide quick access to information needed to fill out reports and generate student lists. Computer programs of this type simulate a grade book and provide more flexible and useful capabilities than the traditional grade book. The instructor begins by entering students' names in each class. Each set of grades for a test, quiz, or assignment is stored according to the name of the respective student. Weight values may be assigned to each type of score. The computer can provide grade averages at any time during the year when the instructor or student needs to determine the achievement level. Another program feature may include a report-generating capability that summarizes individual or small group performances. Statistical summaries are also available that indicate the mean and standard deviation and provide graphic illustrations that represent student performance. As students enroll or withdraw from the class, the list can be alphabetized in seconds. For the instructor who has large groups of students and numerous scores for each student, the computer can be a time-saving tool.

Databases. A number of software programs are available that enable the computer to file information. These programs permit the instructor to record, file, and retrieve information in ways not possible with the traditional system. Instructors can design forms to meet their own needs and then enter specific information. The information can be retrieved in a number of ways. For example, an alphabetical list of names and addresses could be sorted by zip code order. In addition, numeric data stored in the records could be used to provide attendance records, grading information, and tool and supply inventories. Since this technology is changing rapidly, instructors should be alert to the availability of software packages that can best meet their needs.

Graphics Programs

Computer software programs are available that display data in bar graphs, line graphs, pie charts, and so forth. Graphics software packages should be investigated thoroughly so that the selection best meets the instructor's needs.

Graphics programs are either *vector-based* or *pixel-based* (bit mapped). In a vector-based program, lines are single elements drawn point-to-point using geometric principles. For example, computer-assisted design (CAD) programs use vector-based software, which is very accurate and allows for great detail. The electronic files are smaller than comparable pixel-based art files. Popular vector-based programs include, Autodesk®, AutoCAD®, Auto Sketch®, Adobe® Illustrator™, Micrografx® Designer™, and Corel® CorelDRAW™.

In a pixel-based program, lines are composed of individual bits (many elements) drawn by changing pixel colors from point-to-point. For example, paint programs use pixel-based software that allows delicate shading in either gray tones or color and can include electronic photographic images. The electronic files for high resolution, detailed images can become very large. Popular pixel-based programs include Adobe® Photoshop™, Microsoft® Windows Paintbrush, MacPaint, Micrografx® Picture Publisher®, and Corel® PHOTO-PAINT™.

Wordprocessing Programs

Wordprocessing is the generation of words on a computer monitor that can be proofread, revised, printed, and stored. In most educational settings, wordprocessing functions are performed on a computer with specialized software. The computer can perform the wordprocessing functions and still be available for other instructional management and administrative functions.

When using the computer as a wordprocessor, the monitor serves as the blank sheet of paper, and the text is entered using the keyboard or a scanner. Wordprocessing programs allow for insertion and deletion of letters, words, lines, and paragraphs with the touch of a few keys. Various wordprocessing programs have specialized features to facilitate particular functions. At intervals in the inputting process, the save command should be used.

Wordprocessing allows letters to be personalized by changing the greeting and lines or paragraphs within a standard letter. The resulting letter generated for each individual looks as though it has been individually produced. In addition to reports and letters, files of students' names and addresses or parents' names and addresses can be kept up-to-date quickly and easily.

Internet

The *Internet* is a collection of independent computers networked to provide worldwide information resources. Benefits of the massive amount of information available on the Internet have been highly publicized. To the instructor, the Internet is another instructional tool which can provide additional resources for the learner.

The Internet is an outgrowth of a collection of computer networks developed in the 1960s. This large computer network effort was sponsored by the Department of Defense Advanced Research Projects Agency (ARPA), and resulted in the ARPAnet. The original ARPAnet network was developed as a security measure to maintain military communication capabilities in the event that a major communication hub (domain) was destroyed. The ARPAnet allowed the rerouting of communications around a disabled domain. Many domains could be disabled, but the network could still function.

In the early 1980s, educators at colleges and universities realized the value of sharing scarce computer resources. The ARPAnet offered interconnected domains, but the educational needs of unrestricted access conflicted with the military needs of security. The academic community developed their own network named after the National Science Foundation (NSFnet). The NSFnet used interconnected domains of college and university computers around the world similar to the ARPAnet.

Access to information on the Internet has been simplified by the World Wide Web (WWW). The WWW is a user interface to the resources of the Internet. The WWW provides information with links to other data utilizing hypertext links. *Hypertext* is data that is linked through keywords or phrases of related data categories or sets.

World Wide Web information is accessed using a browser. A *browser* is a software program that allows a simplified user interface for access to the WWW. Information on the WWW is accessed at a specific site (home page). A *home page* is a graphic user interface that contains hypertext links for access to related information on the WWW. Specific topics can be researched using a search engine.

A search engine is a computer program that searches through web sites for specific entries and functions like an index in a book. A word or phrase is input, and the search engine searches web sites for matches to the word or phrase. Upon completion of the search, the search engine displays a list of places, or hits, where the word or phrase can then be immediately accessed. A variety of search engines are used for searching web sites to access specific information. Some search engines are hybrids, allowing a user to search with several search engines simultaneously.

Most companies, organizations, and groups have their own web sites. These sites offer a tremendous wealth of information. For example, a learner interested in obtaining information about electrical product safety and certification from the Underwriters Laboratories Inc. (UL) can access this information at the UL web site (www.ul.com). At the UL web site, links are provided to a variety of resources, including information about certification, standards, and UL testing and services. See Figure 11-4.

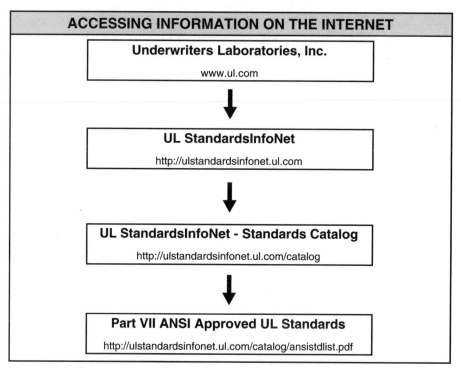

Figure 11-4. Specific information can be obtained on the Internet.

Government publications are available on the Internet. For example, current Occupational Safety and Health Administration (OSHA) standards are included in the Code of Federal Regulations (CFR). The CFR can be accessed at the U.S. Government Printing Office Superintendent of Documents web site (http://www.access.gpo.gov/su_docs). Product information is also available from manufacturers on the Internet. For example, information about Briggs & Stratton engines can be obtained at their web site (http://www.briggsandstratton.com).

The Internet can be useful for the acquisition and dissemination of information. Many rural educational programs are using the Internet for distance learning. For example, assignments are sent on the Internet, completed by the learner, and returned on the Internet. Courses which include laboratory activities require learners to report to a regional lab to complete assignments. Likewise, tests are taken at a proctored regional testing site.

The Internet is an unregulated information resource. A vast amount of information is available. The information available is similar to walking into a huge library. The information desired is somewhere in the library, but must be located. The instructor must provide specific direction in Internet usage to minimize wasted time searching for the desired information.

Current Issues. Responsible telecomputing must be taught to help students understand ethical, as well as security, concerns. Since the Internet is blind to differences in age, gender, ethnicity, behaviors, and prejudices, unsupervised access can pose potential problems for teachers, students, and parents. Teachers should establish rules for responsible telecomputing just as they establish safety rules and procedures for any other laboratory.

Other Applications

The computer applications that can be of assistance to instructors include:

- electronic mailing
- scheduling personal calendars
- charting student performance
- filing advisee records
- entering research data
- preparing manuscripts
- tracking budgets
- organizing and indexing bibliographies
- keeping address files
- searching databases
- checking spelling
- merging address and letter files
- transcribing, editing, and printing correspondence
- developing budgets
- recording and grading student achievement

- updating syllabi and course handouts
- dialing telephone numbers
- scheduling appointments

The following observations are offered to facilitate the work of instructors who use computers:

1. Where two or more individuals within the same unit are using computers, there is value in standardization of hardware and software programs. This results in saving both time and fiscal resources.

2. Develop a working relationship with local computer dealers, school computer specialists, and other computer users outside the instructor's immediate technical specialty.

3. Be a comparative shopper as prices are often negotiable. Software and hardware prices vary; therefore, whenever possible group software items with hardware purchases to increase savings.

4. Always prepare a backup copy of programs and data files.

REVIEW

Questions

1. What major technological development facilitated the production of the computer?
2. What are the essential hardware components of a computer?
3. What are the primary instructional applications of the computer?
4. How can computers be used to aid the instructor in administrative and managerial functions?
5. What are the primary functions of a computer as related to data?
6. How does Windows differ from DOS?
7. What are some of the different forms of computer-assisted instruction?
8. How are drill and practice programs used with a computer?
9. How are correct and incorrect responses used in tutorial programs?
10. How are computer simulation programs used most effectively in vocational subjects?
11. What tasks can computer programs perform in the development of tests?
12. Discuss how computers can be used in grading.
13. What are some of the ways graphics software programs can be used by the instructor?
14. How is wordprocessing used in educational programs?
15. What is the Internet and how may it be used in an instructional program?
16. What are the current issues of concern with use of the Internet?

Activities

1. Describe the components of a computer's central processing unit (CPU).
2. Describe the purpose of a computer program.
3. Differentiate between computer-assisted instruction and computer-managed instruction.
4. Describe the use of a computer in the development of tests.
5. Describe the advantages of using a computer program to manage a class grade book.

6. Describe the forms of computer graphics available to display quantitative data.

7. Explain the advantages of using a wordprocessing program to prepare a manuscript.

8. Search the Internet for specific information to be used for instructional purposes.

9. Shoot photographs of an operation in the laboratory or demonstration in the classroom. Have the film developed into slides which may be used for instructional purposes.

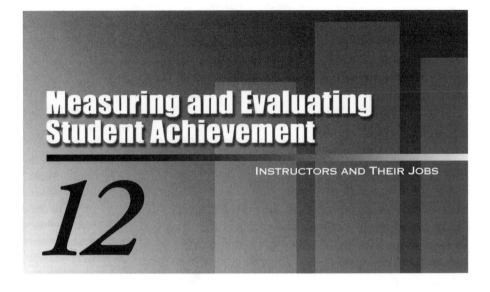

Measuring and Evaluating Student Achievement

12

INTRODUCTION

Written achievement tests and other measures of achievement are used to determine the extent to which students have learned the instructional content. Tests are also valuable in determining the learner's level of knowledge acquired over a longer period of time or may be used prior to a course to determine the level at which instruction should be initiated. Indirectly, tests can indicate the level of instructional effectiveness. Following completion of a course, tests may be used to measure the amount of information students have retained.

Written tests are valuable tools in the learning process; however, even the best tests can measure only part of an individual's achievement. No written test is capable of measuring all of a student's developmental changes that occur as a result of an educational experience. Written tests must be supplemented with performance tests, behavioral observations, attitude scales, and interest inventories to gain a clear picture of a student's development.

Instructors must learn to use achievement tests properly, weigh test results carefully, and combine test results with other evidence of progress and achievement for the best possible evaluation of each student's development.

Measurement is the systematic assessment of a trait or characteristic in quantitative terms. For example, it can be reported that a student answered 8 of 10 questions, or received a rating of 16 on a scale of 20 (20 representing a perfect performance). Evaluation is a qualitative judgment that uses measurement results to assign grades.

CONCEPTS RELATED TO EVALUATION

The development of a systematic plan for determining student achievement must be a part of the course planning process. The course syllabus should describe the instructor's plan for assessing achievement and assigning the course grade. The quality of the decision making depends, in large part, on the instructor's understanding of fundamental concepts of evaluation and associated principles of measurement.

Purposes of Evaluation

Evaluation requires professional judgment regarding a student's knowledge, understanding, skills, or attitudes. The purpose of evaluation is to make decisions regarding a student's progression, placement, and/or course grade. As the instructor engages in the evaluation process, several procedures and/or techniques may be used to obtain information necessary for a sound judgment. Test scores, grades on term papers, research reports, project ratings, and performance tests are a few measurements that might be taken to provide data used by an instructor in the evaluation process. An increasing demand for accountability increases the emphasis on measurement and evaluation procedures used in educational programs.

The primary purpose of achievement tests is to ascertain the extent to which learning has taken place. Well-constructed achievement tests can also serve other purposes in the teaching-learning process. Several of the more important purposes include:

1. Emphasize important content. A test and the discussion that should follow may be used to review, summarize, and emphasize the importance of certain facts, principles, and procedures.

2. Reveal areas of student weakness. A test may identify those parts of a course in which a student should spend more time in study or practice. The test that requires student performance clearly reveals the need for adequate preparation.

3. Identify weaknesses in instruction. A test may reveal areas that were not taught or where another approach or more emphasis might be needed.

4. Hold students accountable. Tests often cause students to feel more responsible for learning. As a general rule, students make greater progress in a course when they are tested over the content presented.

5. Provide a basis for grades and advancement. Tests are used to measure the extent to which students have learned in comparison with known standards and/or the performance of others in the group. Student performance records can serve as a basis for classifying students and placing them in a program at the appropriate level. Student progress is clearly impeded when students lack prerequisite knowledge and skill.

Types of Evaluation

Evaluation is a broad concept that takes into account numerous types of measurements, observations, and judgments that provide the instructor with input as decisions are made regarding the extent to which students have learned. Instructors should be familiar with various forms of evaluation in order to properly assess student achievement.

Criterion-Referenced Evaluation. When an instructional program is directed toward student achievement of specific behavioral objectives, a question to be asked at the conclusion of the instruction is, "To what extent does the student exhibit the competency implied or specified in the behavioral objective?" Tests of knowledge, skills, or attitudes that are formulated to answer this question must contain specific criteria by which judgments can be made. *Criterion-referenced evaluation* is the assessment of student performance that is directly interpretable in terms of criteria or standards of performance.

Test instruments that are criterion-referenced require specific standards for acceptable performance. These standards are set in terms of specifying a performance that either is or is not acceptable. Students whose test scores indicate that they have the ability to perform at or above the established standard are judged to pass, and those who fail to perform at or above the acceptable level do not pass. Using this point of reference for assessment could result in all students passing, some students passing, or no students passing.

Norm-Referenced Evaluation. *Norm-referenced evaluation* compares the performance of each student with other students in the same group. Even though the instruments used in assessing student performance may involve the same elements of knowledge, skill, or attitudes, the basis for determining whether a student has passed or not passed is substantially different when norm-referencing is used than when criterion-referencing is used. Most achievement tests, aptitude tests, teacher ratings, and course grades are based upon a norm-referenced approach to assessment. The primary objective of this type of assessment is to separate students within the group in terms of achievement. Students are ranked from high to low scores, and grades are determined by each student's performance in the group.

Formative Evaluation. When students are assessed to secure diagnostic measures of performance and these measures are used to influence or formulate instructional methods, content, or objectives, the process is *formative evaluation*. The purpose of formative evaluation is to identify inadequacies in student skill, knowledge, or attitudes that may be used in an instructional program. This assessment is also used to identify competencies that students have mastered, thus eliminating duplication of instruction. Assessment can also be used in a formative manner during the instructional process. Questions interjected during the instructional sequence may serve to highlight certain content or give students an opportunity to test themselves.

Summative Evaluation. *Summative evaluation* is the assessment at the conclusion of a course or sequence of instruction. The purpose of summative evaluation is to ascertain the extent to which all students have achieved the established objectives for which the instructional program was designed. For vocational and technical education, this evaluation process communicates to the employer the competence level a learner possesses at the end of the instructional program.

Descriptive Statistics

Descriptive statistics are used to explain to students, parents, and school officials the place of a specific score within the array of scores made by all students. Descriptive statistics describe the distribution of scores in terms of the tendency of scores to cluster together and the extent to which scores tend to be different. The statistics that describe the tendency of scores to cluster together are *measures of central tendency* and include the mean, median, and mode. The statistics that describe the manner in which scores tend to be different are *measures of dispersion* and include the range, percentiles, ranking, and standard deviation.

Measures of Central Tendency. The measures of central tendency are:
1. *Mean* – The average score made by a group of students taking a test. The scores made by students on a test are added together and the sum of these scores is divided by the number of students who took the test.
2. *Median* – The median represents the middle score in an array of scores listed from highest to lowest.
3. *Mode* – In an array of scores on a given test, the score that is made by the largest number of students is the mode.

A frequency distribution of scores on a test is represented in Figure 12-1. The test was completed by 30 students. The frequency column reveals the number of students who earned each of the scores between 3 and 30. The distribution indicates that two students received scores of 30, three students had scores of 27, three students had scores of 24, and so forth. Measures of central tendency for this test indicate that the mean was 19, the median was 21, and the mode was 21.

MEASURES OF CENTRAL TENDENCY

Scores	Tally	Frequency	
30	/ /	2	
27	/ / /	3	
24	/ / /	3	Mean = $\dfrac{\text{Sum of Scores}}{\text{Number of Scores}} = \dfrac{570}{30} = 19$
21	++++ / / /	8	
18	/ / / /	4	
15	/ / / /	4	Median = Middle Score = 21
12	/ / /	3	
9	/ /	2	Mode = Most Frequent Score = 21
3	/	1	
Σ = 570		N = 30	

Figure 12-1. The mean, median, and mode are measures of central tendency.

Measures of Dispersion. Measures of dispersion indicate the distribution of scores. The simplest distribution statistic is the *range*, which is the difference between the highest and lowest scores on a test. To illustrate, consider the performance of two groups of students on a test with 150 possible points. The mean score for each class is 100. The classes, however, are very different, and one class had test scores from 65 to 147, or a range of 82. A second class had test scores from 89 to 108, or a range of 19. In addition to the range, the following measures of dispersion may be used to describe tests:

1. *Percentiles* – The percentiles divide a distribution into 100 parts. Each part contains 1% of the cases. The conversion of raw scores into percentile scores is usually reserved for a large number of cases (1000 or more) or for calculating national normative data. Percentile scores provide specific information about the exact placement of a particular score relative to all other scores within a range of scores. Translating raw scores into percentile scores involves computing the percent of scores in the total distribution that are higher or lower than a specific score. For example, a score at the 50th percentile is equivalent to the

median score, and 50% of the scores in the distribution are higher than the median and 50% are lower. A score that is at the 75th percentile is lower than 25% of the scores in the distribution and higher than 75% of the scores.

2. *Ranking* – The ranking of students from highest to lowest provides an indication of each student's performance in relation to other students in the group.

3. *Standard Deviation* – The standard deviation is a measure of dispersion that indicates the degree to which scores within a distribution deviate from the mean. In a normal distribution of scores, one standard deviation above and below the mean would include approximately 68% of the scores.

Characteristics of Normal Distribution

Many human characteristics and traits follow a normal distribution. For example, intelligence is distributed normally with the largest number of individuals having an IQ of 100 and an equal number of individuals having IQs less than or more than 100.

Instructors should understand that normality holds true for characteristics, traits, and attributes that are taken from a large sample of individuals representing a total population. Most subgroups with which instructors deal are seldom large enough or sufficiently representative of a normal group to approximate a bell-shaped curve on any characteristic trait or attribute measured. This observation would be especially true for achievement test scores for groups of students at the secondary and post-secondary levels since the educational process causes students at the upper levels to be increasingly homogeneous and less likely to be representative of the normal population.

Instructors have often applied the bell-shaped curve of distribution to achievement test scores. See Figure 12-2. Such an inappropriate application would arbitrarily assign a C grade to 34% of the students who scored above the mean and 34% who scored below. The grade of B would be assigned to students who scored between 34% and 48% above the mean, and a D grade would be assigned to students who scored between 34% and 48% below the mean. The top 2% of students would receive a grade of A and the bottom 2% of students would receive a grade of F. While this mathematical approach to the assignment of grades may appear to be very objective, it is based on unwarranted assumptions that cannot be justified.

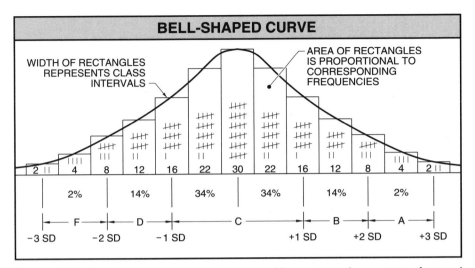

Figure 12-2. Test scores can be graphed as a histogram under a curve of normal distribution with percentages and standard deviations.

ACHIEVEMENT TESTING

Good tests are valuable and necessary measuring instruments, but poor tests may be worse than none at all. Tests that measure the wrong objectives or that measure the right objectives inaccurately may actually detract from the instructional program and discourage students. The fundamental purpose of achievement tests is to ascertain the extent to which students have met the objectives of instruction. These objectives may stem from the cognitive, psychomotor, or affective domains. Depending on the nature of the behavior to be observed, different instruments may be required to assess the extent to which objectives have been met.

Since a student's behavior cannot be observed on a continuous basis over a sustained period of time, the assessment of competence is usually done on a sampling basis. Assessments are taken several times during the course, and it is assumed that the student's performance at each of those times, when averaged, represents the student's level of competence. When achievement in the cognitive domain is being assessed, it is impractical to assess all of the content to which the student has been exposed. Therefore, instructors develop tests that, in reality, include only samples of all the information taught during the class. If these samples represent the student's level of knowledge, the test is said to be a reasonable assessment. If instructors do not complete an effective job of sampling, the assumptions made about the student's level of knowledge or competence could be erroneous.

Tests and other measuring instruments can be grouped as follows:

1. *Oral tests* are used primarily as a spot check of the student's understanding of concepts as a part of the formative evaluation process.

2. *Observation of students* is a vital part of the educational program wherever practical application of learning is an objective. Rating scales can be prepared that list the essential criteria used to make judgments in a more objective way.

3. *Performance tests* require students to demonstrate all or part of a procedure. Performance tests are based on doing elements derived from an analysis.

4. *Written tests* are useful for measuring the students' understanding of facts, principles, and procedures. Written tests can be based on knowing, doing, or attitudinal (cognitive, psychomotor, or affective) content derived from an analysis.

Observation of Students

Direct observation of students as they carry out class assignments and work with other students can provide an assessment of achievement not available by other means. It is rarely possible to evaluate student achievement on the basis of written tests alone. Written tests represent only samples of achievement. Certain attitudes, work habits, and creative abilities are assessed best by observing students at work in daily situations. Both the instructor and the student should know the characteristics being observed and the standards being used to make judgments. When observing, the instructor should look for specific behaviors at each level of achievement. An electronic test bank can be designed to assist an instructor in evaluating students in a specific course. Observation checklists are used by the instructor to make a fair and consistent appraisal of student progress. Observations should be made at predetermined points in the course, and a written record should be maintained. See Figure 12-3.

Performance Tests

If objectives to be assessed relate to a physical act, a performance test should be used. If objectives to be assessed relate to knowledge or information, a written test should be used. If objectives to be assessed relate to affective behavior, a performance test or a written test may be used.

A performance test rates high in terms of validity since it is a direct assessment of the individual's competence. If the performance test is constructed systematically and is administered properly, it also can have a high degree of reliability. Performance tests can be designed to measure skill on such operations as preparing a salad, sharpening a saw blade, inputting a document, or locating the cause of an electrical failure in an automobile.

OBSERVATION CHECKLISTS

	Participation	Care and Use of Tools	Work Procedure
Above Average 3	Makes an effort to learn Always industrious Always prompt in starting to work Always cooperates with others Solves all problems	Repairs and replaces tools Conserves materials and supplies Excellent selection and use of tools for specific job	Always follows standard procedure Always follows safety precautions Always has organized plan for the work Always exceeds requirements
Average 2	Shows average effort to learn Works well with little special attention Usually prompt in starting to work Usually cooperates with others Solves some problems	Generally careful with tools Generally careful with materials and supplies Generally correct selection and use of tools for specific job	Usually follows standard procedure Usually follows safety precautions Shows some plan and organization for working Usually meets requirements
Below Average 1	Puts forth very little effort to learn Wastes time and bothers others Usually slow in starting to work Seldom cooperates with others Unable to solve problems	Continually misplaces and breaks or dulls tools Wasteful of materials and supplies Incorrect selection and use of tools for specific job	Seldom follows standard procedure Seldom follows safety precautions Disorganized Always behind in work Low quality of work Seldom meets requirements

Student	Participation	Care and Use of Tools	Work Procedure		Comments
					Scale of Points Above Average. . . . 3 Average . . . . 2 Below Average. . . . 1

Front and Back of a Student Evaluation

Figure 12-3. Observation checklists are used by the instructor to make a fair and consistent evaluation of student progress.

When developing a performance test, the instructor should describe the criteria by which the student's performance will be judged. Other factors that the instructor must consider in developing and administering the performance test are:

1. Accuracy in following the proper steps of procedure.

2. Speed at which the task can be completed properly.

3. Quality of the completed task.

4. Consideration of safety precautions.

5. Written instructions that describe what students are to do and when they will be observed. Students should be aware if a time limit exists.

6. All necessary tools and materials must be available and in good condition. The student should be allowed to perform the operation without interruption except in the case of a violation of safety practices.

In developing the performance test, it is recommended that the instructor perform the operation to check the appropriateness of the criteria, steps of procedure, and standards by which judgments will be made.

Written Tests

The assessment of cognitive behavior is typically accomplished through written achievement tests. There are certain test construction principles that instructors should know when developing effective achievement tests. Instructors should recognize that written tests can only assess a sampling of the information presented in a class. There is a practical limit to the number of test items that can be completed by students within a class period.

The instructor must ask the question, "What skills, knowledge, and attitudes are essential for students to possess in order to meet the objectives of a lesson or course for which the examination is designed?" Each test item should be evaluated to make certain that it measures essential skills, knowledge, and attitudes. There is a tendency to measure those elements of content that are easy to measure. The instructor must be certain that all elements of important content are tested. The largest number of items in the test should be directed to the most important elements of the lesson or course. Tests should be neither too easy nor too difficult. Generally, the test should not be so easy that everyone gets a high grade. As the instructor makes test development decisions, it is important to consider such factors as validity, reliability, objectivity, comprehensiveness, and practicality. Each of these factors is present in a well-constructed test.

Validity. *Validity*, the most important characteristic of a good test, means the test measures what the instructor wants it to measure as determined by the course objectives. If the test measures elements other than those consistent with the objectives, instructors can never be sure what they have measured. Test validity can be increased by the following guidelines:

1. Include questions which cover important theories, facts, and procedures presented in class. Keep course objectives in mind.
2. Do not include questions that are so general in nature that students can determine the answer with little or no knowledge about the specific subject.
3. Make test items consistent with students' reading abilities. If a student knows the answer but fails to respond properly because of an inability to read and understand the question, the validity of the test question is weakened. Test items using illustrations and photographs may be more valid for certain technical content, depending on the student's reading level.
4. Keep tests free of insignificant information.
5. Avoid tests overemphasizing a learner's ability to memorize facts. This is a common weakness in many tests. The ability to use and apply facts and principles gives a more valid measure of achievement.

The most practical approach to determine validity is to analyze and judge each test item or question to ensure that it reveals a student's actual achievement in the course. After the test has been administered, validity can be judged by comparing the test results with other indications of the student's progress. If a student is an outstanding performer in class but does poorly on a written test, perhaps the test contains items of questionable validity.

Reliability. *Reliability* is the consistency of a test as a measuring instrument. In developing a test, reliability can be increased by using these guidelines:

1. Provide clear test directions for answering each type of item in the test.
2. Reduce or eliminate complicated, ambiguous, vague, and confusing questions that encourage guessing.
3. Increase the length of the test, thus reducing the chance of students guessing correct answers. Students have a better chance of guessing all items correct on a 5-item test than they have on guessing all items correct on a 50-item test.

Objectivity. *Objectivity* refers to tests that can be scored by different instructors with equal results. When creative achievement is to be measured, for example, in writing and design courses, objective tests must be supplemented by other more subjective assessment procedures. When subjectivity enters into the assessment process, the instructor must use written criteria and a numerical scale to record judgments.

Comprehensiveness. A good test samples all parts of a lesson, unit, or course for which the test is designed. A test is *comprehensive* if a proportionate number of test items are developed from several areas of study being assessed. The more comprehensive the test, the greater its content validity and reliability.

Practicality. A test is *practical* if it is easy to administer, read, understand, and score objectively. A test is easy to administer if the instructions to students are clear and concise. Type size and legibility, quality of paper, arrangement of the items, and use of illustrations are all contributing factors. In addition, the test must provide students with adequate time to consider each item.

Test Construction

Written tests are developed to assess the extent to which students have achieved the cognitive objectives specified for a lesson, unit, or course. Even when instructors do not precisely specify student objectives, there is still a delineation of course content that students are expected to learn. In addition to the direct assessment of cognitive behaviors, written tests also serve as indirect indicators of the extent to which students have acquired selected psychomotor and affective behaviors.

Test Length and Coverage. There are a number of variables that must be considered when attempting to match test length to the period of time available. For example, a student can respond more quickly to single sentence true-false test items than multiple choice test items. Completion test items with long sentences and several omitted words are more time-consuming than short sentences with a single word omitted. Short answer test items requiring two or three sentences or a short paragraph require more student time than objective test items. In addition, factors such as student reading ability and intelligence affect the length of time required for students to respond to test items. After the instructor gives several examinations, experience will provide a substantial amount of insight regarding test length.

Regardless of the time available for testing, a test usually includes items that only sample the unit's content and objectives. If all of the unit or course objectives are important, the test should sample the full range of objectives and content covered. The test should be comprehensive. Areas considered to be most important should have more test items than those judged to be of lesser importance. Instructors should plan tests just as they plan instruction.

When developing tests, instructors must also give attention to the levels of learning expected of students in the course. For example, if the test deals with cognitive content, the instructor should decide the levels of cognition included in the instructional program and then develop the test parallel to the levels emphasized. If the unit or course emphasized psychomotor learning and affective learning, the instructor might want the written test to provide indirect assessment of psychomotor and affective areas of learning.

Table of Specifications. A systematic method of developing a test that is comprehensive, represents the various content areas or objectives, and emphasizes the desired levels of learning established by the instructor involves the use of a *table of specifications*. See Figure 12-4. A table of specifications allows the instructor to structure the decision making that is involved in developing an appropriate examination. Decisions related to the inclusion of test items are made by all instructors, either on purpose or by default. Effective instructors can make decisions regarding test items in a systematic and rational way by developing a table of specifications.

TABLE OF SPECIFICATIONS

Content Area to be Tested	(1) Emphasis %	(2) No. of Items	Recall of Facts 10%	Recognition 30%	Application 40%	Synthesis 20%	Actual No. of Items	Total %
1. Principles of learning	10	8	1	3	3	2	9	11.25
2. Selecting and organizing content	30	24	3	8	9	5	25	31.25
3. Instructional aids and devices	15	12	1	3	4	2	10	12.50
4. Developing and using instructional material	20	16	2	4	6	3	15	18.75
5. Measuring and evaluating achievement	25	20	2	6	9	4	21	26.25
Total	100	80	9	24	31	16	80	100.00
Percent	—	—	11.25	30	38.75	20	—	100.00

Figure 12-4. A table of specifications provides a systematic method of developing a test that is representative of the course objectives.

First, the instructor should make decisions about the content areas to be tested and list these areas in the table. Content areas to be tested should be based on predetermined objectives. Next, the instructor should decide the number of total points that will comprise the test. After deciding what is to be tested and the number of total points for a test, the instructor can decide the percent or weight of emphasis to be given to each content area to be tested as shown in the first column (1). The second column (2) specifies the number of items needed to provide the amount of emphasis desired. For example, an instructor who wants to place 10% emphasis on a given content area for an 80-point test would construct eight test items for that specific content area (10% of 80 = 8). The next four columns are used to specify the extent to which the items chosen should measure the student's ability to recall, recognize, apply, or synthesize information. The last two columns reveal the decisions made on the basis of guidelines provided by the other columns in the table. Because some items may yield more than a single point and the use of percents may yield parts of items, the examination will not always yield the exact percent and number of items initially planned in the table of specifications.

Application of a Table of Specifications. Developing a written test based on the parameters established in a table of specifications requires that test items have been developed or will be developed. These steps are suggested when constructing a written achievement test after the table of specifications has been prepared:

1. Select test items that relate to an objective, a content area, or a unit appropriate for the test.
2. Review the selected test items, eliminating those least desirable, and retain the desired number for the test.
3. Repeat this process for the other items to be used in the test.
4. Arrange test items in an order of difficulty.
5. Write directions for the entire test and each test item area.
6. Prepare the final test and answer sheet.

As new test material becomes available, test items can easily be improved. Suggestions for constructing the written achievement test include:

1. Use no more than four or five different types of test items.
2. Include both easy and difficult test items.
3. Arrange each type of test item in order of difficulty, starting with the easier items.
4. Organize test items so scoring is simple, rapid, and accurate.
5. Prepare clear and precise test directions.
6. Prepare and use an answer sheet.
7. Ask other instructors to preview the test.

Developing Test Items

Written achievement tests include true-false, completion, multiple choice, matching, identification, and short answer essay test items.

True-False. A *true-false test item* is a single statement that is either true or false. See Figure 12-5. True-false test items are useful when large amounts of information should be tested in a short period of time. True-false test items are less reliable than other test items because there is more chance for student guessing. True-false test items also tend to measure memory rather than understanding or application. A test composed entirely of true-false items should contain at least 50 items. The more items in the instrument, the less chance the student has of guessing a high percentage of the answers. The following are suggestions for writing true-false test items:

1. Be sure statements are either completely true or false. Do not include items that are part true and part false unless the directions specify that the item must be entirely true to be marked true.

2. Make approximately 50% of the items true and 50% false. Randomly mix items so no pattern of response exists.

3. Keep the language simple.

4. Make the test items as short as possible.

5. Use only test items covering important material emphasized in the objectives.

6. Avoid words that may help students guess the right answer. Words such as always, none, and only should be used with caution. These words are often used with false statements; whereas words such as sometimes, generally, and usually are often used with true statements.

7. Do not write the true statements consistently longer or shorter than false statements.

8. Avoid stating items in negative terms. When negative words such as *NO*, *NOT*, and *NONE* are used, write these words in capital letters and underline them.

Advantages of using true-false test items are that they can be used to assess a wide range of content and they are easy to score. True-false test items are particularly useful for testing knowledge of definitions of terms, facts versus fiction or opinions, and cause/effect relationships. Disadvantages of using true-false test items are (1) students have a 50% chance of guessing correct answers, (2) they may measure students' reading abilities rather than knowledge of subject matter, (3) they require absolute qualifiers, (4) they are difficult to write, and (5) the items may be low in reliability.

Directions: The following statements are true or false. If a statement is true, circle the T at the left. If the statement is false, circle the F at the left and explain why it is false. The first statement is answered as an example.

T   (F)   The WLA model motorcycle has a horizontal engine with opposed cylinders.

Explanation: _The WLA model is equipped with a V-Block engine._

T   F   1. The purpose of the oil bath air cleaner is to clean the oil.

Explanation: _____

Figure 12-5. Some true-false test items require an explanation for all false responses.

Completion. The students' knowledge of principles, procedures, numerical problems, and equations can be tested using completion test items. A *completion test item* is a true statement in which blank spaces are inserted in place of one or two important words that have been omitted. See Figure 12-6. The student must write the proper word in the blank or on an answer sheet.

The following are suggestions for writing completion test items:

1. Write a number of short statements covering the most important information in the unit or course.

2. Review these statements and omit one or two important words. Make sure the meaning of the sentence is clear after the words are omitted.

3. Omit only words that call for specific information. Make sure only one word is correct or, if there is more than one possible word, give credit for all correct answers.

4. Make all blanks the same length to avoid clues regarding the length of correct answers.

5. Omit only those words that test the student's knowledge of specific content learned during instruction, not items of general knowledge. Include the verb in the statement. Use the articles "a" and "an" and singular and plural verbs (is/are) in sets to avoid providing clues to the correct response.

6. Number each blank space and provide a space for answers on a separate answer sheet that has corresponding numbers or in blanks along the margin of the test sheet.

Directions: Complete the following statements by writing the correct word or words in the blank space or spaces. The length of the black space is not an indication of the word or phrase to be used in properly completing the statement. The first statement is answered as an example.

Capacity 1. An important consideration in tool design is the _____ and range of machine tools.

_____ 2. Where shock is an influencing factor in cutting tool applications, it is normally better to use a tool made of _____ steel than a carbide-tipped tool.

Figure 12-6. Completion test items measure a student's ability to recall facts, such as technical terms, tolerances, or exact specifications.

Completion test items are often in the form of a question rather than an incomplete statement. The following is an example of a completion test item question: *A(n)* _____ *is a machine that changes mechanical energy into electrical energy.*

Advantages of using completion test items are (1) there is little chance to guess correct answers, and (2) they are good when students must remember specific facts, words, or symbols. Disadvantages of completion test items are (1) they measure memory rather than judgment, and (2) it is difficult to develop items that call for only one correct answer.

Multiple Choice. A *multiple choice test item* is a statement followed by a series of alternatives, all of which are plausible but only one of which is best. See Figure 12-7. The statement or question, often referred to as the "stem" of the test item, should pose a problem or situation that can be solved by the correct or best response. The stem of the multiple choice test item should focus on a specific learning outcome. A wide variety of outcomes, from simple to complex, may be measured with multiple choice test items. Multiple choice test items are adaptable to most subject matter content, and they can be written to assess different levels of the learning domains. Given the versatility of multiple choice test items, it is not surprising that many standardized tests consist solely of multiple choice test items. The following are suggestions for writing multiple choice test items:

1. Include the best or correct response and three alternatives (distractors) for each test item.

2. Include only plausible alternatives that are approximately the same length as the correct response.

3. Provide appropriate space for responses on the test or on a separate response sheet.

4. Include as much of the test item as possible in the stem of the item. Make the alternatives as short as possible.

5. Avoid test items on trivial facts.

6. Measure only content that has been taught.

7. Use diagrams, drawings, and pictures when necessary.

8. Use *A, B, and C* and *neither A, B, nor C* sparingly as response alternatives.

9. Avoid the use of negative words such as <u>*NO*</u> or <u>*NEVER*</u> in the stem. When it is necessary to use a negative word, underline and capitalize the negative word.

10. Avoid the use of *a* or *an* as the final word in the introductory statement. Instead use *a(n)*.

The advantages of using multiple choice questions include (1) there is little chance of guessing correct answers, (2) objective scoring is facilitated, (3) they may be designed to measure judgment as well as memory, and (4) they can be altered to test many types of subject matter. Disadvantages of using multiple choice questions include (1) it is difficult to construct items that measure judgment, (2) an instructor may be measuring a student's reading ability rather than knowledge, (3) the items often include trivial information, and (4) it is difficult to write plausible alternatives.

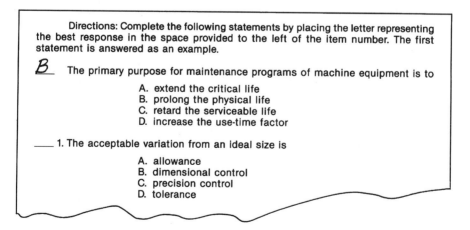

Figure 12-7. A multiple choice test item is a statement followed by a series of plausible alternatives.

Matching. *Matching test items* consist of two sets of related information. See Figure 12-8. In a traditional matching set, items in the first column usually consist of a list of statements or phrases to be matched with the responses, which may be written or graphic. The first column containing the longer items should be placed on the left side of the page to facilitate the ease of reading. The second column containing the shorter responses should be placed on the right side of the page. The student is required to identify the response in the second column that matches the statement or phrase in the first column. For example, the first column might consist of a list of definitions and the second column a list of technical terms. The student reads each definition and selects the appropriate response from the column containing the technical terms. One method of indicating the correct response is to have students write the letter or number corresponding to the correct response in a blank space provided to the left of each item in the first column; thus, making it easy for students to record the correct responses and easy for the instructor to score the items. Graphic materials such as symbols, illustrations, and charts may also be used in a matching set.

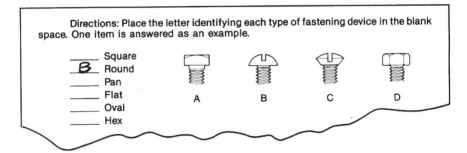

Figure 12-8. A matching test item requires the student to match terms with appropriate illustrations or words.

The following are suggestions for writing matching questions:

1. Use at least five, but no more than 15 items in each matching set.
2. Include at least three (but no more than five) more items in the column of responses than are in the first column. State whether item responses may be used more than once.
3. Include homogenous information in matching lists. Place numbers and dates in ascending or descending order, and arrange names in alphabetical order.
4. Write clear directions as to the method required for the student to record responses.
5. Place the columns side-by-side on the same page.

Advantages of selecting matching test items are that a large amount of information can be tested in a small amount of space, and they are easy to score. Also, matching test items are objective and discriminating. Disadvantages result because matching test items are not the best method for measuring complete understanding of information, and they are difficult to construct properly.

Identification. An *identification test item* helps to measure a student's knowledge of tools, supplies, or equipment. For example, a student may be required to examine drawings and/or photographs and then identify them in the blanks provided. See Figure 12-9.

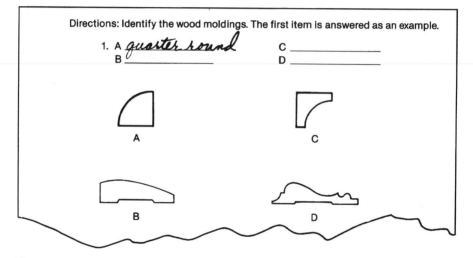

Figure 12-9. An identification test item is used to measure a student's knowledge of tools, supplies, and/or equipment.

An advantage of the identification test item is that it measures knowledge of such factors as the names of tools and materials or the locations of features on a machine. A disadvantage is that since photographs or graphics are necessary in written identification tests, their reproduction may pose a problem for some instructors.

Short Answer Essay. A *short answer essay test item* requires a student to respond to a question in sentence and paragraph form. See Figure 12-10. Essay test items have value in measuring a student's general understanding of a subject. Essay test items are difficult to grade objectively, time-consuming for instructors to read, and may encourage excessive verbalizing on the student's part. Therefore an instructor seldom prepares an entire test composed of essay test items.

The following are suggestions for preparing and scoring essay test items:

1. Ask for specific information that can be given in a short paragraph. Decide what will be accepted as a correct response and determine the value for full or partial response.

2. Make sure the item is clear and that the student knows what is expected.

3. Require the student to explain, describe, or provide reasons for the response.

Directions: Respond to the following items as briefly as possible. Use complete sentences and make your replies clear and direct. The first item is answered as an example.

Describe the procedure to follow in constructing a partition wall for a typical one-story house.

after framing out, nail all headers and cripple studs for the frame openings while the wall is still on the floor. Space all studs 16" on center. After the framework is complete, set the partition in place.

1. Describe the master pattern needed for joists and studs in a typical one-story house.

Figure 12-10. A short answer essay test item measures a student's comprehension of a subject.

Advantages of the short answer essay test item are that they (1) are easy to develop, (2) provide students with an opportunity to organize and express ideas, (3) provide the best indication of students' overall knowledge of certain subjects, and (4) measure written communication skills. The disadvantages of the short answer essay are that they (1) may measure students' communication skills rather that knowledge of the subject, (2) are difficult to grade objectively, (3) measure a limited number of objectives in a specific time period, and (4) may encourage excessive verbalizing.

Before scoring essay examinations, conceal students' names so their identity is not known during the grading process. Read and grade one item on all test papers before proceeding to the next item. This process gives the instructor an overview of the average quality of responses and provides a basis for assigning scores. Some instructors write the expected response for each test item prior to scoring, and assign a proper weight to each response by giving points for significant subject matter described properly by the student.

Electronic Test Bank. An electronic test bank may be developed by using a personal computer to maintain a file of specific test questions. See Figure 12-11. Electronic files are developed for test instructions, test questions in a variety of formats (true-false, completion, multiple choice, matching, etc.), and answers. The files containing questions are named by their particular subject matter. Using the cut and paste function, instructions and questions are selected and imported into the test document. Questions are numbered. Answers for the newly-created test are organized into a test-specific answer key, which the instructor uses to grade the test.

For maximum effectiveness, a file-naming system must be developed that allows questions to be easily selected and pulled into the test being developed. By mixing the questions selected, an infinite number of tests may be developed. Specific software for test development is commercially available.

Test Evaluation and Scoring

An instructor should keep a record of the times each test item is missed. This record provides information necessary for decisions regarding the validity, reliability, and usability of each test item. This information can also be used to identify content that was not learned by students and should be taught a second time.

If an item is missed many times, the following type of analysis should be made:

1. If the test item is missed by both high achievers and low achievers, it probably contains information that is ambiguous and should be rewritten or discarded. If the item is missed by the least capable students but answered correctly by the most capable students in the class, the item is valid, reliable, and discriminating. If an item is generally answered correctly by both high achievers and low achievers, it may mean that the item is too easy.

2. Tests can be used for teaching as well as evaluating. The instructor and students can learn much from studying the results of a good test. Time should be provided in class for a thorough review of the test. Discussion helps to clear up misunderstandings and provides valuable information to the instructor and students.

ELECTRONIC FILES

BASIC WELDING
Question Formats

**1. SELECT TEST
INSTRUCTIONS**

True-False
Circle T if the statement is true. Circle F if the statement is false.

Completion
Determine the response that correctly completes the statement. Write the appropriate response in the space provided.

Multiple Choice
Select the response that correctly completes each statement. Write the appropriate letter in the space provided.

BASIC WELDING

WLDNG10

**2. SELECT AND NUMBER
TEST QUESTIONS**

True-False

T   F   **1.** A back weld reinforces a groove weld and provides complete penetration through the thickness of the joint members.

T   F   **2.** The same weld symbol is used for back welds and backing welds.

T   F   **3.** Mechanical finishing methods used after welding to obtain the desired contour are designated by a letter placed on the right side of the weld contour symbol.

Completion

_____   **1.** Back or backing welds provide additional strength to _____ welds.

_____   **2.** Back or backing welds are made on the _____ side of a groove weld.

_____   **3.** A back weld is completed _____ the groove weld is completed.

Multiple Choice

_____   **1.** Weld A specifies a leg size of _____".
        A. .25   C. .75
        B. .50   D. neither A, B, nor C

_____   **2.** Part 2542738 is _____ in shape.
        A. square   C. round
        B. rectangular   D. neither A, B, nor C

BASIC WELDING
Answers   Ch 10

**3. SELECT ANSWERS AND
DEVELOP ANSWER KEY**

1. **T**
2. **C**
3. **D**
4. **.1542**
5. **finishing**

Figure 12-11. Electronic files of test items make it possible for the instructor to develop a comprehensive test.

Item Analysis. The instructor should complete a careful analysis of student responses to the various items on an examination. It is also important to secure student input regarding the processes used to arrive at both correct and incorrect responses.

Item difficulty and item discrimination are two statistical procedures that have been developed that enable an instructor to make systematic observations and comparisons of test items. An *item difficulty index* represents the percent of students tested who respond correctly to an item. For example, a difficulty index of .75 for an item indicates that 75% of the students responded correctly to that item. A high or low item difficulty index does not, in and of itself, indicate to the instructor that the item should or should not be included in future tests. The instructor may want some items that all or nearly all of the students will answer correctly. Also, an item with a low item difficulty index indicating that a small percent responded to the item correctly does not, in and of itself, indicate to the instructor that the item is either good or bad. The instructor may decide that the item is a good item, but that there must be a better instructional strategy in order that more students understand the content being tested. On the other hand, the item may have been so poorly worded that even students who knew the content missed the test item. If the instructor keeps a pool of items for future use, either in a card file or on a computer diskette, it is helpful to record the difficulty index for the test item each time it is used.

The following procedure is suggested for the calculation of an item difficulty index for a given test item:

1. Separate the test papers into three groups: upper third, middle third, and lower third. Set aside the middle group and work with only the upper and lower groups.

2. For classes with 30 or fewer students, it is recommended that the test papers be separated into two groups: the upper and lower groups; no middle group is used.

3. Record student responses for each group to each item.

4. Add all student responses and place into the following formula to determine difficulty index for each item:

$$Difficulty\ index = \frac{high\ correct\ (6) + low\ correct\ (3)}{no.\ of\ high\ group\ (15) + no.\ of\ low\ group\ (15)} = \frac{9}{30} = .30$$

Another systematic means of analyzing test items is item discrimination. An item discrimination index indicates the extent to which student performance on any specific item correlates with the performance by students on the test as a whole. The following procedure is suggested for the calculation of an item discrimination index for a given test item:

1. For each item, subtract the number of correct responses made by students in the low group from the number of correct responses made by students in the high group. For example, on item one of the test, six students from the high group answered the item correctly, and three students from the low group answered the item correctly. Therefore, the mathematical process would be $6 - 3 = 3$.

2. For each item, the numerical difference between the high and low groups would be divided by the number of students in one of the sub-groups being used. The formula, therefore, would be:

$$Discrimination\ index = \frac{\overset{6}{high\ correct} - \overset{3}{low\ correct}}{\underset{15}{no.\ of\ high\ group}\ or\ \underset{15}{no.\ of\ low\ group}} = \frac{3}{15} = .20$$

The higher the discrimination index, the better. An item which discriminates perfectly would have all students in the upper group answer the item correctly, and all students in the lower group answer the item incorrectly. A negative discrimination would indicate more students in the lower group answered the item correctly than students in the higher group.

The results of an item analysis process do not provide absolute answers. Item difficulty and discrimination indices, however, provide information that the instructor may use to improve test items or the instructional strategy.

ASSIGNMENT OF GRADES

Grades are an inherent part of the educational process. Most instructors expect grades to serve as part of the motivation-reward system, as well as provide documentation of performance or achievement. The evaluation process may involve a number of factors that must be considered as a student's course grade is determined. Typically, there will be test scores, written reports, projects, or other activities, as well as performance test scores and observational ratings made by the instructor. For example, if a point system is used to determine grades, one test may have 80 points while another might have 120 points. A student report may be worth 75 points, and the teacher may assign 40 points for class participation, cooperation with other students, and other attitudinal factors.

It is recommended that the instructor announce grading standards in advance, for example, 90% – 100% equals A; 80% – 89% equals B; 70% – 79%

equals C; 60% – 69% equals D; and below 60% equals F. This standard will provide students with an approximation of their grade at all times.

Translation of Scores into Grades

It is recommended that only raw scores be reported during a course because letter grades on measures of different weight can be misleading. If an instructor accumulates a student's raw scores on several measures during a course, only one translation to a letter grade is required at the end of a course. Most students and parents can understand the translation of raw scores or percents into letter grades. Not everyone will be in agreement with the cutoff point, for example, between A and B or C and D, but there is no substitute for the instructor's judgment based on experience.

The means of arriving at course grades is a compromise between norm-referenced and criterion-referenced grading. The achievement of one student has no bearing upon the grades received by other students. In fact, all students could receive the grade of A if they all had raw scores that could be converted to 90% or higher. Beginning instructors often have difficulty in establishing expected standards of performance and, as a result, may find a flexible standard to be advantageous. With a flexible standard, the instructor would announce that students who receive a grade of 92% or higher would receive an A, and that students who scored between 80% and 91% would receive *at least* a grade of B. In this way, the inexperienced instructor would provide a degree of freedom to allow the norm-referencing concept to be used. For example, if the natural break between a group of high achievers revealed that the *lowest* of the high scores was 89% with the next highest score being an 85%, the instructor might assign the grade of A to all scores of 89% and higher. The B scores might begin at 88%, even though no student received an 88%, and the B range might be dropped down to 77% or 78%, again depending on the natural break in scores within a class.

Many methods are available to assist in the translation of numerical scores (raw scores) into letter grades. The easiest approach to communicate to students and parents is the translation of raw scores into percents. With the development of computer software, much of the laborious calculation of percents from raw scores can be handled quickly and accurately. The use of a computer grade book program also allows the entry of scores from various evaluation items throughout the course.

As instructors make decisions regarding the extent to which students have learned, they must give careful consideration to the standards by which achievement is to be judged. An understanding of fundamental statistical procedures enables an instructor to analyze test data and draw meaningful conclusions related to student achievement and instructional effectiveness.

REVIEW

Questions

1. What is the purpose of written achievement tests?

2. In addition to written tests, what are other systematic means by which an instructor can assess student development?

3. What differentiates criterion-referenced evaluation from norm-referenced evaluation?

4. What are measures of dispersion?

5. What is the difference between a student's raw score converted to percentage and a student's percentile score?

6. What are the most common types of written test items?

7. Why would it be inappropriate to administer a 15-item true-false test?

8. How can item difficulty and item discrimination indices be used in analyzing and modifying test items?

9. How do tests provide a basis for grades and advancement?

10. What differentiates formative evaluation from summative evaluation?

11. What are measures of central tendency?

12. What are the representations of the width and area of rectangles in a histogram?

13. What factors should an instructor consider when developing and administering a performance test?

14. How is validity differentiated from reliability?

15. What are some of the difficulties in writing multiple choice test items?

16. What are some of the advantages of short answer essay test items?

Activities

1. Explain the use of written tests as an indirect assessment of instructional effectiveness.

2. Differentiate between measurement and evaluation.

3. Differentiate between criterion-referenced evaluation and norm-referenced evaluation.

4. Differentiate between formative and summative evaluation.

5. Define the measures of central tendency, which are used to describe student performance on a test.

6. Calculate the mean, median, and mode, and the range and standard deviation for a 50-item test.

7. Explain why it is inappropriate to arbitrarily impose a bell-shaped curve to assign course grades.

8. Explain how an instructor can increase the level of objectivity when assessing student achievement through observation or performance testing.

9. Define the terms validity and reliability.

10. Prepare a table of specifications for an examination to be given over a unit of instruction.

11. Calculate the item difficulty and item discrimination indices for a test administered to a class.

Effective Learning Environments

INSTRUCTORS AND THEIR JOBS

13

INTRODUCTION

Effective classroom management begins with preparation of the classroom, shop, or laboratory. Instructors should be sensitive to the appearance and efficiency of the learning environment. Ignoring the physical appearance of the space in which students and instructor will be interacting is to ignore an important variable in the teaching-learning equation.

The instructor who organizes the physical arrangements of the classroom and laboratory establishes a positive learning environment that facilitates the social interaction between students and instructor, and among students. A carefully laid out physical environment can reduce or eliminate potential problems. Traffic routes for entering and leaving a classroom should reduce bottlenecks and crowded conditions. Instructor planning and organization maximizes the student's time spent on the task and minimizes periods of inactivity. The potentially time-consuming task of distributing materials, taking attendance, or checking out supplies can be done efficiently by the instructor who anticipates needs and delegates authority.

Regardless of the age of learners, the instructor should develop ways to manage student behavior effectively. Students accept a variety of leadership styles as long as a teacher is fair and consistent. Instructors who expect students to succeed and treat them accordingly are likely to see them succeed. Instructors who expect students to fail and treat them accordingly are likely to see them fail. Students who are treated as responsible individuals are likely

245

to become positive learners. Students who are treated as if they are inherently bad and prone to antisocial behavior, whose misconduct is seen as evidence of their "bad nature," will probably turn out to be behavior problems. Instructors should project positive expectations when interacting with students and treat them the way they (the instructor) would like to be treated. Students also should understand the reasons for a rule if they are to accept it. Reasons should be communicated to all students and reinforced individually in private discussion.

INSTRUCTIONAL PLANNING AND ORGANIZATION

Effective instruction demands effective planning and organization. The learning environment established by an instructor sets the tone for student behavior and student learning. Research in the area of instructional effectiveness indicates a high correlation between effective management techniques, a positive learning environment, and student achievement. Instructors must give thought to the efficient and effective arrangement of classrooms and laboratories and make effective use of resources. Instructors should make changes to avoid problems; give careful consideration to rules, regulations, and student expectations; and handle most of the routine housekeeping and paperwork before or after class. The majority of class time should be spent in the instruction and supervision of learning activities.

Effective instructors are well-organized and well-prepared for teaching, making assignments, and monitoring student activities. Instructors should make efficient use of time. During the instructional process, instructors should maintain a high level of interest and keep instruction moving at a lively pace.

Lesson Plans

A key component of effective instruction is instructional planning. The instructor's lesson plan reflects the planning for an instructional period and is essential for establishing efficient and effective instruction. While the instructor must recognize the importance of timing and pacing, a measure of flexibility must be maintained since it is seldom possible to anticipate the amount of time that will be needed for every lesson element.

Management of Time

Scheduling is the process of establishing the timing and sequence of the various phases of an instructional program. Scheduling concerns instructor and student activities, as well as the use of equipment, supplies, and space. It is unrealistic to establish rigid rules of scheduling. Two instructors teaching the same content to the same level of students would not necessarily adhere to the same sequence of instruction. Professional judgment as well as the availability of equipment, nature of classroom and laboratory facilities, instructor's teaching load, and nature of the content to be taught are variables that must be taken into account.

Learner Activities. All types of applications, both mental and physical, are encompassed by learner activities, learner participation, and practical work. For example, solving mathematical problems and typing a letter are forms of practical work. The two activities are different in terms of the amount of mental and physical activity, however, both activities involve the practical application of skills and knowledge.

Long periods of instruction do not promote learner attention unless there is a considerable amount of variety in the presentation. Short periods of lecture followed by discussion, questions, and practical activity provides a stimulating environment, interested students, and greater learning.

Breaks and Rest Periods. Long instructional periods may create problems with student attention or fatigue. The traditional class length of 45 minutes to 60 minutes allows the learner a natural break and a change of pace.

Extra Sessions. While there are advantages of scheduling double and triple class periods, there is a point at which long periods of time devoted to a learning activity is nonproductive even when breaks are provided. Excessive hours at work often waste human energy and do not necessarily increase productivity. In some industries, for example, workers have produced more in a 7- or 8-hour day than they did in a 9- or 10-hour day. It is doubtful whether most students can concentrate on new subject matter for more than five or six hours per day. In addition, longer class periods may result in lack of interest and a noticeably decreased level of learning efficiency. Courses that involve a considerable amount of practical application can sustain student interest over a longer period of time than courses taught primarily through lecture.

TEACHING-LEARNING ENVIRONMENT

Effective classroom management begins with the preparation of the physical facility. The instructor must consider ways of making the classroom and laboratory an attractive and efficient learning environment. The layout of the classroom and laboratory should allow the instructor to monitor instructional areas at all times. In addition, the physical facility should have an instructional area where students can be seated comfortably.

Classroom environments can be improved by careful consideration of the stimuli (color, furniture, displays, arrangement of seats, cleanliness) that affect student behavior. The instructor must be sensitive to the physical environment if learning is to be maximized. If the instructional area is too warm, cold, or stuffy, student learning will be affected adversely.

Prior arrangement of chairs in accordance with the type of instruction planned saves instructional time. For example, a different arrangement of chairs would be required for a film than would be necessary for a group demonstration. The nature of the learning environment affects student interest and attention.

Starting Classes

The way the class period begins often sets the tone of student attention and interest, which has an impact on student learning. The businesslike atmosphere established by the instructor when starting a class has a direct effect upon students' attention and attitude toward the instructional process. Unnecessary delays and distractions, whether caused by the physical environment or the instructor's management style, impact on the teaching-learning process.

Roll Call. An instructor may wish to call students' names out loud in order to identify them more readily during the first several class periods in the school year. Valuable instructional time, however, can be wasted when taking and recording attendance. Attendance can be taken quickly by using a seating chart, which identifies where students sit. In some situations, it may be preferable to distribute a form on which students sign either their name or their initials after their name.

Written Instructions. Instructors should establish ways in which written instructions are distributed and retained by students. If instructional material is not readily available through textbooks or reference materials, instruction sheets should be prepared, duplicated, and distributed to students.

Placing handouts on a table next to the entrance to a classroom or laboratory is an efficient way of distributing instructional materials. When the instructor refers to the material later in the period, students will have the material at hand.

The break between classes may be used to distribute instructional materials to each student's desk or work station. If a large amount of written instructional material is to be used during a course, the material should be placed in notebooks or folders before being distributed to students. Handouts can also be prepunched prior to distribution so they fit into students' notebooks to promote organization.

Oral Instructions. Learning can be made more efficient when the instructor plans the oral presentation. As the instructor provides instruction, a few questions help test the level of understanding among individuals in the class before proceeding to the next part of the lesson. Looking for signs of student restlessness and boredom, the alert instructor recognizes the need to change the pace or perhaps take another approach to the lesson, which may make the difference between a dull or an interesting class session.

Distribution of Tools, Equipment, Supplies, and Materials. When the instructional situation requires the use of tools, equipment, supplies, and materials, it is important that these items be available and in the quantity needed for the learning activity. Frequently used tools should be available at work stations in convenient cabinets or on open panels. Special instruments may be kept in locked cabinets.

The U.S. Naval School in Norfolk, Virginia has used individually-fitted tool drawers with excellent results. In each drawer, the student has all tools required for carrying out an activity, thus enabling the learner to concentrate on the task to be accomplished. By merely glancing at the open drawers at the end of each instructional period, the instructor can see if any tools are missing. If a tool has been broken or misplaced, responsibility can be determined, and the tool can be replaced or recovered. In addition to preventing the loss of tools, this system eliminates confusion and time lost by students and instructors.

IMPACT OF ENVIRONMENT ON LEARNING

Physical conditions within a classroom or laboratory impact on student interest and learning. Teacher interest in students, the subject, and the classroom area helps to establish the tone for student learning. Instructor expectations and modeling can bring about the desired learning environment with a minimum of rules and regulations. Student misbehavior can be minimized by reinforcing expected behavior and quickly extinguishing undesirable behavior. Monitoring student behavior is carried out effectively by instructors who position themselves in a way that permits eye contact with all students. Students who know that the teacher is observing them are less likely to misbehave.

Distractions

Instructors of effective educational programs should attempt to minimize interruptions during a class period. For example, the administration should be careful about the use of intercom devices that interrupt a class period. Also, colleagues should be sensitive about entering another teacher's classroom and distracting the normal learning process. Sending messengers into classrooms to deliver notes and information should also be avoided. Usually, this kind of information can be delivered at the beginning or end of a class period.

Time of Day. Learning is accomplished more easily at certain times of the day. Learning varies with individuals, content, and the amount of activity involved. Some individuals work better later in the day, while others do their best work earlier. Generally, it is better to schedule more complex learning activities during morning hours. Also, the period following a meal is not effective for films or lectures.

Instructional Aids

Instructional aids should be set up prior to the class period. When this is not possible, plan the instructional period so that the equipment can be set up when students are occupied (working a problem, preparing an assignment, planning a learning activity or project).

Instructors should prepare before class and look for ways to save valuable class time. For example, transparencies should be arranged in the proper order prior to class. An instructor can also save time when using the chalkboard. For example, if the lecture develops an idea by using sketches on a chalkboard, it may be desirable to put part of the sketch on the board prior to class. Rough sketches made in advance on paper help the instructor to plan where these will be located on the chalkboard space during the instruction.

Amount of Content to Cover

Instructors must also decide the amount of content to be covered in a period of time. The primary mission of an instructional program is to facilitate the development of desirable attitudes and to assist students in gaining competencies related to both mental and physical skills. The value of an instructional program cannot be measured by the amount of the content in the curriculum. Schedules crowded with lectures and demonstrations often result in little learning when insufficient time is allowed for students to consider and apply the content. Instructors should eliminate nonessential content and allow more time for reinforcement, summarization, and repetition on essential points. Each item of subject matter in the course should be challenged on the basis of whether or not it is needed for the student to achieve competence in the objectives of the program.

Application of Theory

There should always be a planned relationship between informational content and application. As an instructional program is planned, the relationship of theory to practice must be considered. Sound principles of teaching and learning require certain basic and prerequisite knowledge prior to the introduction of new concepts and principles. Also, application should follow soon after the presentation of information to increase understanding and strengthen the associations that are essential for effective learning.

Dividing instruction into small units followed immediately by periods of application is recognized as sound educational practice. For example, mathematics, machine operations, and electrical principles should be taught over a considerable period of time, enabling each element to be applied. Essential principles should be spread throughout the course and applied to practical problems as they occur in the instructional process.

Influencing the Rate of Learning

Experienced instructors realize that the rate of learning decreases rapidly when students are kept in a passive classroom setting with an extensive amount of lecture for periods of time that exceed their attention span. The point at which the rate of learning decreases rapidly may be after as little as 10 minutes or 15 minutes of lecture. If provisions are made for strengthening the learning process by practical application, discussion, summation, questions, and tests, a much longer period of instruction may be used. These periods of application or practical work should follow as closely as possible the presentation of related information, procedure, or concepts. Short periods of application in each period of the daily schedule are desirable. In any event, some practical work should be included in every day's plan.

The effective instructor is an effective manager of facilities, equipment, materials, supplies, and the instructional process. The instructor's behavior and expectations of students establish the environmental conditions that have a substantial impact upon the learner's attitude and interest.

As the instructor considers the establishment of an effective learning environment, some attention should be given to the following:

1. Keep lectures and presentations short. Provide for questions and discussion.
2. Reduce nonessential content in order to allow time for review, discussion, and application of the most important content.

3. Allow breaks between periods for both a change of pace and time to consider instruction. The scheduling of changes of pace and breaks has a positive impact on learning.

4. Keep the instructional day at a reasonable length. This may be supplemented by additional practical application or individual study after the more formal instructional period.

5. Schedule the most complex and demanding intellectual work in the morning. Avoid scheduling lectures and films or other more passive instructional approaches after a meal.

6. Provide for maximum variety in teaching through the use of a variety of teaching methodologies, well-planned applications, and well-selected instructional aids.

In the final analysis, the instructor is most effective when the student takes responsibility for learning and is motivated to seek answers to problems. Ultimately, the instructor becomes a director of learning rather than a dispenser of information.

Questions

1. What is the impact of instructor expectations upon learner behavior?
2. What is the relationship between lesson planning and scheduling of the instructional process?
3. What are the positive and negative relationships between the length of a class period and student learning?
4. How does classroom and laboratory arrangement influence student behavior?
5. How can an instructor minimize the time involved in taking attendance?
6. What techniques can be used to increase efficiency related to the distribution of handouts?
7. If the instructor does not have time to set up instructional equipment prior to the class period, how can this be done during the period without wasting time?
8. What is the relationship between the amount of content covered and student learning?
9. What is the relationship between student attention span and student learning?
10. What are the two basic elements of effective instruction?
11. What are some of the classroom stimuli that affect student behavior?
12. What effect can changing the pace of delivery have on oral presentations?
13. When should instructional aids be set up?
14. What are some approaches an instructor might employ to influence the rate of learning in a positive manner?
15. What are three ways an instructor may take the roll?

Activities

1. Describe the primary components of an effective learning environment.
2. Describe the relationship between planning and time scheduling within a class period.
3. Explain the relationship of learner activities to student interests and learning.

4. List five conditions within the classroom and laboratory that the instructor can control that could have a positive effect upon a student's attitude toward learning.

5. Describe the means by which a seating chart can be used to take roll and facilitate the instructor's learning of student names.

6. Describe a system that can be used to distribute handouts without taking class time.

INTRODUCTION

On-the-job training (OJT) is over-the-shoulder coaching by a supervisor as a trainee works and produces a useful product or provides a service. In one sense, the application step of a lesson is simulated OJT. This may include the application of information following a classroom demonstration or may consist of a more extensive phase of instruction. See Figure 14-1. For example, in a teaching methods class, application is provided when a prospective teacher gives a brief lecture or provides a practice demonstration to the rest of the class. Application of the basic principles of instruction also occurs when a prospective teacher writes a lesson plan, designs a teaching aid, or prepares a test.

Projects and exercises used in a course of study are often designed to provide for the application of knowledge in the development of on-the-job skills. Work on such projects may be similar to actual work on the job.

On-the-job experience is more easily simulated in the classroom with some subjects than with others. Job standards and skills in keyboarding and shorthand can be established in the classroom. It is more difficult to simulate actual working conditions with subjects such as the building trades and production line work involving heavy equipment.

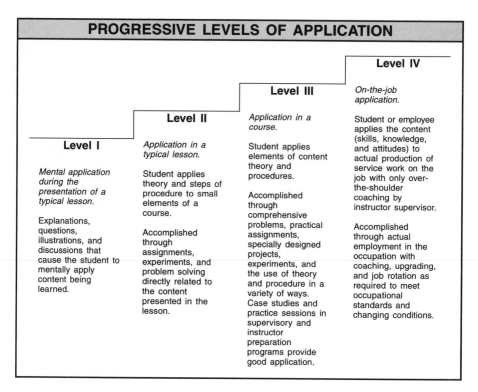

Figure 14-1. Knowledge and skill taught in a course of instruction involves progressive levels of application.

OJT ORIENTATION

OJT is continuous in many work situations. Such factors as turnover of personnel, changes in work tasks, changes in products, reorganizations, and expanding work programs make OJT a permanent part of most organizations' activities. See Figure 14-2. Generally, the supervisor has the major responsibility for OJT although this responsibility may be shared by others. If the individual is to be trained effectively and economically on the job, and at the same time not interfere with the production work schedule, the OJT supervisor should:

1. Provide opportunities for realistic learning experiences. Give less experienced personnel a chance to do the job, perhaps under the supervision of a skilled worker. This technique provides a more versatile work force and better team effort.

2. Use slack periods for instructional programs. Slack periods provide good opportunities for instruction at lower cost. Instruction can be

beneficial if it is carefully prepared, is made known to trainees in advance, is provided fairly to all trainees who need it, and becomes a regular and effective part of the daily work.

3. Provide trainees with new technical information. Knowledge of technological changes being considered broadens the trainee's concept of the job, motivates preparation for new assignments, and facilitates proper use of the new process.

4. Maintain an open attitude toward trainee suggestions. Trainees have many ideas for improving work conditions, tasks, and products. Establish an atmosphere where trainees are encouraged to think, improvise, and improve work methods.

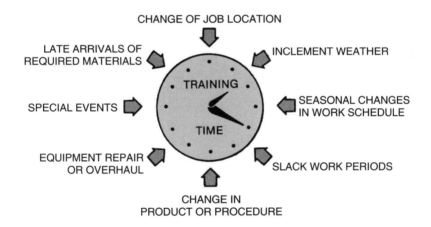

Figure 14-2. Job-related factors allow time for OJT without interfering with the production work schedule.

OJT METHODS

The difference between providing OJT instruction and a more formalized instructional situation is that the former typically occurs in short periods of time when the trainee needs the information. Supervisors who provide instruction must learn flexible instructional planning and instructional execution.

Planning of OJT Instruction

The supervisor who must instruct on the job should analyze the work task to be learned. Steps of procedure are inherent in the process of carrying out any work task, and the supervisor must be able to identify and communicate each step in a manner that allows the trainee to perform successfully. See Figure 14-3. After analysis has been completed, the supervisor develops a plan for teaching the content involved in the performance of the task. For simple tasks, the instruction can be completed in minutes. For complex tasks, instruction may be spread over a period of time. As the supervisor plans for the instructional process, a lesson plan should be developed that includes (1) an overview and rationale for doing the task efficiently and effectively; (2) a list of tools, materials, and aids necessary for explaining the task to be accomplished; (3) an outline of the content to be covered in an efficient sequence; (4) a list of key questions over difficult-to-understand points; (5) an opportunity for the trainee to carry out the procedure under supervision; and (6) a test of key points presented in the lesson. See Figure 14-4. The supervisor should also consider using a trainee instruction sheet that summarizes the process to be learned and provides written material that can be used as a reference when the supervisor is unavailable.

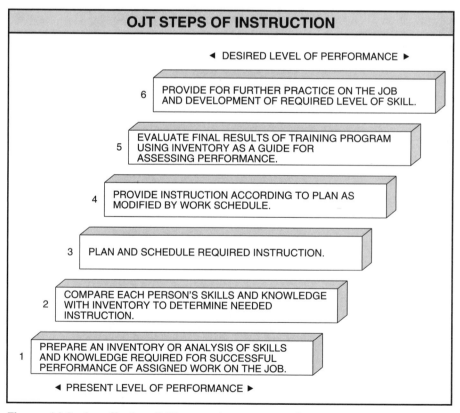

Figure 14-3. An effective OJT supervisor uses a plan to provide instruction to trainees.

OJT LESSON PLAN OUTLINE

Lesson Plan _____

Content from Analysis _____

Supervisor _____

Tools and Equipment Needed

1. _____   4. _____

2. _____   5. _____

3. _____   6. _____

Step 1   Obtain background information and arouse student interest.

Step 2   Present job.

Steps	Key Points
1.	
2.	
3.	
4.	
5.	
6.	

Step 3   Practice job.
          Allow trainee to demonstrate job.
          Ask questions and correct errors.

Step 4   Assign job. Date: _____

Step 5   Follow up. Dates: _____, _____, _____, _____, _____, _____

Figure 14-4. An OJT lesson plan should include a logical progression of key tasks to be discussed by the supervisor.

Execution of OJT Instruction

A supervisor should attempt to put the trainee at ease. If the trainee is under too much tension because of a fear of failure, it is difficult for the communication process to be carried out effectively. The supervisor should be friendly, relaxed, and behave as if on-the-job instruction is a natural event. Supervisors should provide unhurried instruction. They should begin with easy-to-learn information, such as tool and equipment locations, the schedule, or job rules and regulations.

It is helpful if the supervisor is aware of the trainee's initial level of job competence and what experience and skill the trainee has that could transfer to a specific task. The supervisor should set the stage for training by pointing out the relevance of the task to be learned and the advantages from the trainee's point of view.

After the supervisor has all materials and tools and the trainee is ready, the content of the lesson can be presented. One step should be demonstrated at a time, and the steps must be in proper sequence. The supervisor must explain, demonstrate, test, and make provisions for application. It is important to emphasize key points and communicate efficiently and effectively.

In OJT instruction, these suggestions may be helpful to supervisors:

1. Provide the trainee with a chance to devote full attention to the task.

2. Do not be too quick to suggest changes on minor items. The trainee develops a better self-concept if permitted to complete the task even if there are small problems that must be worked out. An overeager supervisor pointing out each performance flaw has an adverse effect on learning.

3. Correction or criticism must be directed at the incorrect act, not at the trainee.

4. Keep emotional control. The supervisor who becomes too tense or egotistic does not help the trainee. Observe and act in a calm manner.

5. Always follow instruction with questions. Ask trainees to explain the procedure or give reasons for their actions.

Follow-Up of OJT Instruction

After periods of independent work, it is important to engage in follow-up activities. The follow-up procedure allows the supervisor an opportunity to provide assistance if needed and to be assured that incorrect procedures do not become habits.

In the initial follow-up phases, the trainee should be observed frequently and provided with encouragement and an opportunity to ask questions or make suggestions. In most situations, the frequency of follow-up and review is needed less as the trainee functions independently.

Job Rotation

Job rotation involves placing a trainee temporarily in another job for the purpose of training. Job rotation tends to slow down production and create some confusion; however, disadvantages are offset by having more than one person capable of doing a specific job.

OJT Coaching

OJT coaching involves analyzing trainees' performances that can be improved, correcting improper or dangerous practices, discussing the work with the trainees to get their points of view, and providing assistance and encouragement as trainees attempt to improve performance. The act of OJT coaching suggests a degree of criticism that the trainee may resent. Even though coaching is difficult, it is a major OJT method to be mastered. Advantages of coaching include:

1. Coaching can be provided at the moment it is needed.
2. Coaching tends to be practical and realistic.
3. Trainees are motivated to learn because of an immediate need to know.
4. Supervisors can easily identify specific performance deficiencies in trainees and take proper action.
5. Results of the training are readily apparent because the trainee is working with actual equipment, and the finished work can be judged.

Perhaps the most vital element in OJT coaching is timing. Trainees must be allowed to develop their own skills, and they must do this by practice. The skilled supervisor analyzes each worker's performance progress continually so that guidance may be given when it is needed. Too much supervision, however, is to be avoided.

Learning is an emotional, an intellectual, and a physical experience, and all learning is affected by human relations on the job. The supervisor should take time to set the standards for the job and make sure those standards are understood. An atmosphere of mutual trust, respect, and approval must be created. Progress should be recognized and a word of encouragement used whenever it is deserved, especially with new trainees.

Questions may be used to focus the trainee's attention on key steps of procedure. A series of questions can lead the trainee through a procedure, thus developing confidence and ability. Questions are valuable when determining an individual's readiness for the next task.

OJT Progress Charts

Individuals involved in OJT have different degrees of skill and knowledge. Some may need instruction in basic elements of the occupation while others may need only specialized instruction. To ascertain the needs of each individual, the skills and knowledge they possess must be compared with the present and future requirements of the task expected.

Time and effort can be expended on unnecessary instruction. This often leads to the neglect of instruction that is vital. A proper use of OJT progress charts is one answer to this problem. An *OJT progress chart* helps spotlight training needs and records trainees' progress.

The objective of an OJT progress chart is to compare the present abilities of trainees against present and future requirements of the assigned job. An OJT progress chart may be made for each block of an occupational analysis, or several blocks may be included in each chart. See Figure 14-5.

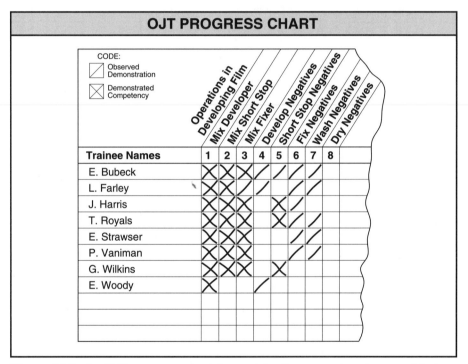

Figure 14-5. An OJT progress chart is used by the supervisor to record trainee achievement of manipulative skills.

OJT progress charts can be used to decide which trainees will be assigned specific tasks as they occur on the job. Similar charts are also used with knowledge elements of content. Records may be kept by indicating results of oral and written tests for each individual.

The analysis of the occupation, as compared with the demonstrated ability of trainees, provides a basic list of OJT needs. Other needs for OJT are revealed whenever undesirable conditions occur such as poor cooperation, harmful rumors, excessive complaints, poor housekeeping, unsatisfactory use of safety equipment, excessive waste of materials, abuse of equipment, absenteeism, insubordination, lack of pride in quality of work, inaccurate records, and time wasted. Instruction alone may not solve all of these problems, but an effective OJT program is usually an essential part of the solution.

FACTORS ASSOCIATED WITH EFFECTIVE SUPERVISION AND OJT

Effective supervision consists of several key factors that should be integrated with OJT. High achievement on the job is attributed to two-way communication between supervisor and trainee, appropriate performance standards, participation in planning and decision making, team spirit, achievement recognition, analysis of underlying causes of errors, good working conditions, constructive criticism, atmosphere of approval, coaching to correct defects, effective delegation, clear instructions and assignments, and effective training. See Figure 14-6.

Figure 14-6. High achievement on the job is attributed to key factors that should be integrated with OJT.

Two-Way Communication

Supervisors should do as much listening as talking. Research indicates that employee motivation grows out of a feeling of worth and self-respect. This feeling is increased when the supervisor takes the time to talk with individuals and to listen to their ideas and concerns. The supervisor who is too busy to talk is not getting the best support and effort from the group. Effective communication is an essential part of OJT.

Appropriate Performance Standards

One of the first steps toward effective OJT supervision is to establish appropriate performance standards against which achievement or work is measured. Occupational analysis provides a method for systematically identifying job-related skills. The degree of proficiency expected on the job can be included in the analysis.

Standards should be explained during instruction so each trainee develops the ability to meet standards. In day-to-day supervision, each trainee should be well-informed about the specific standards for each task. When this is not done, the trainee may spend too much time reaching standards higher than are required, or they may fail to meet desired standards. The result is either increased costs or unacceptable work. Unreasonable standards discourage trainees and they may quit trying.

Participation in Planning and Decision Making

Participation bears a positive relationship to motivation, cooperation, and team spirit, and all are needed for high productivity. Since a feeling of worth and self-respect is essential to motivation and high productivity, participation in planning has a positive bearing on effective supervision. When trainees have a share in planning their work, they are more inclined to:

1. attempt to do what is required;
2. support the need for changes and innovations in the work;
3. provide the supervisor with information needed to take action on problems;
4. provide time-saving suggestions; and
5. work with the supervisor as a willing team member.

Supervisors are responsible for results and at times must make decisions without guidance from the team. In most cases, decisions receive more support if trainees believe their ideas have been considered and a decision is reasonable.

Team Spirit

The importance of good human relationships within a group is often under-estimated. Research has shown that high morale and productivity result more from good human relationships than from increased pay, improved physical working conditions, and other tangible benefits. Supervisors must give careful thought to the relationships that develop on the job.

OJT helps to build team spirit as individuals train together and find a common ground for communication and understanding. Strong friendships and loyalties to the organization come as a natural by-product of the relationships that occur during well-planned and productive educational programs.

OJT facilitates a higher degree of understanding between the members of the unit and the supervisor. Success in an OJT situation and the resulting increase in competence on the job lead to greater job satisfaction and a feeling of belonging to a team.

Achievement Recognition

Trainees often receive little recognition for work well done. When efforts appear to go unnoticed, the trainee is likely to assume that the supervisor judges the work to be of little worth or of poor quality. Direct praise through verbal or written comments should be given immediately for a task well done. Other examples of recognition may include showing interest in the trainee's work and noting progress in developing desirable skills. An OJT progress chart can aid the supervisor in identifying this progress.

When the supervisor takes time to discuss the job and provide OJT coaching, the trainees are more likely to believe that their work is important and that recognition is given when deserved. Encouragement and OJT coaching are important in meeting the trainee's needs for recognition and self-respect.

Analysis of Underlying Causes of Errors

All significant on-the-job errors should be analyzed. Only after the cause of the error is identified can appropriate action be taken. A problem may be the result of many interrelated causes. When analyzing the cause of errors, these factors must be considered:

1. quality or thoroughness of instruction provided;
2. physical working situation;
3. trainees' physical limitations;
4. adequacy of job preparation;
5. relationship between the trainee and others in the work situation;

6. prevailing atmosphere and group morale; and

7. amount of wasted effort caused by changes in organization, rules, regulations, studies, and surveys.

Good Working Conditions

Physical surroundings are important for efficient and orderly work. Such factors as color, light, temperature, and noise have direct effects on productivity. Employee relationships, supervisory relationships, career planning, and job opportunities are also a part of the working conditions.

Constructive Criticism

It is never easy to discuss deficiencies. Supervisors sometimes avoid criticizing a trainee whose performance should be improved. Failure to correct errors and coach for performance improvement results in poor performance, negative attitudes, and low morale.

All facts should be gathered and evaluated before criticizing. Sometimes it is necessary to point out deficiencies in a very direct and forceful manner, but this should be done in an impersonal, fair, and firm manner. The supervisor should criticize the act, not the individual.

Supervisors should use these guidelines when discussing performance with a trainee:

1. Always get the facts. Supervisors who criticize with inaccurate facts find themselves in embarrassing situations.

2. Consider the circumstances and look behind the facts. The circumstances may bring the facts into proper perspective and suggest an approach for improvement.

3. Have a flexible plan. Be prepared with questions to ask and to change the course of action if answers suggest change.

Atmosphere of Approval

Productivity is fostered in an atmosphere where new ideas may be tried. OJT is vital in developing an atmosphere of approval because it

1. helps individuals develop confidence in their abilities,

2. informs trainees about job expectations,

3. recognizes progress and provides a basis for recognition,

4. helps establish work standards and trainee acceptance of standards, and

5. provides the supervisor with a greater perspective on the problems encountered by the new trainee.

Coaching

Coaching is used to correct deficiencies and leave the trainee with a desire to improve. If the trainee's confidence and willingness to try again are destroyed little has been gained.

Effective Delegation

Most supervisors know how to take responsibility, but a smaller number of supervisors know how to share responsibility or how to give responsibility to others without losing control. Delegation is one of the best approaches to high production, as well as to the development of personnel at all levels from trainee to manager.

Delegation provides the supervisor with an opportunity to judge the trainee's ability in areas beyond the present job. Delegation also allows the supervisor to check the trainee's competence and to identify specific needs for OJT coaching or other types of training.

Too many supervisors believe that they cannot delegate a task because it must be finished and other employees are not qualified to do the task correctly. However, responsibility and recognition bring out the best in trainees. Delegation is a priority in an OJT plan.

Clear Instructions and Assignments

The supervisor's goals are of little value to the working team if instructions and assignments are not clear. A supervisor who rushes through the process of assigning work may fail to check for understanding and leave the trainee confused. Clear assignments are required if trainees are expected to work to capacity.

Effective Training

Effective supervision is interwoven with OJT. Supervision without training becomes an unproductive operation with little long-range benefits to the trainee, supervisor, and organization. OJT, whether in a formal classroom or laboratory setting or in a work setting, is vital to the improvement of trainee performance and productivity.

Employee development is recognized as an essential component in the operation of a business or industry. Employee development is costly, but the absence of training may be even more costly. When involved with OJT, the supervisor may change from a teaching role to that of a coach. Individual coaching helps to build a positive relationship between trainee and supervisor, and it helps to develop the trainee's competence and confidence.

Trainees learn faster and remember longer when they understand the reason for learning. When practical, provide trainees with a broad view of the whole process before providing detailed instruction on components of the process. Several short training sessions are more effective than one or two long periods of instruction. This is due to the need for an application period for learners. It is important for the supervisor to realize that skill does not increase at a steady rate. There are plateaus where rapid progress may occur for a period of time and then a slowdown occurs, which may cause the trainee and the instructor to become discouraged.

Instruction is a necessary part of OJT supervision. It helps to reduce employee turnover, conserve materials, reduce training time, reduce machine downtime, increase the quantity and quality of production, decrease production costs, and improve morale. A well-prepared employee who is competent and confident requires a minimum of supervision in the planning and performance of assigned tasks. Competent individuals are the most vital asset of an organization. Effective OJT, through a variety of approaches, develops a competent work force.

REVIEW

Questions

1. What is OJT?

2. Why is OJT considered an important element of an organization's operation?

3. What is the purpose of the follow-up phase of OJT?

4. What is meant by job rotation and how does it relate to OJT?

5. What is the purpose of an OJT progress chart?

6. Why is two-way communication important to OJT?

7. How can the supervisor highlight trainee deficiencies without damaging trainee morale?

8. Why is it important to get the facts before criticizing a trainee?

9. Why do some supervisors fail to delegate responsibility and authority?

10. What are the essential elements of a lesson plan?

11. What are some of the advantages of OJT coaching?

12. How are appropriate performance standards developed for OJT?

13. What are some of the ways in which achievement may be recognized in OJT?

14. What guidelines should an instructor use when discussing performance with a trainee?

15. How does OJT develop an atmosphere of approval?

16. How is delegation a priority in an OJT plan?

17. Where should correction in OJT be directed?

18. What is the first step of instruction in OJT?

Activities

1. List several job-related situations that may indicate a need for OJT.

2. Explain how OJT can be provided in a work setting to minimize interference with employee productivity.

3. List the elements that should be included in a plan for providing OJT instruction.

4. Prepare an OJT lesson plan outline for a simple task.

5. Describe job rotation and its advantage as a means of OJT.

6. Prepare an OJT progress chart and include the skills or procedures for one or more tasks.

7. Observe an instructor during OJT and list the key factors of effective supervision as they occur.

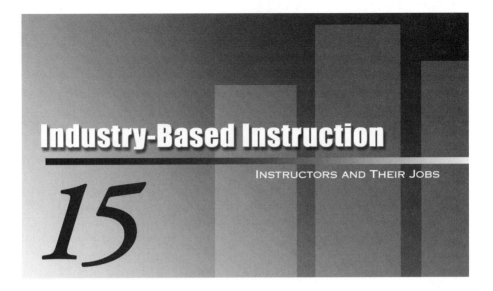

Industry-Based Instruction

15

INTRODUCTION

In industry today, maximum productivity is crucial for success. Costly inefficiency or downtime is unacceptable in a competitive world market. Advances in automated systems, sophisticated processes, and new tools of the trade demand trained employees for a high-performance and safe work environment. Training efforts to maintain and increase employees' level of competence can often be a challenge for companies and organizations. Establishing and maintaining training program quality and consistency requires qualified instructors and quality training materials. Many companies have recognized the need to invest in industry-based instruction. The primary benefit of industry-based instruction is its direct application to job performance, which leads to increased organizational effectiveness.

DIFFERENCES BETWEEN SCHOOL-BASED AND INDUSTRY-BASED INSTRUCTIONAL PROGRAMS

School-based instruction prepares individuals before entering the workforce. Once in the workforce, however, it is often necessary for workers to update and upgrade their skills, as well as to acquire new knowledge, skills, and worker behaviors. Instructional approaches in school settings are fairly standard with set routines and a predetermined teacher-student ratio. Curriculum materials and textbooks are obtained largely from commercial sources. In school-based instruction, the teaching approach varies with the teacher's preferences, educational background and experiences, available resources, and school district goals and policies. For example, a school district may require that a

271

particular textbook be adopted for a course. However, usage of the textbook and supporting materials may vary from teacher to teacher. In contrast, industry-based instruction is prescriptive to meet specific needs.

Industry-based instruction is instruction that is sponsored, planned, designed, conducted, and evaluated at the job site, or at a remote location such as on a college or university campus. The primary purpose of industry-based instruction is to provide immediate upgrading and/or retraining to employees for specific and relevant competencies to enhance job performance. Such instruction is typically offered periodically for varying amounts of time. For example, an instructional program on the operation of a new piece of equipment may require two hours or two days, depending on the existing level of competence and the requirements of the new equipment. This approach is in direct contrast with academic settings in which most of the curricula and the accompanying objectives reflect the notion that education is a long-term enterprise and that results can be known only after years of schooling. In industry, however, curricula are focused and represent specific job skills.

The rapid rate of technological change drives the demand for continuous educational improvement of employees whose performance will impact the productivity of the company. Many employees acknowledge the need to acquire new competencies, as well as to enhance their existing skills, in order to advance on the job. While some industry-based instruction may be required, such as in safety regulations, some instructional programs are optional. Individuals who volunteer to participate in an instructional program are usually goal-directed and want to be involved in practical learning opportunities. They want to be respected for the competencies that they possess and to be challenged. Foremost, employers and employees want to see the relevance between what they are learning and meaningful applications to their jobs.

Some companies hire specialists to facilitate instruction designed to close the gap between the needs of the company and competencies of the employees. These positions may be titled industry trainers, instructors, or personnel development specialists. In industry a title that commonly encompasses all of these titles is human resource development specialist (HRD specialist). An HRD specialist may directly plan and conduct seminars and workshops to update and upgrade employees' competencies, or the company may contract with a state department of education, community college, or technical institute to plan and conduct the instruction.

Employer Needs

Employer needs are focused on the specific capabilities required to support the mission of the employer. The maximum return on investment in training efforts is the primary objective. In addition, employer needs related to personnel are based on the pool of employees and potential new hires. The control of this pool is a major difference when compared with the population typically found in school-based programs. The needs of companies may be grouped as functional skills, soft skills, and technical skills that impact and influence the return on investment.

Functional Skills. *Functional skills* are those minimal abilities such as reading, writing, calculating, and computing that allow individuals to function in normal life situations and on the job. People entering the work force today will probably hold 14 to 15 different jobs in as many as seven or eight different occupations in their working life. Technical expertise alone is no longer adequate to ensure productive and effective workers. Functional skills are becoming an essential complement to technical expertise. Employers expect employees to possess functional skills in reading, writing, speaking, listening, reasoning, and computation.

Functional skills also include computer literacy such as usage of common word processing and spreadsheet software. Functional skills are transferable and portable to different job settings. Oral communication skills and listening are among the most critical skills for successful employees. Oral communication skills are practiced in many settings. For example, technical personnel need to be able to communicate effectively with non-technical people such as end-users inside the company and vendors and customers outside the company.

Asking appropriate questions and providing appropriate responses are required to routinely communicate information to supervisors, management, coworkers, vendors, and customers. Clarity and continuity in all communication prevents interruptions affecting company productivity. For example, employers have established policies related to sick leave to ensure important company tasks are performed throughout an absence. Timely communication regarding a scheduled absence is required as a matter of employee courtesy and responsibility.

Numerous job responsibilities depend on effective communication skills required for selling, working in a team, giving supervisors feedback about progress, or interactions with customers and vendors. For example, a majority of the U.S. labor force is employed in a service industry that requires a great amount of communication. As the service industry continues to grow, the importance of oral communication as a key element to good customer service continues. Persuasion, selling, and marketing help to build good customer relations, which will generate business from returning customers.

Job responsibilities and skills required can be analyzed using the *Developing a Curriculum* (DACUM) process. The DACUM process analyzes occupations to identify specific tasks necessary to work successfully in a particular job or occupational area. For example, DACUM analyses revealed that functional skills common to electronics manufacturing technicians, paper and chemical manufacturing workers, and workers in general manufacturing include technical writing, technical mathematics, communications, reasoning, following instructions, problem solving, and decision-making. Employers value employees who can communicate effectively using both verbal and written skills.

Technical workers are often required to use multiple sources of printed information. While most workers may have learned to read in an academic setting, specific applications of these skills to real-world problems and jobs is generally not taught. For example, following procedures, reading schematic drawings, or reading technical manuals are job specific reading skills. Some high school and postsecondary programs are incorporating technical communications as a requirement in some curricula. This is an advantage for newer workers. However, experienced workers may need to acquire these skills at their employment.

Soft Skills. *Soft skills* can be defined as interpersonal skills, knowledge, and attitudes that are not essential to technical skills or basic functions of the job, but yet impact the work place. Soft skills are non-technical skills in the areas of interpersonal relations, project management, negotiation, and relationship building. These skills are critical to acquiring employment and advancing in the field. In the competitive job market, soft skills are becoming an increasingly essential complement to technical expertise.

Employers continue to seek personnel with technical expertise who also are successful in product-development decision-making, multidiscipline teaming, and customer relations. The rationale is that employees who can utilize their skills in concert with the skills of others will be more productive, leading to increased company profits. Getting along with coworkers, supervisors, customers, and vendors is essential in fostering a pleasant and safe work environment.

Employers seek employees who understand how their work fits into the overall business and who appreciate the role of technology in society and the economy. Current research and literature related to hiring trends and attributes of employees suggest that employers expect workers to possess an array of personal attributes that influence job success. Negative attitudes may result in performance errors that result in loss of time, money, or customers. Attitudes also play a major role in one's work habits that impact safety practices. Workers who have positive work attitudes and who know how to behave professionally and dress appropriately on the job are most desired by employers.

The most successful employees are often those who demonstrate positive attitudes in their body language and speech. The most basic of these attitudes involve simple tasks such as daily informal pleasantries that are important to creating and maintaining a congenial work environment. Positive work attitudes, punctuality, open-mindedness, and cooperation are often more important to job success than technical expertise because these attitudes reflect the way individuals view themselves, their responsibilities, and their coworkers.

Employers want workers who are committed to organizational goals and objectives. This includes meeting deadlines, showing initiative, and demonstrating a team spirit. For example, in order to function effectively as a team member, one needs to be comfortable sharing tasks with others. Along with teaming skills are skills that enhance participation in a group as a team leader or as a contributing member. Negotiation and conflict-resolution skills are also important to being an effective team member.

Employees must understand a broad perspective of the company mission and goals while working in a specific job. Interpersonal skills that are unique to a specific job or work environment may be identified through a task analysis or by consulting the Dictionary of Occupational Titles. For example, DACUM analyses revealed that interpersonal skills for electronics manufacturing technicians include communicating with customers and manufacturers, being responsible, exercising leadership, being a team player, and being a creative problem-solver. Interpersonal skills for workers in general manufacturing jobs include ability to exercise leadership, follow instructions, and solve problems.

Technical Skills. *Technical skills* are task-specific skills that require additional training beyond the functional skill level and usually require in-house pretests to assess. In industry, worker interaction with technology changes rapidly. Such technologies require more skilled and educated workers, who can collect, graph, analyze, and program data and who are able to recognize alternative solutions to problems. Technical skills may require expertise with traditional tools and equipment, or new tools offered by computer software. As tools change, technical skill requirements also change.

Technical skill requirements vary with the type and size of the industry and the specific job. Computer-related technology continues to lead in the type of technical skills most needed in the workplace. The growth in technology has redirected corporate resources from tangible entities such as oil and steel, to intangible entities such as knowledge and the ability to acquire, compute, interpret, and report information efficiently and accurately. Consequently, employers continue to seek employees who have the necessary mathematics and science skills to enable them to address complex technical issues and learn as technology changes. Examples of technical skills needed by companies who hire electronics manufacturing technicians include testing products, analyzing schematics, troubleshooting, diagnosing, and estimating.

A major growth area of technical skills has been related to programming, database management, and utilizing the Internet. With advances in the technical skills required, employers will continue to seek professionals with skills that exceed fundamental knowledge and skills. The companies that use sophisticated equipment will need more highly skilled workers. These workers will benefit by receiving higher wages.

Learner Needs

Assessing learner needs is the first step in the development of any successful instructional plan. This assessment carefully considers the background, experiences, needs, and expectations of the learners. For example, technology literacy must be considered before using a computer in the instructional program. Other required information about the learner includes knowledge of the subject matter to be presented and any special needs a learner may have. Learners must possess certain functional skills, soft skills, and technical skills to perform effectively and efficiently. The HRD specialist assesses learner competency prior to the design of appropriate and meaningful instruction to meet the objectives of the instructional program.

Functional Skills. Functional skills of the learner should be assessed by objective tests. These tests may be developed internally by the HRD specialist to meet a specific company need, such as a test on communication skills. Commercially prepared tests may also be used to assess a person's competency level in a specific skill area such as reading or mathematics. For example, the Kaufman Functional Academic Skills Test (K-FAST), published by American Guidance Service, assesses reading and mathematics abilities, and the California Diagnostic Reading Tests (CDRT), published by CTB Macmillan-McGraw-Hill, assess reading only. Before administering any of these tests, appropriate research must be completed to ensure the tests are suitable for the intended audience and provide meaningful data.

Soft Skills. Soft skills are more difficult to quantify and often assessment occurs through interviews with coworkers. Prior to interaction with other employees, another tool that can be used to assess soft skills is the Myers-Briggs Type Indicator® (MBTI)® assessment tool. The MBTI® assessment tool can be used to identify a personality type by revealing the manner in which people perceive and the way they make judgments (Briggs Myers, 1998). The benefit of the MBTI® assessment tool is that it enables the HRD specialist to maximize the potential of an employee by recognizing and addressing various personality types encountered on the job. Copyrighted MBTI® assessment tools and interpretative information are available from Consulting Psychologists Press, Inc., Palo Alto, CA.

The MBTI® assessment tool is based on the theory that variations in human behavior are not due to chance, but rather to differences in the way that people perceive and make judgments. See Figure 15-1. The MBTI® assessment tool describes four dichotomies, each made up of a pair of opposite preferences. These four dichotomies include Introversion-Extraversion, Sensing-Intuition, Thinking-Feeling, and Judging-Perceiving. Combinations of these four dichotomies result in 16 different personality types. The personality types identified are not interpreted as being better or worse than another. Rather, each type has its strengths and influences needs, values, and interests. Consequently, individuals with common preferences will share some of the same attributes yet also possess some unique attributes. Understanding personality types is key to making appropriate and successful job matches, building effective teams, and maintaining harmonious working relationships.

The 16 MBTI® personality types, made up of groups of four letters, are separated into a preference for Extraversion (E) or Introversion (I). Some individuals are Perceiving (P) types, taking in information, or Judging (J) types, organizing information to arrive at decisions. Sensing (S) types perceive information using the five senses. Intuitive types perceive information using indirect perception or Intuition (N). Some individuals form conclusions through logical Thinking (T), or form conclusions through Feelings (F). For example, an individual who is an ISTJ could have a personality type associated with an analytical executive compared to an individual who is an INFP with a personality type associated with a "people-oriented" executive.

MYERS-BRIGGS TYPE INDICATOR® (MBTI)®
Characteristics Frequently Associated with Each Type

	Sensing Types		Intuitive Types	
Introverts	**ISTJ** — Quiet, serious, earn success by thoroughness and dependability. Practical, matter-of-fact, realistic, and responsible. Decide logically what should be done and work toward it steadily, regardless of distractions. Take pleasure in making everything orderly and organized — their work, their home, their life. Value traditions and loyalty.	**ISFJ** — Quiet, friendly, responsible, and conscientious. Committed and steady in meeting their obligations. Thorough, painstaking, and accurate. Loyal, considerate, notice and remember specifics about people who are important to them, concerned with how others feel. Strive to create an orderly and harmonious environment at work and at home.	**INFJ** — Seek meaning and connection in ideas, relationships, and material possessions. Want to understand what motivates people and are insightful about others. Conscientious and committed to their firm values. Develop a clear vision about how best to serve the common good. Organized and decisive in implementing their vision.	**INTJ** — Have original minds and great drive for implementing their ideas and achieving their goals. Quickly see patterns in external events and develop long-range explanatory perspectives. When committed, organize a job and carry it through. Skeptical and independent, have high standards of competence and performance — for themselves and others.
	ISTP — Tolerant and flexible, quiet observers until a problem appears, then act quickly to find workable solutions. Analyze what makes things work and readily get through large amounts of data to isolate the core of practical problems. Interested in cause and effect, organize facts using logical principles, value efficiency.	**ISFP** — Quiet, friendly, sensitive, and kind. Enjoy the present moment, what's going on around them. Like to have their own space and to work within their own time frame. Loyal and committed to their values and to people who are important to them. Dislike disagreements and conflicts, do not force their opinions or values on others.	**INFP** — Idealistic, loyal to their values and to people who are important to them. Want an external life that is congruent with their values. Curious, quick to see possibilities, can be catalysts for implementing ideas. Seek to understand people and to help them fulfill their potential. Adaptable, flexible, and accepting unless a value is threatened.	**INTP** — Seek to develop logical explanations for everything that interests them. Theoretical and abstract, interested more in ideas than in social interaction. Quiet, contained, flexible, and adaptable. Have unusual ability to focus in depth to solve problems in their area of interest. Skeptical, sometimes critical, always analytical.
Extraverts	**ESTP** — Flexible and tolerant, they take a pragmatic approach focused on immediate results. Theories and conceptual explanations bore them — they want to act energetically to solve the problem. Focus on the here-and-now, spontaneous, enjoy each moment that they can be active with others. Enjoy material comforts and style. Learn best through doing.	**ESFP** — Outgoing, friendly, and accepting. Exuberant lovers of life, people, and material comforts. Enjoy working with others to make things happen. Bring common sense and a realistic approach to their work, and make work fun. Flexible and spontaneous, adapt readily to new people and environments. Learn best by trying a new skill with other people.	**ENFP** — Warmly enthusiastic and imaginative. See life as full of possibilities. Make connections between events and information very quickly, and confidently proceed based on the patterns they see. Want a lot of affirmation from others, and readily give appreciation and support. Spontaneous and flexible, often rely on their ability to improvise and their verbal fluency.	**ENTP** — Quick, ingenious, stimulating, alert, and outspoken. Resourceful in solving new and challenging problems. Adept at generating conceptual possibilities and then analyzing them strategically. Good at reading other people. Bored by routine, will seldom do the same thing the same way, apt to turn to one new interest after another.
	ESTJ — Practical, realistic, matter-of-fact. Decisive, quickly move to implement decisions. Organize projects and people to get things done, focus on getting results in the most efficient way possible. Take care of routine details. Have a clear set of logical standards, systematically follow them and want others to also. Forceful in implementing their plans.	**ESFJ** — Warmhearted, conscientious, and cooperative. Want harmony in their environment, work with determination to establish it. Like to work with others to complete tasks accurately and on time. Loyal, follow through even in small matters. Notice what others need in their day-by-day lives and try to provide it. Want to be appreciated for who they are and for what they contribute.	**ENFJ** — Warm, empathetic, responsive, and responsible. Highly attuned to the emotions, needs, and motivations of others. Find potential in everyone, want to help others fulfill their potential. May act as catalysts for individual and group growth. Loyal, responsive to praise and criticism. Sociable, facilitate others in a group, and provide inspiring leadership.	**ENTJ** — Frank, decisive, assume leadership readily. Quickly see illogical and inefficient procedures and policies, develop and implement comprehensive systems to solve organizational problems. Enjoy long-term planning and goal setting. Usually well informed, well read, enjoy expanding their knowledge and passing it on to others. Forceful in presenting their ideas.

"Modified and reproduced by special permission of the Publisher, Consulting Psychologists Press, Inc., Palo Alto, CA 94303 from **Introduction to Type® 6th Edition** by Isabel Briggs Myers. Copyright 1998 by Consulting Psychologists Press, Inc. All rights reserved. Further reproduction is prohibited without the Publisher's written consent."

Figure 15-1. The Myers-Briggs Type Indicator® (MBTI)® assessment tool classifies combinations of behavior into 16 different personality types.

When personality preferences are ignored in job assignments and the work environment, efficiency may be reduced from negative interaction between coworkers or negative attitudes toward job assignments. For example, thinking personality types tend to respond to information conveyed compared with feeling personality types that respond more easily to values conveyed. Recognizing preferences for perception, judgment, introversion, and extraversion helps HRD specialists to match people with specific kinds of learning materials, management strategies, and work environments.

Repertory Grids. A repertory grid is another tool that can be used for identifying attitudes, feelings, and perceptions. Like a cognitive map, a repertory grid allows one to make visual representations of perceptions. Use of a repertory grid requires individuals to probe into their thoughts about what they actually think, rather than about what they think they should know. A grid may be as simple or as complex as the objective(s) of its use warrant.

Every grid consists of three essential features: elements, constructs, and linking mechanisms. See Figure 15-2. Elements are the objects of thought, places, ideas, or people observed. HRD specialists or workers with supervisory job titles and responsibilities may select the elements for the grid. For example, team leaders may be selected as the elements for observation. The constructs are the positive and negative attributes used to describe and differentiate among the elements (team leaders). Constructs may be generated in different ways. For example, the constructs may be elicited directly from the elements. This is the most effective way of generating constructs. The elements (team leaders) suggest the constructs (attributes) to be observed. This method helps the observer to focus on the demonstrated desirable or undesirable qualities of a person, rather than on ideal qualities.

REPERTORY GRID						
Constructs: (Positive Attributes/Negative Attributes)	**Team Leaders Observed**					
	A	**B**	**C**	**D**	**E**	**F**
Consensus builder/Not consensus builder	+	+	+	+	−	−
Good listener/Poor listener	+	+	−	+	−	−
Accepting/Not accepting	+	+	+	+	−	−
Creative/Not creative	−	+	−	+	−	−
Competitive/Not competitive	−	+	−	−	−	+
Resourceful/Not resourceful	+	−	+	+	−	−
Problem solver/Not problem solver	−	+	+	+	−	−
Prompt/Not prompt	−	+	−	−	−	+

Figure 15-2. A repertory grid for team leaders allows a supervisor to analyze performance based on constructs developed by all team leaders.

Each team leader selected for observation is asked to describe ways in which one team leader is similar to or different from other team leaders. The supervisor collects the descriptions and uses them to develop the constructs (attributes) for the repertory grid. Constructs are listed in brief bipolar terms. After the grid is developed, the supervisor records his or her perception of the leadership attributes of each team leader by using a linking mechanism such as a plus sign (+), or a minus sign (–) in the column corresponding to the team leader. A plus sign means the supervisor perceives the team leader as possessing the positive attribute, whereas a minus sign means the opposite.

Interpretation of the grid is based on the pattern of plus signs and minus signs. A quick glance at the grid allows the supervisor to analyze the perception of all team leaders based on constructs that team leaders provide. The plus signs and minus signs in each column reveal the perceived attributes for a different team leader. The more plus signs a team leader receives, the more positive attributes that are perceived. The supervisor can count the number of plus signs and minus signs across each row to determine the number of matches and mismatches of each construct with the team leaders.

For example, the HRD specialist selected six team leaders for observation. Responses indicate that Team Leader B is perceived as possessing all of the positive attributes except one, resourceful. Team Leader F is perceived as possessing only two of the positive attributes, competitive and prompt. The constructs "creative, competitive, and prompt" have a sporadic pattern, indicating no apparent relationship between them and the elements as a group. Thus, only five of the eight constructs may be useful to discriminate among team leaders. Results of the grid analysis are useful for assessing HRD needs, planning special courses, workshops, or seminars, making promotion decisions, and assigning work groups.

Technical Skills. Technical skills can be assessed using a pretest. A pretest is a written examination or a performance test that documents entry-level technical skills. The pretest includes test items and/or activities that assess learner knowledge and skills related to the proposed instructional program. When performance tests are used, the competencies to be assessed should relate to the skills required for the job. When written tests are used, questions should be written in an objective format. This allows the instructor to score the test quickly by traditional means or by using an electronic scanner answer sheet. Pretest results are used to help determine the amount of content review required and the pace of material to be presented. The HRD specialist may develop the pretest, or it may be one that is commercially available with the instructional materials.

Technical skills assessment can also be conducted using a survey. A survey is an instrument used by the instructor to determine prior experience and level of competency of the learners. The HRD specialist should allow time before instruction begins to review information provided on the survey instrument. Information from the survey is then analyzed along with results of the pretest. Such analysis helps the instructor adjust the content and pace of course material. Supplementary instructional material should be available for learners who have advanced competency level skills.

INSTRUCTIONAL PLANNING

Instructional planning is best conducted after analysis of learner needs. This information provides the tools available to maximize performance of all learners in the program. When assessment information cannot be collected before instruction begins, learner needs assessment must be performed during the first session. Often this process is conducted through formal and informal activities.

The HRD specialist should be aware of individual learning styles and cognitive levels. This will allow appropriate selection of the technologies and instructional methods to accommodate the different learning styles. Learners who are especially adept at using computers will be comfortable with computer-based training activities. In contrast, those who are less experienced with computers may be challenged to simply complete an exercise and submit it electronically. Instructional planning will address the best approach to accommodate individual learning styles.

Course Outline

A *course outline* lists the sequence of the material presented in the course. This allows the instructor to plan the proper pace by which specific course objectives are to be fulfilled. The course outline should be developed based on the course objectives, the length of the course, and the instructional facilities available. The course outline dictates the content that is presented using individual lesson plans.

Lesson Plans

A *lesson plan* details the interrelationships among elements of the teaching-learning process. A lesson plan may consist of a few notes or a detailed outline depending upon instructor experience and preference. Instruction should be tailored to the group based on information provided on a survey instrument and pretest scores. Depending on the time frame, a lesson may require 30 minutes or 3 hours. Lessons should include enough material to allow flexibility if the lesson proceeds more quickly or slowly than planned.

The lesson plan provides a basis for maintaining an instructional pace or rhythm. Learners must be challenged but not overwhelmed in an instructional program. A pace that maintains a variety of learner activities and adequate challenge is desirable. Breaks during instruction are necessary to maintain learner alertness. The instructor also needs occasional breaks to maintain instructional vitality.

Course Announcement

Potential course participants commonly learn about the instructional program through a course announcement. The course announcement lists pertinent course information, and may be included in a company newsletter, magazine advertisement, press release, or published document, or posted on the Internet. A course announcement commonly includes course title, brief course content description, meeting date(s), meeting time(s), meeting location(s), course materials required, instructor(s). Course announcements must be posted early enough to allow ample time for registering for the course.

Preparation for Instruction

Instructional effectiveness is enhanced when momentum is created and maintained by the instructor. Proper preparation for instruction is critical for success. The instructor should review all material relevant to the unit content, assemble the required components for the unit activities, and complete the learning activities following the exact procedures listed. Highlight any information to be emphasized on the resources developed. General tasks for instructional preparation can be compiled on a checklist for verification before instruction. See Figure 15-3.

INSTRUCTIONAL PREPARATION CHECKLIST

Delivery Before Instruction

☐ Order *Digital Multimeter Principles* texts for participants and remove Certificate of Completion.
☐ Order *Components Kits* for participants.
☐ Order/obtain DMMs as required.

Week Before Instruction

☐ Review Instructional Outline.
☐ Review *Digital Multimeter Principles* text chapters.
☐ Review references in *Electrical Principles and Practices* and *Electrical/Electronic Systems*.
☐ Review Electronic Slides.
☐ Review video clips referenced.
☐ Make copies of activities for participants.
☐ Make copies of Worksheets for participants.
☐ Review Activity Answer Keys.
☐ Make copies of Surveys, Pretests, and Posttests for participants.

☐ Review Survey, Pretest, and Posttests.
☐ Obtain personal protective equipment required.
☐ Gather/prepare instructor-provided resources.
☐ Order/obtain multimedia projector with spare bulb.
☐ Verify computer files and software functions.
☐ Develop/make copies of instructor-provided activities.
☐ Review related DMM operation procedures in user's manual.
☐ Develop registration sheet (name, company, title, supervisor, etc.).
☐ Test DMMs for proper operation.

Day of Instruction

☐ Check condition of training room (lighting, temperature, seating, cleanliness, work spaces, equipment condition, etc.).
☐ Review related DMM operation procedures in user's manual.
☐ Test computer and multimedia projector for proper function, and focus in training room setting.
☐ Check screen, whiteboard markers, and other supplies.
☐ Organize handouts, transparencies, reference material, and instructor-provided resources at presentation desk.
☐ Distribute DMMs, *Components Kits*, and handouts.
☐ Distribute registration sheet.

Figure 15-3. An instructional preparation checklist is used to verify tasks required prior to instruction.

A prepared instructor is ready for instruction by making the necessary copies, staging handouts, and checking equipment. For example, computers and multimedia projectors should be turned ON and checked for proper operation. Technical support staff should be accessible. As a precaution, a spare bulb should be available to prevent a long disruption to the lesson presentation. References in books can be tabbed for quick access to information required. All equipment and instructional resources should be located in the training room for maximum efficiency. See Figure 15-4.

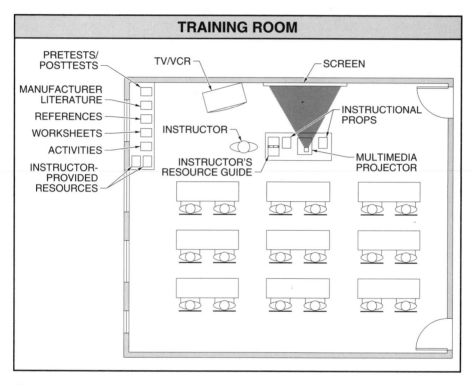

Figure 15-4. A training room is designed and prepared for maximum instructional efficiency in a training program.

Instructor-Developed Activities. Instructor-developed activities can be added to each unit to further reinforce information presented, provide more hands-on activities, and/or offer opportunities for advanced learners. Components supplied by the instructor can be used with components supplied by commercial vendors. For example, in an electrical training seminar on measuring resistance and continuity testing, the instructor may include an activity using a double-pole, double-throw (DPDT) switch, a normally-open (NO) pushbutton, a normally-closed (NC) pushbutton, and a double-pole, double-throw (DPDT) relay.

Instructor-developed activities can provide written explanations, graphic representations, and specific assignments. See Figure 15-5. Activities present an opportunity for the instructor to apply key concepts of the instructional unit. The course format determines the amount of time available. Specific components, tools, and equipment may be required for some activities. When appropriate, the time to remove components, identify the components, and return components must be included in the overall time for instruction.

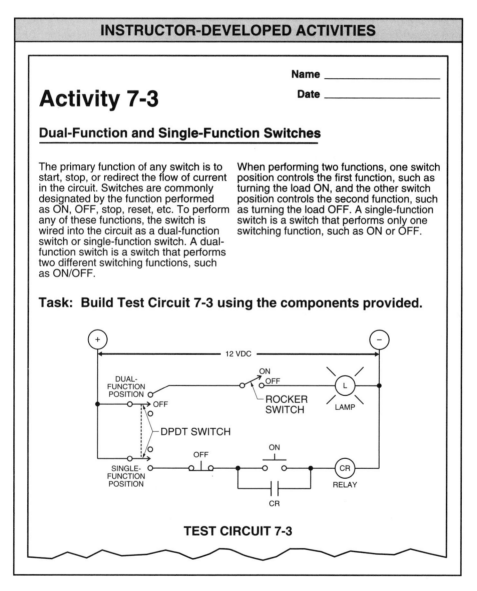

INSTRUCTOR-DEVELOPED ACTIVITIES

Name _____

Date _____

Activity 7-3

Dual-Function and Single-Function Switches

The primary function of any switch is to start, stop, or redirect the flow of current in the circuit. Switches are commonly designated by the function performed as ON, OFF, stop, reset, etc. To perform any of these functions, the switch is wired into the circuit as a dual-function switch or single-function switch. A dual-function switch is a switch that performs two different switching functions, such as ON/OFF.

When performing two functions, one switch position controls the first function, such as turning the load ON, and the other switch position controls the second function, such as turning the load OFF. A single-function switch is a switch that performs only one switching function, such as ON or OFF.

Task: Build Test Circuit 7-3 using the components provided.

TEST CIRCUIT 7-3

Figure 15-5. Instructor-developed activities provide an opportunity to reinforce relevant concepts covered during instruction.

It is important to explain how activities relate to the unit topic. In addition, relevance is imperative when prerequisite knowledge and skills are presented. For example, measuring DC voltage requires a digital multimeter (DMM) to be connected to the circuit with matched polarity. The instructor can demonstrate the activity step-by-step as listed in the procedures. Measurement value variations and particular problems that could occur when completing the activity are noted during the demonstration. For example, if the DMM is set to AC voltage and DC voltage is measured, there is no polarity indicated on the display when reversing the DMM test leads. Differences in equipment must also be addressed. For example, some DMM test leads have alligator clip attachments that slip over the test probe for ease in connection to a circuit.

Training Objectives. Training objectives vary according to the purpose of the training program and the level of the participants. Training objectives should specify the knowledge and skills to be acquired in the course, with consideration given to industrial experience, educational background, and current level of competency. Specific examination and/or certification requirements also have a direct bearing on the training objectives and should be used to develop the course and determine the content of the course outline. Competencies, which detail the intended outcomes and expectations of the instructional unit, are then identified to meet the training objectives.

The instructor should explain the purpose of the instructional unit in context with the new information to be presented. Competencies are prioritized based on importance. For example, safety topics are presented first. Competencies written for specific tasks define the expected learner outcome and enhance successful achievement.

INSTRUCTIONAL METHODS

Instructional methods vary with the content areas to be taught and the learners in the course. The best instruction occurs through the use of several instructional methods. An effective instructor can quickly sense which instructional methods are most and least effective in a given situation. In some cases, the instructional method may be limited by time, facilities, equipment, and/or budget. This challenges the instructor to be creative when faced with potential constraints.

The instructor sets the standard for the way information is presented and how the class is expected to respond. Information should be conveyed efficiently for better comprehension. Key points listed in an instructional outline offer a guide to the content and sequence to follow. It is a good idea to have textbooks and other printed materials available for reference as information is presented. Information presented with personal experiences interspersed, and an obvious passion for the subject matter, will serve to motivate the learners.

HRD specialists are responsible for the delivery of instruction regardless of the instructional design process used. Common instructional methods include lecture, demonstration, hands-on activities, guest speaker, job-site tours, distance learning, cooperative learning, team teaching, problem solving, questions, learner presentations, modular instruction, on-the-job training, self-directed instruction, and individualized instruction. See Figure 15-6.

Lecture

Lecture is an instructional method that uses oral presentation of information. Lecture is an efficient method of disseminating information quickly to a large group. Information is conveyed in a one-directional mode. The primary advantage of lecture is the ability to impact many learners at a given time. Disadvantages of lecture are the limited amount of learner feedback and instructor-learner interaction.

INSTRUCTIONAL METHODS			
Method	**Characteristics**	**Method**	**Characteristics**
Lecture	Presents information to group efficiently but limits learner interaction	Problem Solving	Elicits knowledge and skills through solution of assigned problems
Demonstration	Shows and explains sequential hands-on procedures for completing task		Requires learner prerequisite knowledge and skills
	Requires extensive instructional aid preparation and rehearsal	Questions	Initiates discussion and assesses comprehension
Hands-on Activities	Reinforces desired procedures through physical practice		Raises attention level of learners
	Enhances retention of theoretical concepts	Learner Presentations	Compels thorough learner comprehension of subject matter
Guest Speaker	Provides additional perspective		Provides opportunities for advanced learner investigation in content area
	Offers opportunity to interact with professional in field	Modular Presentations	Allows self-paced instruction using discrete packaged material
Industry Tours	Provides authentic on-site experience to learners		Provides opportunity for instruction in specific topics
	Offers opportunity to interact in setting away from training facility	On-the-Job Training	Delivers instruction in same environment where task will be performed
Distance Learning	Delivers content to remote locations		Utilizes demonstration and hands-on practice
	Provides interaction between students and instructor using Internet	Self-Directed Instruction	Learner-initiated instruction to achieve specific competencies
Cooperative Learning	Uses interaction between learners to acquire knowledge and skills		Often uses learning contract developed by instructor and learner
	Builds on shared collective knowledge of learners	Individualized Instruction	Addresses specific needs of individual learner
Team Teaching	Enhances training capabilities		Tailors individual instruction developed by instructor and learner
	Shares instructor responsibility		

Figure 15-6. Instructional methods should be varied throughout the course for maximum comprehension of content.

Demonstration

Demonstration is an instructional method that uses a combination of lecture and instructor activity to convey information. Demonstration provides an opportunity for the instructor to perform skills acquired in the field. The instructor must prepare for the demonstration in advance and practice the demonstration to reduce the possibility of any unplanned events during the class demonstration.

Hands-On Activities

A hands-on activity is an instructional method that uses physical contact and interaction during a given procedure. Hands-on activities integrate auditory and visual senses with tactile reinforcement to produce greater comprehension. Hands-on activities using experimentation can produce valuable learning experiences. Expected results can serve to confirm a theory or principle. Unexpected results can serve to elicit curiosity and critical thinking. The instructor can use each of these activities to stimulate learning. For example, distributing a defective component or a component with a different rating to selected members of the class can spur a discussion regarding the cause of mixed results.

Guest Speaker

Guest speakers invited to the training programs offer a different perspective, which expands and enhances the content presented. Guest speakers can be arranged through manufacturers, local companies, product service facilities, and suppliers. For example, an electrical equipment distributor can provide current information about new products and capabilities.

Industry Tours

Industry tours provide an opportunity to leave a familiar environment and experience activities in different situations. Some locations may require personal protective equipment such as eye and head protection. Prior to the tour, the instructor should explain what will be seen and how it relates to the material covered in class. After the tour, the instructor should review and summarize information presented during the tour.

Distance Learning

Distance learning is instruction that utilizes communication technologies to provide instruction in multiple locations. A forerunner to distance learning was instruction through correspondence schools. Correspondence schools utilized instructional materials in printed form. Interaction using the printed instructional material occurred via the U.S. Postal Service. Distance learning, or e-learning, builds on this concept using communication technologies such as interactive multimedia, videoconferencing, computer networking, and/or the Internet. These electronic delivery systems create numerous and varied opportunities to provide instruction at multiple remote sites.

Historically, teaching methodologies emphasized the role of the instructor in a live setting with learners in the same room or laboratory. However, the role of the HRD specialist in distance learning can be more demanding than the role of an HRD specialist in a traditional instructional environment. In a distance learning environment, additional lesson planning and other information are needed to properly facilitate the teaching/learning process. The HRD specialist must identify the appropriate use of the various technologies based on the specific learning environment. Logistical information such as operation of the equipment, location of sites, contact persons responsible for scheduling facilities and equipment, and technical resource personnel for troubleshooting equipment problems are required.

It is critical that the HRD specialist selects the medium that best suits learner needs and overall instructional program goals. Research strongly supports the importance of a consistent flow of communication between the instructor and the learners. This requires the HRD specialist to develop strategies and design communication feedback loops and communication structures into the process. Teleconferencing, electronic mail discussions, and videoconferencing are common examples of distance learning environments that provide for multi-directional communication.

The ideal distance learning environment supports multi-directional communication that allows the instructor and students to communicate with one another at one site, and also allows students at different sites to communicate. This communication is vital to create a learning environment in which the learners can interact with the instructor, receive active and timely feedback, and share their ideas at their site, as well as at distant sites. Assignments can be sent on the Internet, completed by the learner, and returned on the Internet. Courses that include laboratory activities require learners to report to a regional lab to complete assignments. Likewise, tests can be taken at a proctored regional testing site.

The instructor must create the atmosphere that fosters the necessary interaction in distance learning. Initially, learners may shy away from appearing on camera or lack the confidence to participate. Given encouragement, and opportunities to interact, learners will gain the confidence needed to fully participate. A general rule of thumb is that the instructor should spend approximately one-third of the time presenting, one-third of the time for comments, questions, and responses, and one-third of the time for practical applications. Presentation time, interaction time, and practice time should be intertwined with no more than 10 to 15 consecutive minutes in any one activity. Depending on the structure of the instructional program, distance learning can be an asynchronous program or a synchronous program.

Asynchronous Programs. Asynchronous programs are programs in which communication between the sender and receiver occurs at different times. Sending e-mail messages is an example of asynchronous communication. The receiver of the e-mail message can also access the message at any time and respond. The original sender of the e-mail message can read the response at any time. This availability of information also occurs in other examples of asynchronous communications such as Listservs, bulletin boards, and newsgroups.

Synchronous Programs. Synchronous programs are programs in which communication between the sender and receiver occurs at the same time (real time). This requires communication between the two via computer, teleconferencing equipment, or other communication technology at the same time. Both the sender and receiver are engaged in communication using data, video, and/or audio. The most common synchronous communication is chat on the Internet. More elaborate synchronous communication is used by the medical profession to demonstrate medical procedures on a patient in a remote location. Synchronous programs more closely represent traditional instructor-led instruction than asynchronous programs because of the spontaneous interaction that can occur.

Blended Learning. Blended learning has become more popular as a variation of distance learning. Blended learning refers to programs that use instructor-led methodologies, and technologies available in distance learning programs. This approach provides the personal interaction with the instructor combined with the benefit of delivering instruction in remote locations. Blended learning can use both asynchronous and synchronous program delivery. Learners respond differently to instructional delivery methods and blended learning provides the vehicle for providing different communication strategies between the instructor and learner. For example, some learners would be more apt to communicate using e-mail messages rather than face-to-face communication with the instructor. Other learners may respond to verbal reinforcement from an in-person instructor rather than an image on a computer screen.

Cooperative Learning

Cooperative learning uses the collective efforts of several learners to acquire and process new information. This method is particularly useful when there is a broad range of knowledge and experience in the group. Cooperative learning requires interaction among all learners in the group. An example of cooperative learning could include a troubleshooting activity that is assigned to a group. The members of the group may be pre-selected to ensure a variety of competencies that can be used in reaching an answer.

Team Teaching

Team teaching is an instructional method that involves the use of more than one instructor. Team teaching offers the advantage of combined technical and teaching experience of the instructors. This can provide a richer instructional experience for the learners. Learner expectations must be consistent among the different instructors. Team teaching also allows an instructor to focus on a particular topic. For example, one instructor may be responsible for safety features, and the other instructor may be responsible for representative applications in the field.

Problem Solving

Problem solving uses commercially prepared or instructor-created problems to elicit logical reasoning to find a solution. Problem solving should be used only with learners having advanced capabilities. For example, prerequisite knowledge of basic electrical principles and safety precautions is necessary before attempting electric motor problem solving. An advanced seminar activity could include common problems contributing to electric motor failure. Knowledge of electrical theory, troubleshooting techniques, and contributing causes is required before determining the ultimate cause of motor failure. Problem-solving activities must be selected carefully to be appropriate for all learners in the class.

Questions

Questions can be used during instruction to initiate discussion, verify comprehension, and raise the level of alertness. For example, the instructor in an electrical maintenance seminar could begin by asking the question, "What is the most important feature of a digital multimeter?" This prompts all learners to organize and focus mental activity on the course topic and subsequent discussion. Learner comprehension can be verified by randomly selecting learners to answer questions related to the topic presented. For example, the question "What is ghost voltage?" could be asked, and a learner is then selected to answer the question. Without knowing who will be asked to answer, all learners are attentive to the question. After a satisfactory answer is given, another question may be asked, such as "What are two sources of ghost voltage?" and a different learner should be selected to answer. Questioning could be continued until comprehension of the basic concepts is assured.

At times, particularly during evening classes or extended seminars, questions may be used to raise the level of alertness in the class. During a demonstration, if a learner appears to lose concentration, a question can redirect the focus of attention. For example, during a troubleshooting procedure, a quick question directed to the learner such as "How does the position of the test leads in this example compare to the other circuit demonstrated?" will alert all learners to the need to remain attentive.

Learner Presentations

Learner presentations reinforce content by compelling the learner to acquire a comprehensive understanding of a subject area. This is especially true if a question and answer session is included in the presentation. Peer learners can ask some insightful questions, and the presenter must be adequately prepared to successfully answer each question. Learner presentations also provide opportunities for advanced learner investigation in a specific content area.

Modular Instruction

Modular instruction uses discrete, packaged materials that can support a self-paced instructional program. Modular instructional packages may be developed by the HRD specialist or purchased from a commercial vendor to address a specific instructional need. Modular instruction is often self-contained with the goals, objectives, supporting materials, activities, and assessment criteria. However, the HRD specialist must maintain an active role in assisting learners with efficient and effective ways to approach the material. Learners who are inexperienced with modular or individualized instruction will need assistance in selecting the appropriate module(s) to meet specific needs. Care must be taken to avoid conditions that may allow learners to feel isolated without the guidance, direction, and feedback from the HRD specialist. These conditions can result in a negative learning experience.

Several major advantages are inherent in modular instructional materials. They provide an opportunity for participants to select areas in which they need instruction, work at their own pace, and self-evaluate throughout the process. The focus of assessment is on whether or not the individual achieved the competency to the desired level of proficiency, rather than on the amount of material covered. In addition, the HRD specialist should be available to answer questions, help clarify materials, provide supplementary materials, and to assist with logistics of individual assignments such as simulations or arranging small or large group meetings.

On-the-Job Instruction

On-the-job instruction is instruction provided to one or more learners while they are at their normal occupation. The advantage of on-the-job instruction is that instruction occurs in the same environment where the task will be performed. This instructional method uses demonstration as the principal method of transferring knowledge and skills.

Self-Directed Instruction

Self-directed instruction is instruction in which learners are self-motivated to seek out instruction to achieve the instructional goals. Learners who see the need for instruction will often volunteer for instructional programs. Although it is true that some adults would prefer not to participate in instructional programs to update or upgrade their skills, many want an active role in establishing the goals and objectives of the instructional program, identifying instructional resources, and choosing and implementing evaluation strategies.

Self-directed learning does not take place in isolation. Learners should have a guide or facilitator who can assist them with their learning. Self-directed learning may be contrasted with school-based learning that is typically teacher planned, teacher directed, and teacher evaluated. On the other hand, the focus of self-directed learning is on the management of learning resources based on mutual agreement of objectives, learning activities, and evaluation processes. Self-directed learning is often carried out through learning contracts, which are developed by the learner and the facilitator.

Individualized Instruction

Few instructional programs have the resources to allow individualized instruction. However, an instructor may use individualized instruction throughout a course to meet the specific needs of learners. For example, a learner with less field experience than the rest of the class may require additional individualized demonstrations of a particular technique. A learner with significantly more field experience than the rest of the class may require more challenging activities to stay engaged.

MODELS FOR INDUSTRY-BASED INSTRUCTION

Models of industry-based instruction have been developed to serve as a guide and frame of reference for industry-based instruction. Common elements such as analyzing needs, designing and developing materials, delivery methods, and evaluation are addressed by most models. The model chosen must serve the needs of the instructional program.

International Board of Standards for Training, Performance, and Instruction

The International Board of Standards for Training, Performance, and Instruction (IBSTPI) developed one of the most comprehensive and universally accepted models. The IBSTPI model competencies, which are essential for instructors, include the following:

1. Conduct needs assessment for training.
2. Assess instructional needs and characteristics of participants.
3. Analyze instructional environment.
4. Determine instructional content.
5. Order and organize instructional content.
6. Identify instructional strategies.
7. Analyze existing and emerging technologies for instruction.
8. Select and modify or develop instructional materials.
9. Evaluate instruction.
10. Design instructional management systems.
11. Plan for effective implementation of instruction.

Instructional System Development (ISD) Process

The Instructional System Development (ISD) process is an organized process for analyzing, designing, developing, and implementing instructional systems used by the U.S. Air Force. The ISD process uses concepts from systems engineering, behavioral and cognitive psychology, and instructional technology to ensure that Air Force personnel are taught the knowledge, skills, and attitudes essential for successful job performance in a cost-efficient way.

The ISD process includes the basic system functions of management—directing or controlling ISD and operations, support—maintaining all parts of the system, administration—day-to-day processing and record keeping, delivery—bringing instruction to learners, and evaluation—gathering formative and summative feedback data, and operational evaluations to assess system and learner performance. System functions support the overall framework of the instructional system. Aspects of the functions are active throughout all phases of the ISD process. The phases utilized in the ISD process are (1) analyze what instruction is needed, (2) design the appropriate instruction to meet the need, (3) develop instructional materials to support the instruction, and (4) implement the instructional system. See Figure 15-7. In the ISD process, evaluation activities are included in every phase within system functions.

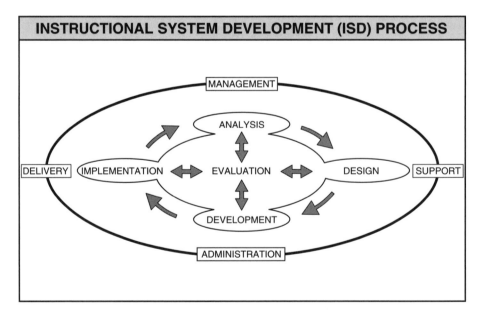

Figure 15-7. Instructional System Development (ISD) is an organized process for analyzing, designing, developing, and implementing instructional systems used by the U.S. Air Force.

INSTRUCTIONAL RESOURCES

A good instructor provides several instructional resources to present information and maximize comprehension. A variety of instructional resources can serve to maintain interest during long sessions. Seamless integration of these resources is a trait of a good instructor. Like methods of instruction, availability of instructional resources may be dictated by facility, equipment, and/or budget constraints. Instructional resources will grow as the instructor presents the material at different times. Some of the instructional resources may include copyrighted reference material.

Copyrighted Reference Material

Reference material used to support content presented in the instructional program may be copyrighted material. Depending on the use of this material, permission may be required. Copyright is the legal ownership of literary, musical, or artistic work that authorizes the right to reproduce, publish, and/or sell the work. Copyright is indicated on a work by the word copyright or ©, the name of the copyright holder, and the year. Additional statements may be used to further define limitations for reproduction. The phrase "All Rights Reserved" is commonly used to specify all derivative use of the work.

Copyright protects authors and publishers, but society also benefits from the creative efforts that are protected. Copyright laws vary in different countries. Copyrighted material may be reproduced within the bounds of fair use for classroom use. Reproduction of copyrighted material beyond fair use is illegal.

Obtaining Permission to Reproduce Copyrighted Material. Permission to reproduce copyrighted material should be requested in writing from the copyright holder. Generally, information in the request should include the definition of material to be reproduced, how material is to be used, and the number of copies to be made.

The copyright holder assesses the request for impact on copyright holder and/or author, impact on the market for the material, and the value of the copyrighted material reproduced. The copyright holder has the right to grant or deny permission to reproduce the copyrighted material and to charge a fee for the use of copyrighted materials. The copyright holder may require a specific credit line to be used with the copyrighted material reproduced.

Some reference material is in the public domain. The public domain is a term used to describe "property of the public." Public domain material is the property of the public and free from copyright restrictions. For example, pamphlets, books, or other material published by the U.S. government is public domain material.

Computer Software

Instructors have become increasingly reliant on computer software to support instructional activities. Computer software varies in complexity from simple drill and practice programs to comprehensive multimedia tutorial software that utilizes links to supporting text, sound, video clips, and Internet resources. Computer software must be carefully reviewed to ensure appropriateness and return on the total investment. Computer software is expensive, and illegal use may seem attractive. However, computer software is also copyrighted material and is subject to the license agreement for specific use. The terms and conditions of the software license agreement are commonly listed on the CD-ROM or diskette package that comes with the software. Usage of the software on more than one computer or on a network of computers may violate the software license agreement. When using computer software, the instructor must apply the same guidelines as those for printed copyrighted materials.

Visual Aids

Visual aids enhance instruction by allowing learners to view information, procedures, processes, or components of equipment. A visual aid can be as simple as a manufacturer's technical data poster, or as complex as a detailed cutaway of an industrial control and its internal components. Visual aids are useful when presenting operational principles that are not evident during normal operation. For example, improper usage of electrical test equipment such as a digital multimeter (DMM) can result in internal damage to the DMM and/or injury to the user. A severely damaged DMM is best illustrated by exposing affected components. Component cutaways can also be used to expose critical parts. Cutaway models and information may be obtained by contacting the manufacturer.

Videotapes/Video Clips

Videotapes allow the presentation of information with or without the instructor present. Videotapes can present operations or activities that are difficult to replicate in a classroom setting. For example, troubleshooting industrial circuits is best illustrated by showing footage of a typical industrial application. An additional benefit of videotapes is the ability to view sections of the videotape individually and/or repeatedly as required.

Portions of videotape footage can be saved as digital files in the form of video clips. Video clips are short videotape segments saved in files that can be used in computer software. This provides great flexibility for the instructor when accessing specific content areas. Any additional supporting materials (workbooks, guides, etc.) can be used to reinforce videotape/video clip material presented and test for comprehension. A common practice is for the instructor to capture videotape footage of procedures specific to the course or facility. As with any instructor-led demonstration, special care is required to depict proper procedures and safety precautions.

Presentation Software

Presentation software requires a computer and a multimedia projector and can be used to develop an organized collection of text, photographs, illustrations, video clips, audio clips, and other elements for enhancing instruction. Revisions and presentation customizing for specific classes are easily accomplished using presentation software. In addition, presentations created by the instructor allow for photos and video clips of the specific training program to be depicted, which provides greater topical relevance. Different presentation software products are available for purchase such as Adobe® Acrobat® and Microsoft® PowerPoint®. The navigational functions of presentation software allow the instructor to focus on specific items for greater clarity and emphasis during instruction.

Reference Materials

Reference materials include books, periodicals, trade journals, technical service bulletins, company newsletters, and other print and non-print materials. Reference material may be available as a printed document or in an electronic format on the computer. A variety of reference materials should be accessible to all learners in the program. In addition, many companies invite the opportunity to have information distributed to potential customers. Codes and standards organizations can also be contacted for specific information. See Figure 15-8.

CODES AND STANDARDS ORGANIZATIONS		
NFPA National Fire Protection Association Batterymarch Park Quincy MA 02269 www.nfpa.org	Provides guidance in assessing hazards of products of combustion
	Publishes the National Electrical Code®
	Develops hazardous materials information
ANSI American National Standards Institute 11 W 42nd St New York NY 10036 www.ansi.org	Coordinates and encourages activities in national standards development
	Identifies industrial and public needs for standards
	Acts as national coordinator and clearinghouse for consensus standards
NEMA National Electrical Manufacturers Association 2101 L St NW Suite 300 Washington DC 20037 www.nema.org	Assists with information and standards concerning proper selection, ratings, construction, testing, and performance of electrical equipment
MSHA Mine Safety and Health Administration 4015 Wilson Blvd Room 601 Arlington VA 22203 www.msha.gov	Develops and ensures compliance with safety and health standards
	Investigates accidents and assesses civil penalties for violations
NIOSH National Institute for Occupational Safety and Health 4676 Columbia Pkwy Cincinnati OH 45226 www.cdc.gov/niosh	Acts in conjunction with OSHA to develop recommended exposure limits for hazardous substances or conditions located in the workplace
	Recommends preventive measures to reduce or eliminate adverse health and safety effects
UL® Underwriters Laboratories Inc. 333 Pfingsten Rd Northbrook IL 60062 www.ul.com	Tests equipment and products to verify conformance to national codes and standards
CSA Canadian Standards Association 178 Rexdale Blvd Rexdale ON M9W 1R3 www.csa.ca	Tests equipment and products to verify conformance to Canadian national standards

Figure 15-8. Codes and standards organizations provide information and reference materials for learners.

Overhead Transparencies

An overhead transparency includes instructional material reproduced on a transparent film. Overhead transparencies can be used in lighted room conditions, which provide an environment for learners to take notes, use reference materials, and interact with the instructor. Information presented can be revealed in stages by uncovering relevant portions of the transparency.

Training Stations

Training stations allow hands-on activities on live or simulated equipment. Training stations usually permit a variety of tasks in less space than the actual equipment in industry. An instructor can create some of the best training stations. For example, a security alarm system training station can be constructed with circuit components mounted on a display board. This allows the learner to see all system components that would normally be located in different parts of a building.

LEARNER EVALUATION IN INDUSTRY-BASED INSTRUCTION

Industry-based instructional programs are effective to the extent that participants are able to apply newly gained knowledge and skills to their jobs. An essential part of measuring instructional effectiveness is learner evaluation. Learner evaluation must be considered early in the process by job supervisors and managers. Factors considered include objectives, content, materials, and activities of the workshop.

Program Content Review

Program content review prior to evaluation typically is performed in a group. The instructor can lead a discussion asking learners to recall information they learned during the instructional program. Learners can work individually or in groups to prepare for the review. Learners can write questions and their corresponding answers for review, and share these with the group. The instructor can form groups and have each group provide a review of a specific topic related to the workshop. Group discussions of ways in which the learning experiences can affect the learner can be based on individual and group reviews. "Quiz show" games and exercises can be used to facilitate reviews of facts, concepts, and procedures learned.

Posttest

A posttest is a written examination or a performance test that documents exit skills and can serve as a record of the training received. A posttest includes test items that assess learner knowledge and skills after instruction related to the objectives of the specific workshop. Like a pretest, questions are written in an objective format for grading efficiency by traditional or electronic means. Many employers require verification of attendance and performance in the training program. In addition, some employers may use posttest results as a record of employee development for compensation and advancement.

Worksheets

Depending on the course, the questions on worksheets can be answered with or without instructional references. With the textbook or other instructional materials, worksheets reinforce key concepts presented. Without reference materials, a worksheet can function as a quiz for specific content areas. Other assessment means can be used. For example, questions on slides in presentation software or transparencies can be projected. Learners can then answer the questions. When time permits, questions can be used to lead into discussion topics after testing is completed.

Competency Verification

Checklists may be used to indicate mastery of specific competencies. Checklists may be included as part of an instructional program or they may be developed by the instructor. See Figure 15-9. All competencies listed on the checklist should be derived from the skills, knowledge, and attitudes related to the occupational area or job task for which the learner is preparing. The checklist can serve as a record of competencies demonstrated for the instructor. All competencies may not be achieved depending on the competencies presented in the instructional program. The instructor should sign and date the checklist before giving it to the learner or appropriate company representative.

Self-Assessment

Checklists, questionnaires, open-ended questions, and short essays are effective tools to help learners assess their strengths and weaknesses. Self-assessment should include areas in which the learners would like additional information, as well as areas in which they feel competent. A list of these areas can be compiled for sharing with the group. In addition, individual learners can solicit feedback from other group members and develop a personal profile based on the feedback and their own assessment.

Learner Recognition

Learner recognition at the completion of the instructional program is an integral part of some training programs. The instructor may recognize learner achievement individually. However, recognition is enhanced when additional personnel, such as the learner's supervisor and/or coworkers, are present. A Certificate of Completion can function as an opportunity to document professional growth efforts by an employee. Some instructional programs include awarding of a Certificate of Completion at a banquet following completion of the training program.

ELECTRONIC SYSTEM COMPETENCY CHECKLIST

Name _____ Date Completing Instruction _____

Unit III. Microprocessors

_____ 1. Identify memory circuits

_____ 2. Identify and test data input and output circuits

_____ 3. Verify parallel-to-serial conversion

_____ 4. Verify digital-to-analog conversion

_____ 5. Remove/replace circuit boards

---

4 = Skilled–Learner can do independently without supervision

3 = Moderately Skilled–Learner can do with limited supervision

2 = Limited Skilled–Learner requires instruction and close supervision

1 = No instruction in this area–No experience or knowledge in this area

Instructor _____

Figure 15-9. A competency checklist can be used to document mastery of specific competencies.

HUMAN RESOURCE DEVELOPMENT (HRD) SPECIALIST REQUIREMENTS

The role of the human resource development (HRD) specialist will vary depending on the setting. The HRD specialist may be responsible for identifying instructional needs, developing curriculum, and/or may be directly involved with instruction. Those HRD specialists who are directly involved with instruction may be hired on a full-time or part-time basis. Instructors may also be first-line supervisors or managers who conduct individual and small group on-the-job training. By contrast, teachers in school-based instructional programs are required to hold certain credentials to meet state teacher certification requirements. Generally, these requirements include a baccalaureate degree in a major field of study with a host of general education courses. Industry-based instruction does not typically require specific credentials, and instructors often may take courses specializing in educational techniques to augment technical expertise.

Instructor Requirements

The instructor must have an in-depth knowledge of the subject matter to be taught and the appropriate teaching methods to convey information efficiently and effectively. Experience in the field is an absolute requirement. Teaching skills involve the effective transfer of knowledge and experience using appropriate instructional methods and resources. Successful instructors continually seek to improve their skills in all of these areas.

Subject Matter Knowledge. Subject matter knowledge is acquired through field experience and formal training. Field experience is necessary for establishing instructor credibility. Most instructors have a variety of experiences, but may have a void in a particular skill area. In addition, as technology advances, new voids may be created. The instructor can fill voids through proactive efforts to acquire new knowledge and skills.

Many companies allow "shadowing" of employees by instructors to gain firsthand experience. Technical update seminars and workshops sponsored by recognized companies present new products, tools, and equipment. Conferences offer a wealth of new information from industry professionals and equipment vendors. These opportunities usually provide time to share common problems and solutions with peer professionals in the field. For example, the American Society for Training and Development (ASTD) provides information through publications and conferences for training professionals. Other sources of information include trade publications, special classes, and professional organizations.

Local business and industry representatives can be excellent resources for an instructional program. An instructor can utilize such resources by establishing an advisory committee. An advisory committee can offer support and program direction from an industry perspective. Local business and industry representatives are usually very supportive of collaborative instructional efforts.

Teaching Skill. Teaching skill, like any technical skill, is improved with practice. Formal courses that present learning theory and teaching methods are available. In addition, successful instructors acquire many teaching skills through trial and error, and by emulating other successful instructors. The instructor must utilize sound instructional methods and resources to achieve maximum effectiveness.

Safety Information. Safety information is the most important information conveyed by the instructor. The instructor must identify potential risks and minimize the potential for injury, equipment damage, or both. Some activities involve greater risk than others. For example, measuring AC voltage at a wall outlet has a greater potential for injury than measuring DC voltage in a flashlight battery. Consequently, more time should be spent reviewing safety considerations when working with AC voltage.

The subject of safety should be emphasized. The instructional program should serve as a model of safe work practices. The instructor, as an example, must demonstrate all safety practices and procedures to be followed. In addition, it is the responsibility of the instructor to maintain a safe learning environment. This responsibility varies depending on the facility used for training. For example, a seminar in a hotel conference center may pose fewer safety hazards than a training setting within the production facility. Clearly defined safety precautions and procedures must be provided to help the instructor reduce hazards that could lead to an accident.

Equipment from different manufacturers may not have the same safety features. In addition, some testing equipment may be damaged from previous work. Before any tests are performed, the learner must have properly operating tools and equipment. Depending on the instructional program, it may be the responsibility of the student to provide test tools. The instructor must not assume that all tools and equipment brought to the course are in safe operating condition. Tools and equipment provided to students must also be tested for proper operating conditions before the class begins.

CHALLENGES TO HUMAN RESOURCE DEVELOPMENT (HRD) SPECIALISTS

Work and the workplace are changing rapidly. Recent studies by Merrill Lynch and the Hudson Institute have investigated trends that will help to shape work and the workplace in the first years of the 21st century. The changing nature of work and the workplace will influence the instructional and development needs of industry. American society underwent major changes in the last half of the 20th century. Globalization, technology, and workforce demographics represent major changes that influence work and the way in which companies will respond to training needs.

Global Markets and the U.S. Economy

Increased globalization is a major concern that influences the way industry responds to competition and instructional needs to update and upgrade worker skills and knowledge. Barriers to communication and transportation once imposed by distance are disappearing, thus preparing the way for a more global marketplace. International trade and world markets are easily accessible. Advanced technologies and instantaneous availability of information, data, services, and goods create the need for highly-skilled workers who can function effectively in this environment. Employers must have experienced workers to remain competitive. Training will be required for workers who lack the technical skills needed to adapt to changes in the workplace. Workers will also need higher levels of functional skills in subjects such as reading, writing, mathematics, and foreign languages. The HRD specialist will be challenged to design, facilitate, and deliver up-to-date instructional programs that develop and enhance these worker skills and attitudes.

Technical Skills and the Workforce

In industry settings, skills related to database management, programmable controllers, computer-automated design, computer-controlled machines, and other kinds of factory-automated technologies are frequently used technologies. Information technologies such as computers and networks alter a production process and associated work tasks. The standard of living created by a skilled workforce will be maintained by continual growth of worker capabilities and productivity. In contrast, unskilled workers will not experience the same growth in job opportunities and high standard of living. This disparity will be magnified with the need for more skilled workers in the future. Individuals who have a high level of functional, soft, and technical skills will continue to be the most desirable in the workplace.

Population Demographics

Better health care, diet, and lifestyle have contributed to longer life expectancies for people in the U.S. Nearly 83 million Americans now living were born in the two decades following World War II. People are not only living longer, they are working longer. In turn, there will be an increase in demand for goods and services, especially in the health care industries. Older consumers spend more annually for services than for products, which will create a demand for a broad range of services. This range will include highly skilled services in the medical profession, to moderately skilled services in home maintenance, to low-skilled services in home health services. As Americans work longer in industry, instructional programs will be needed to upgrade their skills.

Working with Diverse Groups. The ability to work effectively with individuals from all groups is required now and in the years ahead. The workforce will continue to change. For example, a century ago, workers in industry were predominantly male, but now according to the U.S. Bureau of Labor Statistics, women make up 60% of the total workforce and are also employed in nontraditional occupations. Nontraditional occupations are those in which women comprise 25% or less of the total employed. Today, women are working as welders, engineers, and electrical technicians. As the workforce changes, HRD specialists will be challenged to meet the needs of the workers and production demands.

REVIEW

Questions

1. What are some major differences between school-based and industry-based instructional programs?
2. What are the four dichotomies which result in the 16 different personality types identified by the MBTI® assessment tool?
3. What information is commonly included in a course announcement?
4. How can a pretest and posttest be used to increase the effectiveness of an instructional program?
5. How is permission to reproduce copyrighted material obtained?
6. What are some advantages and disadvantages of using distance learning in an instructional program?
7. What is the difference between functional, soft, and technical skills?
8. How can videotapes be used to support instructional activities?
9. What are some common instructor requirements in an instructional program?
10. How is copyright indicated on a work?
11. What are two methods used for assessing soft skills in new employees?
12. What are factors which must be considered when selecting an instructional methodology?
13. How is blended learning different from distance learning?
14. How can a learner self-assessment be used in an instructional program?
15. What are three factors which will affect the role of the HRD specialist in the future?

Activities

1. Develop a list of web sites that can be used as a reference for a first-time instructor.
2. List five ways in which the MBTI® assessment tool can be used in increasing instructional efficiency.
3. Compare and contrast five instructional methods to be used in an instructional program.
4. List 10 questions which must be addressed when developing a math curriculum for an auto manufacturer.
5. Prepare a summary report which explains the rationale for an in-house training program for a software development company.

BIBLIOGRAPHY

Americans with Disabilities Act of 1990. U.S. Public Law 101-336. 101st Cong., 2nd sess., July 1990.

Anderson, J.R. (1996). Situated learning and education. *Educational Researcher, 25*(4), 5–11.

Bloom, B.S. (1956). *Taxonomy of educational objectives: The classification of educational goals.* New York: David McKay.

Bloom, B.S. (1982). *Human characteristics and school learning.* New York: McGraw-Hill.

Brandt, J.R. (1998, February 16). Technical skills overrated? *Industry Week/IW, 247*(4), 7–9.

Briggs Myers, I., & Myers, P.B. (1998). *Gifts differing.* Palo Alto, CA: Consulting Psychologists Press.

Brown, A.L. (1994). The advancement of learning. *Educational Researcher, 23*(8), 4–12.

Brown, R.G. (1993). Multimedia boxes are more than just fun. *Clearing House, 66*(5), 315–317.

Carl D. Perkins Vocational and Applied Technology Education Act of 1990. U.S. Public Law 101-392. *101st Cong., 2nd sess., September 1990.*

Clark, D. (1995). *Internet essentials* (2nd ed.). Indianapolis, IN: Macmillan Computer Publishing.

Copyright Revision Act of 1976. Act 17 USC. 94th Cong., 2nd sess., 30 September 1976.

Costlow, T., & Leopold, G. (2000, May 8). Airing the high-tech work force debate. *Electronic Engineering Times.* No. 1112, 169–170.

Crawford, T. (1996). *The writer's legal guide.* New York: Allworth Press.

Cuevas, V. (1998, August 31). What companies want: The 'whole engineer.' *Electronic Engineering Times.* No. 1023, 130–131.

Curry, L. (1995). *Learning styles in secondary schools: A review of instruments and implications for their use.* Madison, WI: Wisconsin Center for Educational Research.

Dastoor, B., & Reed, J. (1993). Training 101: The psychology of learning. *Training and Development, 47*(6), 17–22.

Dejardin, C. (1989). Proper use of audio-visual aids: Essential for educators. *Community Services Catalyst, 19*(3), 21–22.

Department of the Air Force. (1993). *Instructional system development.* Washington, DC: Author.

Domeyer, D. (2000, March/April). New positions emerging: How you can prepare for them. *Women in Business, 52*(2), 30.

Doms, M., & Dunne, T. (1997, February). Workers, wages and technology. *Quarterly Journal of Economics, 112*(1), 254–290.

Easterby-Smith, M., Thorpe, R., & Holman, D. (1996). Using repertory grids in management. *Journal of European Industrial Training, 20*(3), 3–30.

Eidgahy, S.Y. (1995, February). Management of diverse HRD programs: Challenges and opportunities. *Manage, 46*(3), 15–19.

Ellsworth, J.H. (1994). *Education on the internet: A hands-on book of ideas, resources, projects, and advice.* Indianapolis: Macmillan Computer Publishing.

Ely, D.P., & Plomp, T. (1996). *Classic writings on instructional technology.* (ERIC Document Reproduction Service No. ED 394 517).

Emmer, E.T., Evertson, C.M., Clements, B.S., & Worsham, M.E. (1997). *Classroom management for secondary teachers* (4th ed.). Boston: Allyn & Bacon.

Farrell, A.M. (1996). Roles and behaviors in technology-integrated precalculus classrooms. *Journal of Mathematical Behavior, 15*(1), 35–53.

Flechtner, B. (1996). Shocking discoveries: Developing internet use policies for the computerized classroom. *Communication: Journalism Education Today, 29*(3), 11–13.

Furst-Bowe, J. (1992). The utilization of instructional technology by beginning technology education teachers. *International Journal of Instructional Media, 19*(3), 229–234.

Gagné, R.M. (1985). *Conditions of learning.* New York: Holt, Rinehart & Winston.

Gagné, R.M., & Briggs, L.J. (1988). *Principles of instructional design.* New York: Holt, Rinehart & Winston.

Galler, B.A. (1995). *Software and intellectual property protection: Copyright and patent issues for computer and legal professionals.* Westport, CO: Quorum Books.

Gibbs, W.J., & Lario-Gibbs, A.M. (1995). *TestMaker: A computer-based test development tool.* (ERIC Document Reproduction Service No. ED 387 097).

Gipps, C.V. (1994). *Beyond testing: Towards a theory of educational assessment.* Washington, DC: Falmer Press.

Golas, K.C., & Montag, B.C. (1996). The new media: Interactive 3D. *Journal of Interactive Instruction Development, 8*(3), 21–30.

Gordon, E.E. (2000). *Skill wars: Winning the battle for productivity and profit.* Boston: Butterworth-Heinemann.

Gribas, C. (1996). Creating great overheads with computers. *College Teaching, 44*(2), 66–68.

Griffith, S.C. (1990). Cooperative learning techniques in the classroom. *Journal of Experiential Education, 13*(2), 41–44.

Gronlund, N.E. (1985). *Stating objectives for classroom instruction.* New York: Macmillan.

Gronlund, N.E. (1993). *How to make achievement tests and assessments.* Boston: Allyn & Bacon.

Grusec, J.E. (1992). Social learning theory and developmental psychology: The legacies of Robert Sears and Albert Bandura. *Developmental Psychology, 28*(5), 776–786.

Gruskey, T.R. (1990). *Using mastery in the regular classroom to help learning disabled and at-risk students.* (ERIC Document Reproduction Service No. ED 335 840).

Haladyna, T.M. (1997). *Writing test items to evaluate higher order thinking.* Boston: Allyn & Bacon.

Hamber, A. (1994). The challenge of digital imaging technologies: A practical view of the future. *Information Services and Use, 14*(3), 243–251.

Hicks, S. (2000, May). Successful global training. *Training & Development, 54*(5), 95.

Holpp, L. (1995, March). New roles for leaders: An HRD reporter's inquiry. *Training & Development, 49*(3), 46–50.

Individuals with Disabilities Education Act of 1990. Section 504 of Rehabilitation, Comprehensive Services, and Developmental Disabilities Act of 1973. U.S. Public Law 112. 93rd Cong., 2nd sess., September 1973.

International Board of Standards for Training, Performance, and Instruction. (1998). *2000 Competency standards.* Retrieved from http://www.ibstpi.org/98comp.html

Jasmine, J. (1996). *Teaching with multiple intelligences: Professional's guide.* (ERIC Document Reproduction Service No. ED 400 512).

Johnson, L.M., & Johnson, V.E. (1995, January/February). Help wanted—accountant: What the classifieds say about employers' expectations. *Journal of Education for Business, 70*(3), 130–134.

Judy, R.W., & D'Amico, C. (1997). *Workforce 2020: Work and workers in the 21st century.* Indianapolis, IN: Hudson Institute.

Kate, N.T. (1998, February). Improving worker skills. *American Demographics, 20*(2), 39–40.

Klimes, R.E. (1994). *Learn in brain-friendly ways: How to succeed with quality learning styles.* (ERIC Document Reproduction Service No. ED 370 468).

Kraska, M.F. (1996). Trade and industrial teachers' knowledge related to special populations. *Journal of Industrial Teacher Education, 33*(2), 47–59.

Kuchinke, K.P. (1999). Adult development towards what end? A philosophical analysis of the concept as reflected in the research, theory, and practice of human resource development. *Adult Education Quarterly, 49*(4), 148–162.

Laurillard, D. (1995). Multimedia and the changing experience of the learner. *British Journal of Educational Technology, 26*(3), 179–189.

Library of Congress Copyright Office. (1995). *Publications on copyright.* Washington, DC: Library of Congress.

Lipman, M. (1993). Promoting better classroom thinking. *Educational Psychology: An International Journal of Experimental Psychology, 13*(3–4), 291–304.

Mager, R.F. (1997). *Preparing instructional objectives* (3rd ed.). Atlanta, GA: Center for Effective Performance.

Markham, R. (1995). *The super information highway: Developing your child's communication skills with new technologies.* (ERIC Document Reproduction Service No. ED 378 607).

Marrelli, A.F. (1995). Writing multiple choice test items. *Performance and Instruction, 34*(8), 24–29.

Marshall, D.M. (1989). Relational databases–Are you ready? *Cause/Effect, 12*(4), 3–4, 7.

Maslow, A. (1970). *Motivation and personality.* New York: Harper & Row.

Mendelsohn, D.J. (1989). Testing should reflect teaching. *TESL Canada Journal, 7*(1), 95–108.

Miller, W.R., & Miller, M.F. (1997). *Handbook for college teaching.* Sautee, GA: Pine Crest Publications.

Morain, A., & Neves, I. (1991). *Towards a sociological theory of instruction: Pedagogic practices and power and control relations.* (ERIC Document Reproduction Service No. ED 343 814).

Moursund, D. (1993). *Problem-solving models for computer literacy: Getting smarter at solving problems.* (ERIC Document Reproduction Service No. ED 367 287).

Mulford, C. (1994). Spotlight on technology. *Vocational Education Journal, 69*(7), 54–56, 68.

National Audio-Visual Supply. (1992). *How to prepare effective overhead projector presentations: One picture is worth a thousand words.* East Rutherford, NJ: National Audio-Visual Supply.

Nickisch, R. (1992). Teacher anxiety toward computer technology. *Illinois School Research and Development Journal, 29*(2), 16–17.

Norton, R.E. (1985). *DACUM handbook.* Columbus, OH: The Ohio State University, The National Center for Research in Vocational Education.

Oosterhof, A. (1996). *Developing and using classroom assessments.* Englewood Cliffs, NJ: Merrill.

Petterson, K.D. (1995). *Teacher evaluation: A comprehensive guide to new directions and practices.* (ERIC Document Reproduction Service No. ED 386 825).

Piaget, J. (1977). *Science of education and the psychology of the child.* New York: Penguin Books.

Piaget, J. (1983). Piaget's theory. In P. Mussen (Ed.), *Handbook of child psychology* (4th ed.). New York: John Wiley & Sons.

Reiger, R.C., & Stang, J. (2000). Management and motivation: An analysis of productivity in education and the workplace. *Education, 121*(1), 62–66.

Sarkees-Wircenski, M., & Scott, J.L. (1995). *Vocational special needs.* Homewood, IL: American Technical Publishers.

Shapiro, B.C. (1994). Assessing America's best and brightest teachers: The national board for professional teaching standards. *Professional Educator, 17*(1), 41–48.

Shwalb, B.J., & Shwalb, D. W. (1995). Cooperative learning in cultural context. *International Journal of Educational Research, 23*(3), 191–300.

Sitley, A.M. (2000, November/December). How to act professionally on the job. *Career World, 29*(3), 15–17.

Squires, D., & McDougall, A. (1994). *Choosing and using educational software: A teachers' guide.* (ERIC Document Reproduction Service No. ED 377 855).

Steen, M. (1998, August 24). Skills lead to success. *InfoWorld, 20*(34), 77–78.

Sternberg, R.J., & Grigorenko, E.L. (1993). Thinking styles and the gifted. *Roeper Review, 16*(2), 122–130.

Storm, G. (1993). *Managing the occupational education laboratory* (2nd ed.). Ann Arbor, MI: Prakken Publications.

Sugrue, B. (1995). A theory-based framework for assessing domain-specific problem-solving ability. *Educational Measurement: Issues and Practices, 14*(3), 29–36.

Swanson, L.J. (1995). *Learning styles: A review of the literature.* (ERIC Document Reproduction Service No. ED 387 067).

Sweeters, W. (1994). Multimedia electronic tools for learning. *Educational Technology, 34*(5), 47–52.

Sykes, L., & Uber, N. (1995). *Reflections on teaching in a computerized classroom: Knowledge, power and technology.* (ERIC Document Reproduction Service No. ED 388 984).

Tanner, D.E. (1995). The competency test's impact on teachers' abilities. *Urban Review, 27*(4), 347–351.

Terman, L.M., & Merrill, M.A. (1973). *Stanford-Binet intelligence scale manual* (3rd ed.). Boston: Houghton Mifflin.

Thach, L. (1993). Exploring the role of the deliverer in distance education. *International Journal of Instructional Media, 20*(4), 289–307.

Thorndike, R., & Hagen, E. (1986). *Measurement and evaluation in psychology in education.* New York: Macmillan.

Tobias, A. (1998, August 31). Technical skills aren't enough for engineers. *Electronic Engineering Times.* No. 1023, 8–10.

Tyrrell, R. (1995). Colored overlays, visual discomfort, visual search and classroom reading. *Journal of Research in Reading, 18*(1), 10–23.

U.S. Department of Labor. (1991). *Dictionary of occupational titles* (4th ed.). 2 vols. Washington, DC: U.S. Department of Labor.

Wertsch, J.V., & Sohmer, R. (1995). Vygotsky on learning and development. *Human Development, 38*(6), 332–337.

Whitehead, B., & Santee, P. (1994). Using standardized test results as an instructional guide. *Clearing House, 67*(6), 320–322.

Williams, J.M. (1991). *Writing quality teacher-made tests: A handbook for teachers.* (ERIC Document Reproduction Service No. ED 349 726).

Willrodt, K., & Claybrook, S. (1995). *Effects of inclusion on academic outcomes.* (ERIC Document Reproduction Service No. ED 389 102).

Wissick, C.A. (1996). Multimedia: Enhancing instruction for students with learning disabilities. *Journal of Learning Disabilities, 29*(5), 494–503.

INDEX

A

ability, 42–43
achievement, 43
  testing, 223–241
affective behavior, 75
Americans with Disabilities Act (ADA), 41–42
American Society for Training and Development (ASTD), 299
analysis, 70
aptitude, 42
arithmetic-logic unit, 204
assignment sheets, *105*–106, 124–127
Ausubel, David, 18

B

behavior, 75
  affective, 75
  cognitive, 75
  determining, 79
  psychomotor, 75
bell-shaped curve, 222–*223*
Bloom, Benjamin, 84
Bloom's *Taxonomy of Educational Objectives*, 75, 84
books, 116–120
brainstorming, 159
Briggs, Leslie J., 92–94

C

California Diagnostic Reading Tests (CDRT), 276
California Test of Mental Maturity, 44
central processing unit, *204*
characteristics, student's personal, 38–52
  ability, 42–43
  achievement, 43
  aptitude, 42
  diversity, 38–39
  individual differences, 38–42
  intelligence, 43–46
  needs, desires, and interests, 47–52
  physical characteristics, 46–47
    age, 47
    sex, 47
cognitive behavior, 75
cognitive learning, 20
communication skills, 135–138
  articulation, 137–138
  attending, 135
  clarity, 136
  correct English, 138
  focusing, 135

mannerisms, 136
pacing and pausing, 135–136
speaking rate, 138
vocabulary, 137
voice, 137
competency areas, 2–14
  personal, 7–14
    behavior, 10–14
    characteristics, 7–9
  professional, 5–7
    instructional delivery, 6
    instructional evaluation, 6–7
    instructional planning, 5–6
  technical, 3–4
    benefits, 3
    limitations, 4
computer-assisted instruction, 205–206
computer-managed instruction, 205–206
computers, personal, 203–205
  hardware, 204
    arithmetic-logic unit, 204
    central processing unit, *204*
  software, 205, 293
  Windows, 205
computers, use in education, 205–214
  classroom management, 208–214
    databases, 209–210
    grades, 209
    other applications, 213–214
    tests, 209
  computer-assisted instruction, 205–206
    tutorial CAI programs, *207*–208
  computer-managed instruction, 205–206
    drill and practice, 206
    graphics, 210
    industrial management systems, 205–206
    simulation, 208
    wordprocessing, 210
  computer software, 293
  Internet, 211–213
conceptual framework, 92–94
conditions, 84
contiguity, 31
cooperative learning, 157–158
  activities, 158
Copyright Revision Act of 1976, 119–120
copyrighted reference material, 293
  permission, 293